Baruch Nevo and Reinhold S. Jäger (Eds.)

Educational and Psychological Testing:
The Test Taker's Outlook

Studien zur Pädagogischen Psychologie

Edited by Bernhard Kraak

Volume 28

Educational and Psychological Testing:
The Test Taker's Outlook

edited by

Baruch Nevo and Reinhold S. Jäger

Hogrefe & Huber Publishers
Toronto · Lewiston, NY · Bern · Göttingen · Stuttgart

Educational and Psychological Testing: The Test Taker's Outlook

edited by

Baruch Nevo
University of Haifa
and
Reinhold S. Jäger
University of Koblenz-Landau

Hogrefe & Huber Publishers
Toronto · Lewiston, NY · Bern · Göttingen · Stuttgart

The first edition of this
volume appeared under the title
Psychological Testing:
The Examinee Perspective

BF
176
.P79
1993

Printed in Germany
Published on commission by
Hogrefe · Verlag für Psychologie
Göttingen · Toronto · Zürich

ISBN 0889370575
ISBN 3801703967

Introduction

In 1986 Nevo and Jäger edited a book entitled Psychological Testing - The Examinee Perspective. The present book is an extended and updated version of the 1986 edition. We would like to start this introduction by quoting several paragraphs from the 1986 introduction.

Every day many thousands of people around the world undergo psychological and educational tests of one kind or another. Students, job applicants, university candidates, counselees, patients, just to mention a few, are among the vast and diverse clientele of the psychological testing enterprise. How much do we, the constructors and users of psychological and educational tests, know about the attitudes and feelings of the examinees toward tests both before and after them? How much information do psychologists, psychometricians and examiners actually possess about the way the examinees perceive tests, testers and the test situation?

Currently, we seem to know very little about the questions raised above, and what little knowledge we do in fact possess, is unsystematic.
Feedback is often communicated to us only when a scandal associated with testing occurs. Public attacks on the psychological and educational testing estabishment in the mass media or in legislative procedures (on issues such as the invasion of privacy in testing, fairness in personnel selection, openness in testing) may actually be viewed as feedback of a sort on testing. This is also true for the claims about tests which have been brought before courts. However, the overall picture we get through these feedback channels is fuzzy, distorted and inconsistent. Feedback from our clients can be - and ought to be - communicated through channels other than political, journalistic or legalistic ones. Better ways can be sought and utilized in order to provide more systematic and certainly more representative feedback. Information can be obtained from examinees by preplanned and direct techniques that are methodologically sound.
Since the days of Binet and Yerkes, educational and psychological tests have been designed and modified on the basis of statistical data yielded by examinees' responses to the tests and to measurable tasks which they were required to do (criterion). This book establishes the fact that there are additional methods of obtaining information which can be used for

the purpose of improving the tests. Although feedback from examinees can be subjective, we trust that this information will prove to be instructive to the process of test construction and test modification. Towards that end, several examinee feedback models are described in the following chapters.

The contributors to this book share the common professional belief that the examinee's perspective on testing is both important and relevant, and, as such, should be incorporated into the improvement of specific tests and testing in general.

Four years later, when this second edition is about to be published, the field of testing is in even greater need of reorienting towards the individuals' attitudes, opinions and feelings.

The first of the five parts of this book includes chapters that deal with aspects of psychological tests in general.

In the first chapter ("Representative Democracy, 'Men of Zeal' and Testing Legislation") Barbara Lerner reviews ten opinion surveys dealing with attitudes of the public towards testing and points to the discrepancy between the public's views and the claims and statements of non-professional spokespersons on the issue.

In the second chapter ("Face Validity Revisited") Baruch Nevo deals with examinee perception of test validity, and the measurement and practical significance of that perception.

In the third chapter ("Examinees' Feedback Interview"), Ofra Nevo and Baruch Nevo describe a group interview technique designed to extract information from examinees concerning their attitudes and feelings towards taking a particular test.

The second part of the book deals with aspects of tests in the school system.

The major purpose of the fourth chapter ("Situational Bias -the Examinees' Perspective"), by Moshe Zeidner, is to compare the affective dispositions of middle-class and lower-class elementary school students in regard to ability tests and teacher-made examinations. In addition, the frequently claimed relation between test attitudes and test scores is investigated.

In the fifth chapter ("Essay versus Multiple-Choice Classroom Exams: The Student's Perspective") Moshe Zeidner reports student's attitudes towards these two types of tests used in the educational system.

Chapters appearing in the third part of the book examine the testee's perspective and its measurement in college and university entrance examinations.

In the sixth chapter ("The Practical and Theoretical Value of Examinee Feedback Questionnaire (EFeQ)"), Baruch Nevo describes the EFeQ that was devised for systematic study of examinee reactions and presents examples of its actual use.

E.T.S. staff members present their way of collecting feedback from test takers and test supervisors in order to standardize test administration and to help test supervisors become more sensitive to the pressures felt by examinees, in the seventh chapter ("Supporting Peak Performance: Standardizing and Humanizing the Testing Environment").

David Budescu, in the eighth chapter ("Self-evaluation of Success in Psychological Testing") reports on the within- and between- person comparisons of self-evaluation of success in a series of ability tests.

Günter Trost reports in the ninth chapter ("Attitudes and Reactions of West German Students with Respect to Scholastic Aptitude Tests in Selection and Counceling Programs") on test takers' attitudes and reactions with respect to scholastic aptitude tests.

In the tenth chapter ("Correlates of Student's Reactions to their Testing Environment) Oluf Davidsen and James Maxey report students' responses to a questionnaire about aspects of the physical conditions under which they took College Entrance Examinations.

The fourth part of this book deals with aspects regarding occupational and selection tests.

Roger Davis in the eleventh chapter ("When Applicants Rate the Examinations: Feedback from 2000 People") reports rates of satisfaction with tests as measured by reported feelings of fairness and job relatedness of the testees.

In the twelfth chapter ("Is there a Dilemma between Validity and Accpetance in the Employment Interview?") Heinz Schuler discusses different aspects of the occupational interview. Amir Rozen stresses the importance of assessing testees' attitudes toward psychological selection tests (occupational and higher education admission) and presents a method for approaching the testee for that aim in the thirteenth chapter ("Psychological Selection Tests as Viewed by the Testees Five Years Later").

The fifth and last part of this book carries the subject into the realm of psychodiagnostics.

Reinhold S. Jäger ("Measuring Reactions of Examiner and Examinee to Each Other and to the Psychodiagnostic Situation") in the fourteenth chapter and Hagit Benziman in the fifteenth chapter ("The Psychodiagnostic Experience: Reports of Subjects") claim that the introduction of feedback mechanisms into the psychodiagnostic process may add important elements to the understanding of the psychodiagnostic procedure in general as well as to increased insight into the individual's experience.

The fifteen chapters cover a specific range of tests (ability tests, teacher-made examinations, projective techniques) and refer to specific test situations. The contributors to this book, however, believe that the conclusions drawn here may be generalized to other types of tests and to other testing situations.

Some of the chapters have an empirical orientation, others are theoretical and conjectural. While some of the ideas presented may have direct application, others may not.

As in the 1986 edition, no effort has been made to integrate the fifteen contributions (and the several dozen themes) into one comprehensive model, because it is felt that at this stage of conceptual development and research any further attempt at formalization would be artificial.

We hope that some of the ideas introduced in this book will be of interest and of use to the professional in the field of testing.

Baruch Nevo, Haifa
Reinhold S. Jäger, Landau
(editors)
January, 1990

Acknowledgements

We would like to thank Professor Dr. Kraak of the Deutches Institut für Internationale Pädagogische Forschung for his continuous support of this project.
Mr. Ted Goralick and Mrs. Dina Keidar did an excellent editing job. Due to the fact that this book is multinational, their mission was not easy. We would like to thank them both.
The Alexander Von Humboldt Foundation in Bonn and the Research Authority at the University of Haifa partially subsidized the production of this book and we are grateful to these two organizations for their support.

Baruch Nevo, Reinhold S. Jäger

Contents

VIII

The Editors and Authors

Reinhold S. Jäger, Ph.D.
Professor of Psychology, in Zentrum für empirische pädagogische
Forschung, Universität Koblenz-Landau, Germany.

Baruch Nevo, Ph.D.
Associate Professor of Psychology, University of Haifa, Israel.

The Contributors Hagit Benziman, Ph.D.
Senior Lecturer, Department of Psychology, Hebrew University,
Jerusalem, Israel.

David Budescu, Ph.D.,
Associate Professor, University of Haifa, Israel.

Oluf Davidsen, Ph.D.
Former President of the American College Testing Program,
Iowa City, USA.

Roger Davis
Chief Examiner, King Country, Washington, USA.

Barbara Lerner, Ph.D.
Independent Consultant in Law and Psychology, Princeton, USA.

James Maxey, Ph.D.
Assistant Vice President, Research Division, American College Testing
Program, Iowa City, USA.

Ofra Nevo, Ph.D.
Head, Vocational Guidance Center, University of Haifa, Israel.

Richard Noeth, Ph.D.
Executive Director of Admission and Guidance Programs, Educational
Testing Service, Princeton, USA.

XIV

Amir Rozen, M.A.
Occupational Psychologist, Management School, Israel Electric
Company, Haifa, Israel.

Heinz Schuler, Ph.D.
Professor of Psychology, University of Hohenheim, Germany.

Günter Trost, Ph.D.
Director of Institute for Test Development, Bonn, Germany.

Moshe Zeidner, Ph.D.
Lecturer, School of Education, University of Haifa, Israel.

Part 1:

General Aspects

1

Representative Democracy
"Men of Zeal" and Testing Legislation[1]

Barbara Lerner

Abstract

The author reviews data from 10 opinion surveys dealing with attitudes of the public toward standardized testing and analyzes the discrepancy between the public's views and the claims and legislative demands of self-appointed spokespersons on this issue. She considers the implications of this discrepancy and of other similar ones for representative democracy in sight of contemporary obstacles to the realization of the intent of the framers of the U.S. Constitution regarding the relationship between Congress and the American people.

Introduction

The Constitution of the United States opens with this sweeping categorical statement: "All legislative Powers herein granted shall be vested in a Congress of the United States, which shall consist of a Senate and House of Representatives." Early efforts to give the judiciary a role in legislative policymaking were decisively rejected. The grounds were that in a government based on the consent of the governed, only elected officials answerable to the people at frequent intervals should have power to pass laws limiting the freedom of action. In this way, our founding fathers hoped to minimize gaps between the wishes of the majority and the law of the land, saving only those laws necessary to protect unpopular minorities. Are unpopular legislatures and laws, then, a contradiction in terms? Hardly. Public opinion poll data show that American government in general and

1   This article was originally published in the American Psychologist, 1981, 36, p. 270-275.

the U.S. Congress in particular suffered a precipitous decline in popular esteem in recent years. Janowitz (1978, p. 111) indicates that in 1958, 62 percent of the population reported a high level of trust in the government; in 1970, only 35 percent did. Miller (1974) reports that between 1964 and 1970 alone, trust in the government in Washington dropped 25 percent, belief that the government habitually wastes money rose by more than 20 percent, and confidence in the competence of government officials dropped by 17 percent. Data from both the Harris and Gallup polling organizations show that much of this disesteem is focussed on Congress itself. Harris survey data show that positive public ratings of Congress declined from 59 percent in 1964 to 26 percent in 1970 (Mayhew, 1974, p. 166) and that whereas 42 percent of the population expressed confidence in Congress in 1966, only 13 percent did in 1975 (Janowitz, 1978, p. 112). A Gallup survey, using a 3-point rather than a 2-point rating scale, also found a significant drop (Janowitz, 1978, p. 111), as did the Committee on Government Operations of the U.S. Senate. [2] What has gone wrong? How did so great a gap develop between the people and that branch of government designed to have what James Madison called "an immediate dependence on and an intimate sympathy with the people"? (Madison, 1961, p. 165).

Representation: The Structural Problem

The answer most often propounded by serious students of the political process is that social interest groups have a disproportionate influence on legislators and on the regulatory bureaucracies they create (Fiorina, 1977; Mayhew, 1974). Infrequent instances of outright corruption aside, special interest group domination of the legislative process is generally perceived as a structural problem. Lobbyists and lawyers for business, labour, and other special interest groups represent concentrated interests, organized for political action on a permanent basis. The public at large, in contrast, is an unorganized and, at best, sporadically mobilized group whose interests are too diffuse to facilitate effective political action in

---

2   US Senate, Committee on Government Operations. Confidence and Concern: Citizens View American Government. Hearings, December 3, 1979.

most instances. Agreement that this is the essence of the problem is wide-spread; agreement about potential solutions to it is much less so, but in the last two decades, many intellectuals embraced the notion that what was needed was an organized counterforce, a great new growth of law firms and lobbying groups dedicated to serving the public interest on a permanent basis by representing broad, general interests like those of the consumer in the halls of Congress.

As every member of Congress knows, we have had just such a growth - public interest lobbyists and lawyers are more numerous now than at any time in our history; their power is such that they are afforded extremely frequent and respectful hearings by legislators and agency bureaucrats alike, and their success in getting new legislation passed and in breathing new life into old legislation through increased regulatory activity has been little short of amazing: 21 new federal regulatory agencies were es-tablished between 1966 and 1976 alone, and the number of "Federal Reg-ister" pages needed to record their output more than doubled, from 16,850 pages in 1966 to 36,487 pages in 1978. Not surprisingly, in light of these facts, the number of government bureaucrats employed in regula-tory activities tripled from 28,000 in 1970 to 81,000 in 1979; and the direct cost of their activities quintupled, from less than 1 billion dollars in 1970 to about 5 billion dollars in 1979 (Friedman & Friedman, 1980).

Yet, as indicated above, this enormous outpouring of money and effort on behalf of public interest has been accompanied by a precipitous de-cline in popular approval and trust in the government. What accounts for this apparent paradox? Justice Brandeis provided an early clue in his 1928 dissent in "Olmstead vs. United States". He wrote,

> "Experience should teach us to be most on our guard to protect liberty when the government's purposes are beneficient. Men born to freedom are naturally alert to repel invasion of their liberty by evil-minded rulers. The greater dangers to liberty lurk in insidious encroachments by men of zeal, well-meaning but without understanding."

The public is not yet as prescient as Justice Brandeis was, but it has slowly come to share his view and to fear "men of zeal, well meaning but without understanding", even more than it fears the traditional special interests those men of zeal sprang into action to protect it from. In January 1977,

39 percent of the population named "big government" the greatest threat to the nation, a higher percentage than named big labor (24 percent) or big business (23 percent) (Janowitz, 1978, p. 549). Overall, public opinion poll data show that popular anger and frustration with a perceived excess of government regulation and with its enormous and increasingly burdensome indirect costs - current estimated to be between 100 and 200 billion dollars annually (Boren & Levin, 1980; Weidenbaum, 1977)[3] - are at an all time high and may be great enough to foreshadow the first major shift in electoral coalitions since the election of Franklin D. Roosevelt in 1932.

The problem, it seems, is that public interest lobbyists and lawyers do not, in actual fact, represent the public interest as the public defines it any more than special interest lobbyists and lawyers do, and no wonder. The public that is too diffuse and unorganized to monitor effectively the activities of its elected representatives is, by definition, even less likely to be able to monitor the activities of self-appointed spokespersons who are not answerable to it, through the electoral process or in another way.

As a result, the growth in public interest lobbying groups and law firms could increase the representativeness of the government only if they were to voluntarily make themselves answerable to the public by paying close attention to the data from public opinion polls and acting in accordance with them. Few public interest lobbyists or lawyers have chosen to do this, and as a result, it is not at all uncommon for members of these groups to press for definitions of the public interest that stand in striking contrast to the definitions actually favoured by overwhelming majorities of the very citizens they claim to represent.

So-called consumer legislation directed at the testing industry is an especially obvious case in point. Given the increasing negative climate of opinion toward further extensions of government interference into previously unregulated areas of our national life and the increasingly disturbing economic realities underlying it, proposals for such legislation would make sense only if there were clear evidence that in this specific instance, public dissatisfaction with unregulated practice was pervasive and profound. In fact, all of the available evidence points in the opposite direction.

---

3   Weidenbaum, M.L. The Costs of Government Regulation (Pub. No. 12) St. Louis, Mo. Washington University, Center for the Study of American Business, February, 1977.

In a recent article (Lerner, 1980), I reviewed seven opinion polls dealing with attitudes of the public and various sub-groups of it, toward standardized testing. Since then, I have discovered three more unpublished surveys, using much larger national samples of the opinions of both teachers and students and including some fascinating data on the misperception of their views by professional specialists in educational measurement. In what follows, I briefly summarize the results of all 10 studies and then focus, in as much details as space permits, on misperceptions of public opinion by professionals and others, and on the causes and consequences of such misperceptions.

Vox Populi: Ten Opinion Surveys

The best available data on the attitudes of the American public as a whole toward standardized testing are those provided by the Gallup organization. Despite a wealth of scientific data to the contrary, (Lerner, 1979, 1980), self-appointed public interest spokespersons have tried hard to convince the public that standardized tests have little or no utility for Americans in general, and that they are especially unfair to minorities and women. Data from the three separate Gallup polls show that they have not succeeded. In 1979, Gallup pollsters asked a national sample of American parents what they thought of standardized tests. Eighty-one percent thought they were "very useful" or "somewhat useful"; only 17 percent rated them as "not too useful". Non-white parents were, if anything, even more satisfied. Of this group, 85 percent saw standardized tests as useful (Educational Testing Service). [4]
Data from two other Gallup polls make it clear the public perceptions of the utility of standardized tests do not change when the test takers are women or minority group members. In 1977, Gallup pollsters asked a representative sample of American adults whether "ability as determined by test scores should be the main consideration" in allocating jobs and places in college or whether women and minorities should be given preferential treatment. Eighty-one percent endorsed the use of test scores, 8 percent had no opinion, and only 11 percent rejected test scores in favour of preferential treatment (Gallup).[5] In 1979, Gallup pollsters asked the same

---

4   Educational Testing Service, Press Release, January 4, 1979.

5   Gallup, G.H. Press Release, November 20, 1977.

question again, this time using a representative sample of American college students. Results were essentially the same: 80 percent endorsed the use of test scores, 7 percent had no opinion, and only 13 percent rejected test scores in favour of preferential treatment (Gallup).[6]
Do the views of teachers diverge from those of the public as a whole? Leaders of the National Edcational Association (NEA) who are lobbying for new legislation to regulate standardized testing claim they do, insisting, among other things, that teachers are being forced to teach the tests, with resultant gross distortions in the contents of educational programs. However, in the December 1962 issue of the NEA's own Research Bulletin, teachers themselves told a very different story. Asked whether naionwide testing programs such as merit scholarship exams and college entrance exams were exerting an influence on the instructional programs in their schools, 41 percent answered "Yes, and the influence is desirable". Only 5.4 percent said "yes, and the influence is undesirable." Of the remainder, 32 percent could detect no influence at all, and 21.3 percent were undecided.
Leaders of the American Federation of Teachers (AFT) have taken a much more positive stance toward standardized testing in general and toward minimum competence testing in particular, arguing against the adoption of new legislation in this area. Results from a recent AFT survey (Ward)[7] suggests that most members agree with them. Fewer than half of all AFT teachers surveyed complained that test content failed to match their curricula or that test materials were inappropriate or biased for any of their students. Thirty-Seven percent had favourable or very favourable attitudes toward minimum competence testing, 34 percent were neutral and only 20 percent expressed unfavourable attitudes toward it. Thus, results from both surveys suggest that the AFT is right about teachers' views, the NEA is wrong. However, because these surveys were characterized by suboptimal sample sizes and/or response rates, considerable room for doubt remained.
It no longer does because, recently, a team of researchers from the Psychological Corporation (Beck & Stetz,[8] Stetz & Beck,[9]) used semantic dif-

---

6   Gallup, G. H. Press Release, April 5, 1979.

7   Ward, J. G. Teachers and Testing: A Survey of Knowledge and Attitudes. Washington, D. C.: American Federation of Teachers, July, 1980.

8   Beck, M. D. & Stetz, F. P. Standardized Testing as Viewed by Test Specialists and Users. Paper presented at the meeting of the National Council on Measurement of Education. Boston, April, 1980.

ferential scales to elicit the opinions and feelings of a national sample of some 3,300 public and private school teachers of kindergarten through Grade 12, giving them 11 separate items on which they could express negative attitudes toward standardized tests. The percentage of teachers who chose to do so ranged from 2 percent to 13 percent (with only one exception) - 22 percent thought standardized tests were "hard" rather than "easy", an ironic finding in light of the fact that 59 percent of their students rate teacher-made tests harder than standardized ones.

"Hardness" aside, teachers generally rated standardized tests as helpful, fair, useful, and unbiased and described themselves as calm, comfortable, and knowledgeable about as well as supportive toward the tests. More than two thirds thought the amount of standardized testing in their own school system was "about right"; the remainder were split between those who thought there was too much and those who thought there was too little. And although the NEA has been calling for a moratorium on all standardized testing since 1972 and has expressed even greater hostility to minimum competence testing, only 16 percent of the teachers they claim to represent favour such a moratorium, and a clear majority - 62 percent - endorse the use of competence tests to determine high school graduation.

The NEA is not alone in misrepresenting its constituency. Leaders of the National School Boards Association (NSBA) recently joined leaders of the NEA in their campaign against standardized testing, but data (NSBA, 1977) on the opinions of more than 1.000 NSBA members who attended the 1976 NSBA convention show that only 14 percent agreed with their statement: "It would be wise to eliminate standardized testing." In contrast, 69 percent agreed with this one: "Teacher groups (e.g. NEA) who call for the elimination of standardized testing are only trying to avoid being held accountable."

What is true for the public as a whole and for the school board members and teachers is true for students as well. Ralph Nader and his nationwide network of Public Interest Research Group lobbyists claim to represent

---

9   Stetz, F.P. & Beck, M.D. Comments from the Classroom: Teachers' and Students'
     Opinions of Achievement Tests. Unpublished Manuscript, 1979.

10

students, but on the basis of available data, this claim too, must be rejected as false. Specifically, the Naderites insist that the tests are unfair, that they have an excessive influence on college admissions decisions, that they blight students' lives, and that advanced information on what sorts of test questions to expect is grossly inadequate.

Results from a survey of some 3000 students conducted in 1977 by the Response Analysis Corporation[10] for the College Entrance Examination Board indicate that although only 30 percent of the students expected to do well on the Scholastic Aptitude Test, 79 percent believed that SAT scores should have "a great deal" or "a fair amount" of influence on the decisions of college admissions officers. Students who regarded the elimination of the SAT as a poor idea outnumbered students who thought it a good idea by a margin of about two to one. The most frequently chosen reason for retaining the exam was its perceived fairness and objectivity. Large majorities rated both sections of the test as either "very fair" or "pretty fair" (81 percent felt this way about the math section and 73 percent about the verbal section).

Prior to taking the test, more than half of the students reported only mild anxiety about it, approximately a quarter reported none, and only about a fifth described themselves as very anxious. Afterwards, fewer than a quarter reported doing better than they had expected to do, approximately a third reported doing worse, and only 13 percent said they had set their sights lower as a result of their test scores. Sixty-two percent said they had no strong feelings about the SAT experience; the rest were about evenly divided between those who enjoyed it and those who disliked it.

Most students did not begin preparing for the test more than a few weeks in advance, did not answer all of the sample test questions available to them, and did not feel that the preparation helped much. However, because some students did indicate a desire for more information in general and more sample questions in particular, the College Board has developed a new, longer, and more detailed test booklet containing a full length sample test along with the correct answers to each question.

In 1978, the College Board explored students reactions to the booklet, using a sample of some 2000 high school juniors (see Powers & Alderman)[11] These students generally rated the new booklet as more helpful

---

10   Response Analysis Corporation. High School Students View the SAT and College Admission Process. (Report No. 4056): Princeton, N.J. Author, July, 1978.

than the old one and believed that taking the sample test was "very good" or "pretty good" preparation for the exam.

Nonetheless, only 38 percent reported reading the entire booklet, and only 36 percent claimed to have tried to answer all of the sample questions; 23 percent answered none of them. Twenty-nine percent of the students who received the new booklet also felt that way, but data analysis revealed that there were no differential effects on actual scores.

Data on student attitudes toward testing from the previously cited Psychological Corporation study are generally consistent with the above findings and have two advantages: they are derived from a study based on a very large national sample of students 72,000 in all - and cover the entire range from kindergarten through Grade . Students in this study were questioned immediately after taking the Metropolitan Achievement Test (MAT) in the spring of 1978. The younger ones, in kindergarten through Grade 4, were queried about whether they felt nervous before taking the test and were asked to pick happy, neutral, or unhappy faces to describe their feelings toward the test before and after taking it. Fifty-six percent reported feeling some pretest nervousness, but 78 percent chose happy or neutral faces to represent their feelings toward the test prior to taking it, and 82 percent did so afterwards.

Students in Grades 5 through 12 were also asked about pretest nervousness. Thirty percent reported such feelings prior to taking the MAT, but interestingly enough, 64 percent reported such feelings prior to taking the teacher-made tests. These older students were also asked whether they thought the questions on the standardized tests they had just taken were fair: 75 percent thought they were, 11 percent were just unsure, and only 14 percent thought them unfair.

The Psychological Corporation team followed up their initial study by asking a random sample of the membership of the National Council on Measurement in Education (NCME) to respond to both their student and their teacher questionnaires as they thought a random sample of students and teachers would. Their results are congruent with an earlier analysis based on the speeches and writings of measurement specialists (Lerner, 1979), showing that members of this group have had a consistent tendency to overestimate the frequency of negative attitudes toward standardized tests and to underestimate the frequency of positive ones.

In addition to being consistent in their biases, NCME members made a number of very large misestimates. They expected that some 60 percent of the teachers would feel that the amount of testing in their schools was excessive. In fact, as indicated above, fewer than 20 percent felt that way.

NCME members also thought that more than 60 percent would favour a moratorium on state-mandated achievement tests and that only 42 percent would favour the use of competence tests to determine high-school graduation. In fact, the pattern was just the opposite: Only 31 percent favoured a moratorium, even on state mandated tests, and 62 percent endorsed the use of competence tests for high school graduation.

Similar discrepancies show up in NCME members' estimate of student attitudes. These measurement specialists predicted that only about half of the students would rate standardized test questions as fair and that about two thirds of them would find standardized tests harder than teacher-made ones. In fact, as reported above, three quarters of the students thought standardized test questions were fair, and almost 60 percent considered teacher-made tests harder than standardized ones.

The Structural Problem Reconsidered

All in all, the data summarized above show that public dissatisfaction with the unregulated practice of standardized testing cannot be fairly described as either pervasive or profound. Such dissatisfaction as exists is confined to a small, atypical minority, hardly a justification for imposing burdensome government regulations in yet another area of our national life and for forcing all citizens to pay the cost of those unwanted and unneeded regulations, as consumers or taxpayers or both.

Yet, as we have seen, many measurement specialists have very exaggerated notions about the extent of public dissatisfaction with unregulated practice. These notions have already caused some of them to make excessive concessions to self-styled public interest lobbyists in the mistaken belief that they are responding to the wishes of the majority when in truth, they are helping the few to flaunt representative democracy by imposing their will on the many.

Measurement specialists, in the NCME or in any other organization, are hardly alone in this. Many other specialists in other areas and many legislators have made the same mistakes in this area and in others, for the same essential reasons, and the price to our troubled economy and to the "intimate sympathy" our founding fathers hoped to create between the people and their representatives, has been enormous.

Why does this happen, again and again, and what, if anything, can be done to prevent it? Part of the problem, as noted previously, is that organized, concentrated interests tend to defeat unorganized, diffuse ones, allowing special interests to prevail over the public interest as the public defines it, time and time again. Concentrated, organized interests can do this because they are poised to offer prompt rewards to those who concede to their demands and prompt punishment to those who do not. The public at large, in contrast, is a vast amorphous group whose rewards and punishments are almost always slower, more uncertain, and less precisely targeted.

Stated in this way, the problem seems discouragingly intractable, particularly in light of the fact that it is fundamental to our system to give all citizens and groups of citizens the right to petition their government for a redress of grievances, no matter how atypical or unfounded some of those petitions and grievances may be. Perhaps, however, there is another way of approaching the problem, a way of analyzing and effecting rewards and punishments, that offer at least a partial redress of the balance between thepublic interest and the special interests of groups who claim to represent the public while lobbying for positions that it rejects. The sort of rewards and punishments that matter to the people who are dependent on the good will of the general public - elected officials and private citizens engaged in selling goods or services to the public - are, of course, manifold and diverse. Still, it seems reasonable to suggest that a publication and dissemination of facts supportive of their position is a major reward for all of them, and that a suppression and distortion of facts is a major punishment for all of them. If this is so, then it may be that what we need is truth-in-lobbying legislation, a law that would leave lobbyists free to advocate any cause but that would make it more difficult and more costly for them to make patently false claims about the representativeness of their views.

Perhaps, on the other hand, the cost of new legislation and regulation would outweigh the benefits, in this area as in so many others. If so, we need not despair. Private citizens and their remaining free institutions, notably, the press, are often more resourceful and resilient than they first appear, once the nature and significance of a problem becomes clear to appear, once the nature and significance of a problem becomes clear to them, as any serious problem tends to do given sufficient time. Currently, there are signs that this is happening and that both the public and the press are becoming increasingly leery of self-appointed spokespersons for the public interest.

Extreme forms of advocacy journalism still exist, but many responsible investigative reporters and other media people are increasingly unhappy about the role some of their fellows have played, wittingly or unwittingly, as conduits for false claims put forth by new special interest groups, who confuse arrogance with idealism by insisting that they are not special interest groups at all, but representatives of a public whose views they scorn. A more critical attitude toward such claims on the part of the media could help a great deal, particularly if it were coupled with readier and more systematic access to the facts about the actual status of public opinion as revealed by competent polling organizations.

Facilitations of such access would be a good thing in a democracy such as ours, and it would be especially welcome if it were provided by one or more private foundations, without extending the reach of a government sector that Democrats and Republicans alike now see as overextended and without adding to the burdens of that most longsuffering of all consumers, the American taxpayer.

References

Boren, D.L. & Levin, C. (1980, May 28). Regulating Federal Regulators, *New York Times*.

Fiorina, M.P. (1977). *Congress: Keystone of the Washington Establishment*. New Haven: Conn.: Yale University Press.

Friedman , M. & Friedman, R. (1980). *Free to Choose: A Personal Statement*. New York: Harçourt Brace Janovitch.

Janowitz, M. (1978). *The Last Half-Century: Societal Change and Politics in America.*Chicago: University of Chicago Press.

Lerner, B. (1979). Test and Standards Today: Attacks, Counterattacks and Responses. In: R.T. Lennon (Ed.), *New Directions for Testing and Measurement*. San Francisco: JosseyBass.

Lerner, B. (1980). The War on Testing: David, Goliath and Gallup. *The Public Interest, 60,* 119-147.

Madison, D.R. (1961). Paper No. 52. In: R.P. Fairfield (Ed.), *The Federalist Paper.* Garden City: N.Y. Doubleday.

Mayhew, D.R. (1974). *Congress: The Electoral Connection.* New Haven, Conn.: Yale University Press.

Miller, A.H. (1974). Political Issues and Trust in Government: 1964-1970. *American Political Science Review, 68,* 951-972.

National Education Association. (1962). What do Teachers Think? *NEA Research Bulletin,40,* 120-125.

National School Boards Association, (1977). School Board Attitudes Toward Standardized Testing. *NSBA Research Report, 1,* 25-29.

2

Face Validity Revisited 1.[1]

Baruch Nevo

Abstract

The literature of the concept of face validity is surveyed. A definition of face validity involving four facets is proposed. Empirical data suggesting that face validity is characteristic of tests that can be validly and reliably measured are presented. Implications for research and for practical use are discussed.

Introduction

The purpose of this paper is to address the long ignored topic of face validity (FV) and attempt to give it some new theoretical and applied meanings. This is done by (a) reviewing the literature on face validity; (b) defining face validity in the form of a mapping sentence which includes a proposal for measuring face validity; (c) presenting empirical evidence that face validity can be measured reliably; and (d) presenting some implications concerning possible research and possible applications of face validity.

Survey of the Literature

During the 1940s and early 1950s the term face validity carried several meanings and was a source of confusion. The term was discussed by Mosier (1947) in the following way:

---

1   This paper was originally published in the Journal of Educational Measurement, 1985, 22, 287-293.

> The term 'face validity' implies that a test which is to be used in a practical situation should, in addition to having pragmatic or statistical validity, appear practical, pertinent and related to the purpose of the test as well; i.e., it should not only be valid, but it should also appear valid (p. 192).
> The frequency of its use and the emotional reaction which it arouses – ranging almost from contempt to highest approbation – makes it desirable to examine its meaning more closely. When a single term variously conveys high praise or strong condemnation, one suspects either ambiguity of meaning or contradictory postulates among those using the term. The tendency has been, I believe, to assume unaccepted premises rather than ambiguity and beautiful friendships have been jeopardized when a chance remark about face validity has classed the speaker among the infidels (p. 191).
> Since the term has become overlaid with a high degree of emotional content and since its referents are not only highly ambiguous but lead to widely divergent conclusions, it is recommended that the term be abandoned. (p. 205)

An examination of Mosier's (1947) description as well as other manuscripts of that period (English & English, 1958; Freeman, 1950) makes evident the fact that conceptual differentiation between *all* types of validity, including face validity, had not yet been clearly made. Fortunately, Cronbach (1949, p. 47), Anastasi (1954, pp. 121-122), and the first *Standards for Educational and Psychological Tests* (American Psychological Association [APA] 1954) clarified the issue to such an extent that abandonment of the term was no longer necessary. These texts and many others (Anastasi, 1982; Anderson, Ball & Murphy, 1974; Beam, 1953; Cronbach, 1970; Ebel, 1972; Thorndike & Hagen, 1961) emphasized two basic points:

1. Face validity should be separated from criterion-related, content, or construct validity. Face validity should not be confused with the other types of validity and it cannot replace them. Some writers have carried the point even further by placing face validity within quotation marks, implying that it is not really a type of validity.

2. Face validity is an important feature of any psychological or educational test intended for practical use. According to some textbooks (Anastasi, 1982; Brown, 1983; Cronbach, 1970) and according to our

own experience, a test with high face validity may have a better chance than an equivalent test with low face validity of (a) inducing cooperation and positive motivation among subjects before and during the test administration; (b) attracting potential candidates; (c) reducing dissatisfaction and feelings of injustice among low scorers; (d) convincing policymakers, employers, and administrators to implement the test; and (e) improving public relations, including relations with the mass media and the courts.

In view of the importance of these issues, it is surprising to note how little has been done in the area. In fact, a theoretical framework and a measurement procedure with recommendations for its application have never been suggested. Not even one research study has been dedicated to the study of the relations between face validity and psychometric characteristics of tests. No efforts have been reported by publishers or commercial users of tests to measure in a direct way the attitudes of testees toward the test. The few polls reported by the College Board (Response Analysis Corporation, 1978) and by the National Council on Measurement in Education (Stetz & Beck, 1979) are exceptions which only prove the rule. One can speculate regarding the reasons for this state of affairs: that psychologists, having differentiated face validity from other validities, felt that face validity was too trivial to merit serious attention; that the *Zeitgeist* was set against introspection in the fifties and sixties; that testing experts were securing their role as "knowers"; or that experts in testing have been negligent.

The current issue of the *Standards for Educational and Psychological Tests* (APA, 1974) mentions "face validity" twice: first on page 26, where it is asserted that face validity does not really belong to the validity group, and second on page 29, where a distinction between face validity and content validity is drawn. One would expect that after the uniqueness of this term had been established a serious analysis would follow. Unfortunately, this did not happen.

Mapping Sentence for Face Validity

I would like to propose the following formal, facet-type operational definition (Guttman, 1980; Shye, 1978) for face validity:

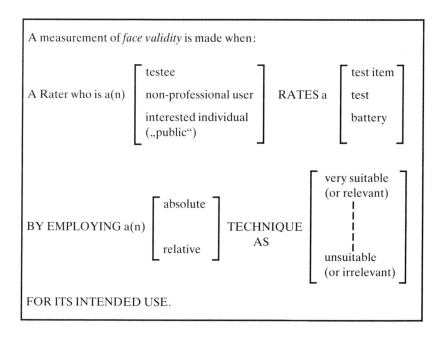

The key terms of this definition merit further discussion.

Rater

A direct measurement of face validity is obtained by asking people to rate the validity of a test as it appears to them. The question then arises as to who this rater should be. Generally, there are three groups of raters whose attitudes toward the test (or the item, or the battery of tests) would be of interest: (a) the persons who actually take the test (e.g., job applicants, participants in experiments, school pupils, etc.); (b) the nonprofessional users who work with the results of the test (e.g., personnel administrators, employers, admissions officers, chairpersons of university departments, psychiatrists, etc.); and (c) the general public (e.g., newspaper readers, newspaper reporters, parents of testees, judges, politicians, etc.). It is suggested that the term *face validity* should be avoided when the rating is done by "experts". When psychologists rate personality questionnaire items as to their subtlety (Gynther, 1979; Holden & Jackson, 1979) or when language testing specialists consider the relevance of oral examinations to language proficiency testing (Stevenson, 1981), *content validity* seems the appropriate term. When researchers are using their intuition and experience to judge if a given test or test item has high probability of being empirically valid (Friedman, 1983; Spence & Helmreich, 1983; Turner, 1979), the term *hypothesized validity* is perhaps more appropriate.

Object of Rating

The term test is used here in its broad meaning and includes ability tests, personality questionnaires, projective techniques, interviews, and school examinations. Raters could be asked to evaluate individual test items, tests as a unit, or batteries of tests. For convenience, test in this paper will refer to all three levels – items, tests, and batteries – unless otherwise specified.

Method of Measurement

The direct approach should be adopted in face validity measurement. In other words, the people who are involved with the test taking should be asked to do the rating. They cannot be replaced by psychometricians, just as, conversely, professionals cannot be replaced by laymen when content validity or construct validity are being investigated.

The general approaches to the measurement of FV are described best as "absolute" and "relative." In the absolute technique, the rater is asked to rate a test or an item on the following 5-point scale: 5 – the test is extremely suitable for a given purpose; 4 – the test is very suitable for that purpose; 3 – the test is adequate; 2 – the test is inadequate; and 1 – the test is irrelevant and therefore unsuitable.

In the relative technique, the rater simultaneously judges the face validity of several tests by comparing them with each other. In our experience, as well as Carter's (1955), raters are usually "rather pleased at having the opportunity to express their opinions in this matter" (p. 63), and they are comfortable with either technique of face validity measurement.

Other Considerations

When measuring FV one may need to consider other variables besides those detailed in the mapping sentence. For instance, testees' attitudes towards the test may depend on the particular time in which the rating takes place. We can ask applicants to rate the face validity of a test immediately after the test has been administered while the testees' impressions are still fresh. Another possibility is to carry out the face validity study in a more remote point in time, perhaps several weeks or several months after the test administration, and after the results have been reported. Another factor that may bear on the measurement of face validity is if responses are anonymous.

Empirical Results

The following report of empirical findings is divided into three parts: interrater agreement, reliability, and discriminant validity data. The data base for the analysis reported here is a file of the responses of 1385 examinees who filled out an Examinees' Feedback Questionnaire (EFeQ) (Nevo & Sfez, 1983). The items comprising the instrument deal with examinees' feelings, attitudes, and opinions about a test they have just taken. The respondents had taken the Haifa and Tel Aviv Universities Entrance Examination. The examination consisted of six tests: General Knowledge, Figural Reasoning, Mathematical Reasoning, Vocabulary, Verbal Reasoning, and English Reading Comprehension (as a foreign language). Two face validity sections were included in this version of EFeQ. In the first one, examinees were asked to rate each of these tests separately, and also to rate the battery as a whole. Absolute ratings were made on the previously defined 5-point scale of „relevance and relatedness to university studies." In the second section, examinees were asked to rate various selection tools (e.g., scholastic aptitude test, personality questionnaire, high school GPA) on the same 5-point scale. In what follows reference is made mainly to results of the first face validity section. Practically all the major findings of the first face validity section were replicated in the results of the second section.

Interrater Agreement

The face validity of a test can be considered a coherent construct only if a reasonable level of agreement exists among raters. Smith (1936) asked 62 students to rate seven types of achievement tests as to their suitability for determining grades in an education course. The average interrater correlation was found to be .31. Similarly, Adams (1950) asked 39 personnel administrators to rank-order seven tests on the basis of their desirability for use in the selection and promotion of people for personnel officer positions. Adams' estimated correlation among the subjects was .33. Carter (1955) asked students to evaluate each of 100 test items on a 5-category scale as to their relevance to the tested subject. When he correlated (over 100 items) the summed ratings of two randomly selected groups of five raters each, he got an average correlation of .46. The average correlation was raised to .62 when he correlated two groups of 10.
In the Haifa face validity study an intraclass correlation was calculated for all males who expected to study Social Sciences at the University (N = 246). The typical interrater reliability as reflected by the intraclass correlation was .44 (significantly higher than .00; p< .01). Considering the fact that the six tests were all scholastic aptitude tests with little variance in the ratings, this correlation reflects a reasonable level of agreement among raters.

Intrarater Reliability

A measurement of intrarater reliability was available; one rating scale, that of the face validity of the Entrance Examination as a whole, was repeated twice in the same questionnaire (EFeQ), with slightly different phrasing and within a different context. Both times the 5-category response scale was used. The product moment correlation between the two ratings across 1385 respondents was .63 (p< .001).

Discriminant Validity of Face Validity

Comparison of tests' means: Dissimilar tests should be judged differently by raters as to the face validity for a particular purpose. If all tests, regardless of their type and nature, receive approximately the same face validity ratings, then face validity is a concept that does not possess discriminant power. Several designs could be employed here. The simplest would be to ask raters from K (random) samples to rate K different tests (each group rates one test) using identical measurement techniques. If the tests are detectably different from one another, then the differences will appear in a one-way analysis of variance. If, by another design, the same subjects rate all K tests, then an analysis of variance with repeated measures is needed. If instead the K tests are rank-ordered by every subject (the relative method), then a nonparametric analysis of variance is required. The third design was employed by Adams (1950). He processed the rankings from 39 raters using Mills' (1939) analysis of variance method. The results „showed the between (tests) variance greater than the within (tests) variance at a probability within the one percent level" (p. 324), and thus supported the discriminant validity of FV.

In the Haifa FV study we employed the second design, namely, an analysis of variance with six repeated measures (Harris, 1975). The six repeated measures were the face validity ratings given by 1385 examinees to the six tests of the Entrance Examination battery. The between-tests effect was highly significant ($F = 64.5$; $N = 1385$; $df = 54,6920$; $p < .001$), with means for face validity ratings of the six tests as follows: General knwledge, 3.19; Firgural Reasoning, 3.54; Mathematical Reasoning, 3.32; Vocabulary, 3.19; Verbal Reasoning, 3.62; English, 3.62. The standard deviations were all in the 1.05-1.15 range. The means are quite close to each other; but if we bear in mind these tests were similar to each other, all being group tests, composed of multiple-choice items, administered in a paper-and-pencil format, and assessing ordinary scholastic abilities of one kind or another, the above results can be considered encouraging.

Comparison of sample means: A high degree of similarity of means across samples of raters should be expected when the samples are randomly drawn from the same population. FV ratings should be stable in spite of minor changes in testing conditions or in the characteristics of the examinees taking the test. If FV measurement is intended to be useful, it must be insensitive to irrelevant factors. If, however, the samples differ significantly, a difference in their rating behavior should appear. Consider a simple example. Two groups of candidates are asked to rate FV of a mathematical mastery test as to its value for selection purposes. If the two groups are both random samples of the same population, we should get very similar results, even when these two groups are examined in different rooms by different examiners. On the other hand, if one group consists of candidates for an Engineering School and the other of candidates for a Law School, we should not expect identical results. This case of two samples and one test could be generalized, of course, to any number of samples and any number of tests. Absolute or relative techniques could both be used, even though the statistical tools for the analysis may differ.

Only one study was found where stability of results across two equivalent subsamples was investigated. Stable results were reported by Turner and Fiske (1968, p. 304) who employed a Process Interrogation Questionnaire to elicit information regarding the inner processes experienced by subjects who take a personality inventory. In our Haifa face validity study an additional sample of 165 people took the Entrance Examination and EFeQ 3 months after the main sample. Members of this sample were examined at different times of the day, in different rooms, and were supervised by different examiners. Nevertheless, their ratings were statistically no different from those of the main sample. On the other hand, a result of inconsistency across samples was found when the original 1385 persons were divided into 10 subsamples, according to their intended major field of study. A multivariate analysis of variance using the method described by Harris (1975) was performed on the data of all subsamples, with sex and age partialled out; the 10 profiles of the average face validity ratings of the six tests were found to be significantly different from each other ($F = 3.21$; $N = 1385$; $df = 54, 6992$; $p < .01$).

Conclusion

FV, as a measure of the quality of a test, can apparently be established statistically. People with similar backgrounds rate test FV similarly, and they rate the FV of different tests differently. These ratings are relatively insensitive to irrelevant effects, and they possess a reasonable degree of measurement reliability. Consequently, it is possible for any test constructor to measure the FV of his instrument and/or its constituent elements prior to finalizing the device. If the need for improvement of FV is indicated, appropriate action can be taken. When a test is published, it is neither facetious nor trivial to report routinely quantitative as well as qualitative evidence regarding the face validity of the test in the manual.

References

Adams, S. (1950). Does face validity exist? *Educational and Psychological Measurement, 10*, 320-328.

American Psychological Association. (1954). *Standards for educational and psychological tests.* Washington, DC: Author.

American Psychological Association. (1974). *Standards for educational and psychological tests (3rd ed.).* Washington, DC: Author.

Anastasi, A. (1954). *Psychological testing.* New York: Macmillan.

Anastasi, A. (1982). *Psychological testing (5th ed.).* New York: Macmillan.

27

Brown, F.G. (1983). *Principles of educational and psychological testing (3rd ed.)*. New York: Holt, Rinehart & Winston.

Carter, H.D. (1955). Importance and significance of objective test items. *California Journal of Educational Research, 6,* 61-71.

Cronbach, L.J. (1949). *Essentials of psychological testing.* New York: Harper & Row.

Cronbach, L.J. (1971). *Essentials of psychological testing (3rd ed.).* New York: Harper & Row.

Ebel, R.J. (1972) *Essentials of educational measurement.* Englewood Cliffs, NJ: Prentice-Hall.

English, H.B. & English, A.C. (1958). *Psychological and psychoanalytical terms.* New York: McKay.

Freeman, F.S. (1950). *Theory and practice of psychological testing.* New York: Holt, Rinehart & Winston.

Friedman, H.S. (1983). On shutting one's eyes to face validity. *Psychological Bulletin, 94,* 185-187.

Guttman, L. (1980). Integration of test design and analysis: Status in 1979. *New Directions for Testing and Measurement, 5,* 9398.

Gynther, M.D. (1979). Do face validity items have more predictive validity than subtle items? The case of the MMPI and Pd scale. *Journal of Consulting and Clinical Psychology, 47,* 295-300.

Harris, J.R. (1975). *A primer of multivariate statistics.* New York: Academic Press.

Holden, R.R. & Jackson, D.N. (1979). Item subtlety and face validity in personality assessment. *Journal of Consulting and Clinical Psychology, 47,* 459-468.

Mills, F.L. (1939). *Statistical methods.* New York: Holt, Rinehart & Winston.

Mosier, C.L. (1947). A critical examination of the concepts of face validity. *Educational and Psychological Measurement, 7,* 191-206.

Nevo, B., & Sfez, J. (1983). *Examinees' feedback questionnaire (Research Rep. No. 61).* Haifa: University of Haifa.

Response Analysis Corporation. (1978). *High school students review the S.A.T. and college admissions process.* Princeton, NJ: College Board.

Shye, S. (Ed.). (1978). *Theory construction and data analysis in the behavioral sciences* (A volume in honor of Louis Guttman). San Francisco: Jossey-Bass.

Smith, F.T. (1936). The relationship between objectivity and validity in the arrangement of items in rank order. *Journal of Applied Psychology, 20,* 154-160.

Spence, J.T. & Helmreich, R.L. (1983). Beyond face validity: A comment on Nicholls, Licht and Pearl. *Psychological Bulletin, 94,* 181-184.

Stetz, F.P. & Beck, M.D. (1979, April), *Comments from the classroom: Teachers' and students' opinions of achievement tests.* A paper presented at the annual meeting of the National Council on Measurement in Education. San Francisco.

Stevenson, D.K. (1981). Beyond faith and face validity. In A.S. Talner (Ed.), *Proceedings of the 1979 Teaching English as a Foreign Language Symposium.* Federal Republic of Germany, Munich.

Thorndike, R.L. & Hagen, E. (1961). *Measurement and evaluation in psychology and education (2nd ed.).* New York: Wiley.

Turner, C.B., & Fiske, D.W. (1968). Item quality and appropriateness of response processes. *Educational and Psychological Measurement, 28,* 297-315.

Turner, S.P. (1979). The concept of face validity. *Quality and Quantity, 13,* 85-90.

3

The Examinee
Feedback Group Interview

Baruch Nevo and Ofra Nevo

Abstract

The group interview is an important technique for studying examinee feedback. This chapter presents a guide for the use of the interviewer. The guide consists of recommendations concerning the necessary equipment and preparations for the interview, the opening announcement, interviewing skills, and the management and manner of terminating of the interview. Statistics based on 12 such group interviews are cited, and the potential of this technique is discussed.

Introduction

A structured questionnaire such as the EFeQ is only one of the techniques available to the researcher for obtaining information regarding the opinions, attitudes, and feelings of examinees in regard to a particular test. A number of other methods can be used as well, such as letters of evaluation from testers, individual interviews of examinees immediately following their completion of a test or sometime thereafter, and group interviews.

It was assumed that group interviews offer a useful complementary source of information to the EFeQ. While the group interview is of course less structured and quantifiable than a closed questionnaire, it has the advantage of being more dynamic, flexible and open - and is in a sense more "innovative" as well. The group interview allows for a free and spontaneous exchange of ideas, and also furnishes nonverbal information. Examinees usually participate willingly in sessions of this kind. Studies of productivity (Show, 1976) have indicated that groups usually produce more and better solutions to problems than do individuals, and are also more effective than individuals in tasks involving a variety of information. Therefore it is productive to try to enrich examinee feedback gathered through the EFeQ with that which is obtained through a group interview.

From the point of view of examinees, the group furnishes an occasion for sharing feelings and ideas, so that a sense of solidarity is created among people who have been exposed to the same "threatening" situation. One can derive a great deal of support and comfort from sharing the experience of the pressures of the test situation with other examinees. Frustrations are an unavoidable aspect of test taking, since tests by definition present difficulties for the majority of people.

During 1981, 1982, and 1983 we successfully experimented with several versions of the group interview. After we had selected the final version, an Interviewer's Guide was prepared in which the procedure for such a group interview was described in detail. The procedure is specifically intended for use in large-scale testing programs. However, with slight changes, this feedback group-interview can easily be adapted to other testing situations as well.

The Interviewer

A basic requirement for interviewers is that they should be familiar with all of the details of the examination. In principle, many examiners can also serve as interviewers. But a good examiner does not necessarily have the skills of a good interviewer. Good examiners have to be strict, maintain their distance from examinees, and prevent the flow of communication. A good interviewer, on the other hand, must behave in an almost diametrically opposed manner. Since the interviewer aims at facilitating communication in order to elicit the subjects' responses to the test, he should be warm, accepting, and genuinely concerned (Carkhuff, 1967). He must encourage the free expression of ideas and feelings, both negative and positive. The interviewer should not be defensive or critically evaluative; better results are achieved by a nonevaluative approach (Meadow, Parnes and Reese, 1959; Sappington and Farrar, 1982). This can be accomplished by following the suggestions of Dinkmeyer and Muro (1971) and of Ivey (1980). (See Interviewer's Guide below.) The training of interviewers should include the following elements: careful reading the "Interviewer's Guide"; observing two or three group interviews by an experienced interviewer; and, finally, conducting two or three sessions under supervision.

Interviewer's Guide

Equipment: tape recorder, name tags, light refreshments.

Preparations
a) Make certain that you know the location of the designated test room, whether it is suitable[1], and whether the examiner has been notified about the interview.
b) A few minutes before the examination is scheduled to end, enter the room and identify yourself to the examiner. Then wait, without interfering with the testing process, until the examination is concluded. Ask the examiner to introduce you, and wait until he/she leaves the room.

Opening Announcement

Take a position in front of the class and say: "The committee in charge of this testing project[2] wishes to learn about examinees' reactions to the test. We think that such feedback could be of great value in improving our tests. One good technique to achieve this goal is to have a group discussion. My task here today is to listen to your responses, ideas, and suggestions regarding the test you have just taken. I would like to ask some of you to volunteer to remain for the discussion. It will take about half an hour. We do not need everyone: 10 or 12 people will do.[3] Those who are willing to stay, please remain seated while the others leave."

---

1   An ideal room will seat 20-25 examinees, and allow for the possibility of rearranging the chairs in a circle.

2   Or other responsible group.

3   Optimal group size is 8-10 persons. A smaller number is acceptable. It is difficult to conduct a productive discussion in a group that exceeds 20 people.

Beginning of the Interview

a) With the help of the interviewees rearrange the seats to form a circle, so that all of the participants (including yourself) can face one another.
b) Distribute name tags and ask the participants to write their first names only on the tags.
c) Invite the participants to help themselves to the refreshments.
d) Now say:
"I would like to assure you that your participation in this discussion is not connected in any way to your test results. This is why I have asked you to write your first names only. Please feel free to say whatever is on your mind, whether it is complimentary or critical. As to the content of our group discussion, I would appreciate it if you openly expressed your attitudes, opinions and feelings about the test's format and content, the clarity of the instructions, the registration process, and so on. May I suggest that the meeting be informal. In other words there is no special procedure, and anyone can speak up at any time. I would like your permission to use this tape recorder. I do not want to trust my memory regarding all the details of our conversation. However, if there is any objection I will turn it off. O.K., let's begin now!"

Interviewing Techniques

As an interviewer you should employ the techniques described by Ivey (1980) and by Dinkmeyer and Muro (1971), namely:
a) Maintain direct eye contact with the interviewees.
b) Sit in a relaxed position that communicates attention and acceptance.
c) Follow the content suggested by examinees.
d) Ask open questions rather than closed ones.
e) Paraphrase the main themes raised by examinees in a way that reflects content and feeling.
f) Summarize the main points raised by one or, preferably more, of the interviewees. (Once a good summary is achieved, the group will move on to another topic.)
g) Make generalizations from one person's remarks in the hope that others will see the relevance of the discussion to their own ideas.

h) Emphasize similarities or differences in the responses of two or more
    interviewees. This will result in more involvement and particpation
    among the group.

The Interview

Normally, a group will furnish abundant information within 20 to 30
minutes of conversation, and with minimal intervention on your part.
You may however encounter some problematic groups in whose case, unwanted developments threaten to interfere with the interview. The following are the most frequent instances of this kind:
a) The group may spend too much time on only one small issue.
b) One or two participants may try to dominate the group, thereby pre-
    venting others from expressing their ideas.
c) The group may seem to be apathetic and to lack involvement. It is
    best to tackle the first two problems by employing a direct approach -
    that is, by openly stating what the source of the difficulty is. In situ-
    ations in which lack of interest appears to be the problem, you may
    try to stimulate the group with provocative questions, such as "Every-
    thing about this test was fine, wasn't it?" Or you may read out a list of
    possible topics for discussion (see next item).
d) It is recommended that you carry with you a list of topics which are
    considered to be important, and to merit being examined in group in-
    terviews. Such a list may include the following subjects: the registra-
    tion process, testing conditions, clarity of instructions, appeal of sub-
    tests, sources of anxiety, face validity, cultural characteristics of
    items and subtests, cheating. If the participants fail to respond to
    these themes, you may mention them again once or twice. But you
    should be careful not to impose your own preferences on the feed-
    back process.

Summing Up

It is your job to terminate the interview. Do so when you feel that the participants are tired, or when they begin to repeat themselves. Before send-

ing them away, it is a good policy to summarize what has been said in the meeting and, of course, to thank them for their cooperation.

Some Encouraging Statistics

Twelve interviews were conducted during 1982 and 1983. Each began after a routine request was put to the examinees to remain in the classroom after the test in order to take part in a group interview. An average of 70 percent of the examinees responded to the invitation, and the average number of participants per interview was 12.6. About one-third of those who took part in the interviews did not speak at all, but the remainder (about two thirds) contributed at least one comment each. In all twelve groups, it was the interviewer who terminated the meeting. No initiatives of this kind came from any of the other participants.

Examples

Examiners, designers of tests, and test users who participated in the interviews as observers or interviewers considered that the meetings were interesting and informative. A review of content of the interviews reveals great similarity to the feedback obtained from the questionnaire. However certain issues surfaced in the group context. Here are two examples:
a) In the interview people tended to be much more open about their anxieties and fears concerning the examination. Such openness usually develops in group interviews, once the interviewees discover that their emotions are not exceptional or abnormal. For many examinees it was of great value to learn that others, too, omitted items or were unable to finish the test on time.
b) Some of the participants commented in considerable detail about particular items. They recalled sentences, words and numbers, and also cited instances of what they believed were ambiguities and contradictions among the test items. In several cases these comments were useful in helping to revise the tests.

References

Carkhuff, R.R. (1964). Toward a comprehensive model of facilitative interpersonal processes. *Journal of Counselling Psychology, 14,* 67-72.

Dinkmeyer, D.C., & Muro, J.J. (1971). *Group counseling: Theory and practice.* Itaksa, IL: Peacock.

Ivey, A.E. (1980). *Counseling and psychotherapy: Skills, theories and practice.* Englewood Cliffs, N.J.: Prentice-Hall.

Meadow, A., Parnes, S.J., & Reese, H. (1959). Influence of brain-storming: Instructions and problem sequence on a creative problem solving test. *Journal of Applied Psychology, 43,* 413-416.

Sapington. A.A. & Farrar, W.E. (1982). Brain-storming vs. critical judgment in the generation of solutions which conform to certain reality constraints. *Journal of Creative Behavior, 16,* 68-73.

Show, M.E. (1976). *Group dynamics: The psychology of small group behavior* (2nd ed.). New York: McGraw-Hill.

Part 2:

The Educational System

4

Situational Bias, The Examinees' Perspective

Moshe Zeidner

"They said, 'We will call the maiden and ask her'."
Genesis 24:57

Abstract

The affective dispositions of middle-class (m.c.) and lower-class (l.c.) elementary school pupils were compared with respect to conventional psychometric tests. The frequently claimed relationship between test attitudes and test scores was also investigated.

Data was gathered on an incidental sample of 229 sixth graders of varying social backgrounds (m.c. = 101; l.c. = 128).

An inventory designed to gauge perceptions and attitudes towards conventional tests was given to a student sample soon after their experience with psychometric testing admiministered by test authorities under standardized conditions. Few meaningful group differences in affective reactions towards conventional tests were apparent, with m.c. and l.c. children largely alike in their perceptions and attitudes towards psychometric as well as school tests. Also, the correlations between verbal ability test scores and attitudinal measures for both m.c. and l.c. groups were largely negligible.

Hopefully, the present study will make a useful contribution to the test bias literature, since hardly any of the bias studies have examined the student's perception of the test under investigation.

Introduction

The charge that standardized psychometric test content and procedures are biased when applied to socioculturally different or disadvantaged subgroups in the population, is one of the most recurrent and dominant criticisms directed against the standardized testing enterprise. In fact, the issue of cultural bias in psychological testing, which has received considerable scientific as well as public scrutiny over the past 15 years, may be appropriately regarded as a proper subset of the test controversy domain (Jensen, 1980; Vernon, 1979).

A variety of different facets of test bias (e.g., content, situation, usage, etc.) have been differentiated in the literature (cf. Berk, 1982; Flaugher, 1978; Jensen, 1980; Sattler, 1982) and a wide variety of methods have proliferated for assessing the divergent types of test bias identified in the literature. It seems that research applying the various criteria of bias to available psychometric tests has flourished to such an extent that it is truly a feat for the interested student of bias to keep abreast of the deluge of publications on the topic.

An entire array of aversive factors in the test context, independent of the test content per se, are often said to act as intervening variables in differentially debilitating ways, thus biasing the test scores of socially disadvantaged groups. Numerous situational factors (e.g., time, test atmosphere, incentives, rapport, etc.) are claimed to interact with social group characteristics, thereby contaminating the test performance of disadvantaged groups, though largely irrelevant to the assessed trait or predicted criterion.

Unfavorable test attitudes as well as negative emotional reactions towards the test context have figured prominently in the literature among the claimed sources of situational bias (cf. Cole and Bruner, 1971; Eckberg, 1979; Evans, 1974; Epps, 1974; Feuerstein and Rand, 1979; Ginsburg, 1972; Samuda, 1975). Accordingly, it has been hypothesized that differential attitudes, perceptions, and motivations with respect to standardized test context as a function of social group membership, may serve as a major source of systematic error variance in assessing the parameters of between-group differences in psychometric test scores. Thus, it is argued that varying social groups may respond differently to the dimensions of the test context, attributing to them varying degrees of ecological significance and meaning. As Cole and Bruner (1971) have convincingly pointed out, while the test situation may indeed be held constant and be uniform from the perspective of the examiner, it may nonetheless be interpreted and responded to differently by examinees of different social groups. If indeed contextual features interact with social group characteristics in affecting the level of test performance, the practice of making inferences about the lower-class examinees' underlying cognitive competence from the level of test attainment in the conventional setting is suspect and perhaps unwarranted.

A review of the literature in search of the specific affective or motivating factors possibly summating to produce deficits for lower-class children reveals a bewildering array of specific factors hypothesized to be operative in the test context. Anastasi (1976), for example, suggests that the negative test attitudes attributed to lower class minority groups may reflect a lack of interest in the abstract test contents as well as expectancies of low achievement on the cognitive task, which in concert may result in lowered test performance.

Scarr (1981) has hypothesized that socially disadvantaged children may truly desire to perform maximally on psychometric tests and may indeed possess the necessary competence to succeed. However, disadvantaged examinees may be handicapped since they have not been trained to apply their cognitive skills to the maximum in an "artificial" test situation. Thus the interpretation of test scores for disadvantaged groups ought to be restricted to statements about their performance under specified test conditions. Hence, social group differences in the interpretative structuring of the test situation may moderate the relationship between cultural factors and testing ability.

Indeed, a positive attitudinal and motivational disposition towards the test context is often assumed to be a necessary although not sufficient-condition for positive test performance. Consequently, lower-class children who are said to be significantly less motivated on the average to perform well on standardized psychometric tests, will also be less likely to succeed in the conventional test taking situation. Thus, observed group differences in level of test performance, it is argued, may be partially attributed to between-group differences in test attitudes and degrees of test motivation (Barnes, 1972; Eells, 1951; Havighurst, 1970; Katz, 1967; Riessman, 1974; Samuda, 1975; Stahl, 1977). Among the most commonly mentioned intervening variables in the literature are the following: poor intrinsic interest in the task (e.g., Deutch et al., 1967; Eells et al., 1951), lack of meaningful contingent reinforcements (e.g., Havighurst, 1970; Riessman, 1974), poor self-esteem and low expectations of success (e.g., Samuda, 1975), and heightened degree of tension and test anxiety (e.g., Katz, 1967; Williams, 1972).

With respect to the Israeli research context, Feuerstein and Shalom (1967) have claimed that the relatively poor performance of lower-class oriental children on psychometric ability measures may reflect their negative affective dispositions towards the test and test situation no less than their cognitive ability. In their opinion, the assumed "neutral" examiner may actually be evaluated by the lower-class child as being cold and aloof. As a result, the socioculturally different examinee, in Israel, may show a total lack of interest in the task and react to the test context by withdrawing or expressing outright hostility.

In view of the commonly held assumption that differential attitudinal dispositions associated with social group membership contribute meaningfully to the explanation of between-group variance in psychometric test performance, the paucity of empirical research directly aimed at sociocultural group differentials in test attitudes and motivations is indeed regrettable. In addition, little research has been conducted on the relationship between test attitudes and the level of test performance.

It is important to bear in mind that the identification of affective dispositions towards psychometric test taking as potential sources of situational bias and possible situational determinants of between-group differences in test attainment rests on two major premises:[1]

1) meaningful sociocultural group differentials in test attitudes and motivations,
2) a meaningful association between test attitudes and level of test attainment.

In view of the serious research gaps in the situational bias literature, the primary objective of the present study is to test the validity, within the Israeli research scene, of the frequently cited assumption that the poor performance of lower-class children on standardized mental ability tests is due, in part, to affective dispositions towards the test taking situation, systematically disadvantageous to their test performance (cf. Cole & Bruner, 1971; Eells et al., 1951; Ginsburg, 1972; Labov, 1970; Severson, 1970; Riessman, 1974).

It is noteworthy that the issue of bias in the test situation has typically

---

1   Let A = Social group; B = test attitudes; C = level of test scores; R = relationship. The observed relationship between social group and test scores (ARC), attested by numerous studies, may be explicated by 2 intermediate generalizations, according to the situational bias hypothesis, namely: A (R')B and B(R")C.

been studied via two main research paradigms: (1) in situation systematic observation of the behavioral styles and motivational reactions of testees from varying social and ethnic groups during test taking (cf. Hertzig et al., 1968); (2) the experimental manipulation of various situation-specific variables (e.g., atmosphere, incentives, expectations etc.) in order to test for the magnitude of interaction between the situational parameters under consideration and sociocultural characteristics (e.g., cf. Schmeiser, 1982; Zeidner, 1983). To date, few studies have approached the issue of situational bias from a "phenomenological viewpoint", focusing on the degree of bias in the various dimensions of the test context as perceived from the examinees' perspective. Interestingly enough, while "judgmental" approaches to the study of bias in the test content per se have gained currency over the past decade and have often even become an integral part of the test preparation process (cf. Berk, 1982), the judgmental method has not faired as well in the study of "situational bias".

Thus, since hardly any of the test bias studies have examined the student's perception of the test situation under investigation, the present study hopes to make a useful contribution to the test bias literature by comparing the affective dispositions of middle-class and lower-class elementary school children towards psychometric tests and test situation following their experience with conventional psychometric measures. In addition, this study hopes to shed light on the commonly assumed covariation between test attitudes and test scores.

Methodology

Sample Characteristics:

Data was gathered on an incidental sample of 229 pupils drawn from eight 6th grade classes, comprising the entire 6th grade student population of four secular elementary schools in the Israeli northern school district. Included in the sample were all 6th grade students, within the respective schools, who were administered standardized psychometric ability tests by the Psychoeducational Testing Service during the academic year 1982. The schools were chosen to represent socioculturally divergent student populations for purposes of comparing the test attitudes of students of varying social backgrounds.

Independent Variable and Criterion Measures:

Social status, dichotomized as middle-class (=m.c.) and lower-class (=l.c.), served as the primary independent variable in partitioning attitudinal data and was gauged by two indicators considered jointly: (1) fathers' occupational status, and (2) fathers' educational level.[2]
The sample distribution by social class (m.c.=55%; l.c.=45%) allowed us to draw comparisons between the attitudinal dispositions of students of varying social background. The social class subgroups were each divided about evenly by sex. However, while the majority of lower-class students (about 3/4) were of oriental extraction, the majority of middle-class students (about 3/4) were of western background, thus reflecting the overlapping of social class and ethnicity in the Israeli population as a whole.
The attitudinal data were collected via a student feedback inventory including 2 main measures briefly delineated below:

A) Association group response test (cf. Szalay and Deese, 1978): The test format consisted of the stimulus object (="Psychometric Test")[3] printed on a sheet ten consecutive times, each followed by an underscored blank space. Subjects were instructed to write down all associations that came to mind upon perceiving the stimulus during a two-minute period.
On the basis of previous research (cf. Szalay and Deese, 1978) showing that earlier associative responses are usually more central to the subjective meanig of the stimulus than later ones, we decided to weight the associative responses in inverse relationship to their serial position on the format. Two types of quantitative indices were utilized to sum data:
a) response frequency, which designates the total number of times a particular association was offered by the group/subgroup as a whole;
b) response scores, designating the total weight for each response

---

2   M.c. students were defined as those whose father (or major breadwinner) was engaged in a "white-collar" occupation and had at least a high school education; l.c. students were defined as those whose father was engaged in a "blue-collar" vocation (or unemployed) and had less than 9 years of schooling.

3   The "Psychometric test" is technically referred to as "Psychotechnic test" in the Israeli context, and it was the latter concept which appeared throughout the inventory.

summed over the individual group members.

The associative data were organized by grouping responses according to common themes or aggregates of related responses referred to hereafter as "meaning components". The individual associations were categorized into predetermined meaning components by two independent coders who reached the level of 90% agreement.

B) Semantic Differential Rating Scale (cf. Osgood et al., 1957):

The instrument consisted of a series of 18 bipolar adjectives on a 7-point continuum against which students were required to make repeated judgement of the two stimulus objects, namely, "Psychometric test" and "Classroom test". Following a short practice session, the stimuli and bipolar adjectives were orally presented to the students in order to pace the subjects and assume scale comprehensibility. The instructions suggested by Osgood et al. (1957) for administering the scale were simplified and adopted to the age level of the subjects.

The specific scales chosen to represent the various semantic differential factors the measure aimed to evaluate (i.e., evaluation, potency, activity, subjective anxiety and comprehension), were selected on account of their seeming relevance to the judged concepts as well as evidence of their utility in past research (cf. Nunnally, 1978; Osgood et al., 1957).

While Osgood et al. (1957) have provided evidence in support of the reliability and validity of the semantic differential as a measure of group attitudes, the scale's validity may often vary as a function of the attitude object. However, examination of the inter-correlations among the items by stimulus and assessed dimension revealed moderate to high correlations for scales assessing a given dimension, thus lending support to the choice of items to represent the various dimensions or "factors" included in the present study.

In addition, students were asked to rate their overall expected level of performance on the psychometric test on a 10-step scale (from 1 = very low to 10 = very high).

Inventory Administration

The inventory was group administered during regular class hours by this investigator and one female research associate shortly after psychometric test administration. Students were told that the information collected would be used for research purposes only, and that their individual responses would be anonymous and would not be seen by school or test authorities. In addition, students were asked to complete a short personal inventory aimed at gathering demographic data (e.g., sex, father's occupation and level of education, ethnic origin, etc.) for purposes of data analysis.[4]

Verbal psychometric test scores were later kindly made available to us by school or testing authorities for research purposes.

Research Findings

The "Pychometric Test": Psychological Meaning Components

What are the major subjective components of meaning attributed by students of varying social group characteristics to the conventional psychometric examination? In order to arrive at a satisfactory reply to the question above, the associative responses elicited by students to the stimulus "psychometric test" were content analyzed in search of predominant themes and categorized into relevant semantic categories. The major meaning components derived will be described briefly below (see Table 1, for responses score distributions by social group):

1) Negative affect: includes aversive emotional reactions to the test situation such as "fear", "anxiety", "tension" and general states of arousal (e.g., "excitement");
2) school context: encompasses associations centering on specific school frameworks (e.g., "track", "lesson") as well as specific school subjects (e.g., "language", "math");
3) test format and material: includes associations dealing with item formats (e.g., "odd man out", "completion", "vocabulary") as well as

---

4   Only part of the attitudinal data gathered during the course of the research will be presented in this paper. The bulk of the findings appear in Zeidner (1983), upon which, in part, the present is based.

particular test modes (e.g., "figures", "verbal test") and accompanying test paraphernalia (e.g., "pen", "eraser", "test booklet");

4) achievement: centers on test outcomes or results (e.g., "grade", "success", "failure");

5) questions and answers: reference to what may very well be one of the major critical attributes of a test, namely, test "questions" or "problems" and test "responses" or "replies";

6) intellect: allusions to thought processes (e.g., "thinking", "understanding", "remembering") as well as to the construct or ability the test is assumed to assess (e.g., "IQ", "intelligence");

7) "time": includes all references to the tests' speeded administration (e.g., "time", "speed", "finishing on time");

8) test situation: includes characteristic features of the group testing situation and environment such as "sitting apart from other classmates", "lack of preparation for exam", "silence" as well as test-specific behavior such as "solving problem", "concentrating", etc;

9) test difficulty: contains associations characterizing the tests' perceived level of difficulty or facility (e.g., "easy", "difficult", "complex", etc.);

10) test attributes: reflect the positive features (e.g., "interesting", "important", "far-reaching") as well as negative features (e.g., "dumb", "odd", "waste of class time") attributed to the psychometric test;

11) test personal: includes all persons perceived to be involved in the test administration procedure in one way or another (e.g., "examiner", "psychologist", "school counsellor", "classroom teacher");

12) positive affect: expression of positive dispositions towards the psychometric test (e.g., "happy", "self-confident of success", "positive feeling");

13) miscellaneous: contains all residual responses not classifiable by the existing coding scheme.

Table 1

Subjective Meaning Components of the Psychometric Test – By Social Group

Social Class	Middle-Class (n = 127)		Lower Class (n = 102)		Total	
Meaning Component	Response %	Score	Response %	Score	Response %	Score
1. Negative affect	459	16	454	17	913	16
2. School context	487	16	377	14	864	16
3. Test Format & materials	358	12	376	14	734	14
4. Achievement	283	10	249	09	532	09
5. Questions & answers	126	04	389	14	515	09
6. Intellect/ Cognition	247	08	165	06	412	07
7. Time	193	07	181	06	374	06
8. Test situation	181	06	163	06	344	06
9. Difficulty	169	06	167	06	336	06
10. Attributions	193	07	70	03	263	05
11. Personnel	147	05	43	01	190	03
12. Positive affect	24	00	54	02	78	01
13. Miscellaneous	91	03	61	02	152	03
Total	2958	100	2749	100	5707	100

The component response score is obtained by summing over individual association response scores within given meaning category.

The most prominent single meaning component of the group as a whole centered on the negative emotional or affective dispositions towards psychometric tests, accounting for about 16% of the total response score. Similarly, the two most salient individual associative responses for the sample, namely, "fear" and "emotionally aroused" were contained in this category.

Moreover, the affective meaning component appears to be of comparable significance for middle-class (16% of response score) and lower-class (17% of response score) students. Thus, both social groups, in effect, show considerable preoccupation with the emotionally charged meanings and "negative affect" associated with conventional testing. Accordingly, within both middle and lower-class groups, "fear" and "emotional arousal" appeared among the three most salient individual associations elicited. In direct contrast, the "positive affect" component comprised only 1% of total response score for the group as a whole, and both social groups contained a negligible meaning category when compared with the "negative affect" component, which was tied more closely to the psychometric test.

An inspection of the distribution of meaning component response scores by social group (cf. Table 1) suggests that students of both social groups associate the psychometric test mainly with the following psychological components of meaning: negative affect, school context, test format and materials, achievement, intellect, time, test situation and difficulty. There also appears to be a reasonably high degree of similarity between the distributions of meaning component response scores for middle and lower-class groups which are also strongly correlated ($r_s = .67$).

In addition, there appears to be a great deal of overlap among the principal lexical responses elicited by middle-class and lower-class children to the stimulus "Psychometric test". In fact, 11 out of the 12 most salient responses elicited by middle-class and lower-class groups respectively (i.e., 92%) are common to both groups, namely: "fear", "emotional arousal", "examination", "pages", "time", "arithmetic", "thought", "difficulty", "success", "figures" and "questions". Given the assumption that the average rate at which groups process associations to a stimulus object may be taken as a gross index of concept meaningfulness for that group (cf. Szalay and Deese, 1978), it appears that the concept under consideration is almost equally meaningful for both social groups. While the lower-class subgroup (x = 8.55, S.D. = 2.17) elicited a greater number of associative responses, on the average, relative to the middle-class subgroup (x = 7.83, S.D. = 2.64), the differences were not shown to be statistically reliable. In summary, when comparing the single associative responses as well as relative meaning component response scores for middle-class and lower-class groups, we find a striking concurrence of response patterns for the two groups with relatively few major differences in qualitative responses or in their relative distributions. In fact, no meaningful differences between groups emerged for a number of critical dimensions where one would perhaps not be surprised to find group differences such as: affective reactions, perceived facility, time factor and achievement. Hence, it would be safe to say that middle-class and lower-class groups share common meaning components and seem to think alike with respect to most dimensions of their affective reactions towards conventional psychometric testing.

Semantic Profile of the "Psychometric Test"

In order to test for the significance of social group differences in perception of the stimulus "Psychometric Test" as gauged by the semantic-differential scale, a T_2-test[5] was carried out on the observed factor score centroids (cf. Tatsuoka, 1971). The multivariate analysis yielded nonsignificant results ($F=2.3$, d.f.$=5.223$, $p= .06$) at the $p= .05$ critical level, suggesting that m.c. and l.c. student groups are not significantly differentiable along the dimensions assessed by the semantic differential factor scores (see Table 2 for factor score means).

---

5   Hotelling's T_2 test yields identical results to that of a discriminant analysis suggested by Osgood et al. (1957) in analyzing group attitudinal differences in n-dimension space.

Table 2
Social Group in Differences in Perceiving the "Pschometric Test"
-Semantic Differences Mean Ratings, S.D.s and t-Values

Dimensions	Middle-Class			Lower-Class			
and Scales	N	x̄	S.D.	N	x̄	S.D.	t values
EVALUATION	127	5.53	.9	102	5.72	1.0	1.51
Pleasant-Unpleasant	126	5.52	1.7	101	5.69	1.6	2.00*
Pretty-Ugly	124	5.52	1.5	101	5.84	1.4	1.69
Good-Bad	126	5.68	1.3	98	6.13	1.2	2.69**
Fair-Unfair	124	5.84	1.7	101	5.58	2.1	-.99
Valuable-Worthless	124	6.14	1.4	101	5.97	1.8	-.77
Sweet-Sour	123	4.76	1.5	101	5.09	2.0	1.39
POTENCY	127	3.91	1.2	102	3.79	1.3	-.71
Strong-Weak	125	4.78	1.5	101	4.78	1.9	.00
Heavy-Light	124	2.94	1.6	98	2.71	1.6	-1.03
Hard-Soft	124	3.91	1.7	100	3.85	2.2	-.26
ACTIVITY	127	4.91	1.0	102	5.22	1.2	2.12*
Fast-Slow	126	4.97	1.7	99	5.55	1.8	2.50*
Hot-Cold	124	4.35	1.7	100	4.48	2.0	.54
Active-Passive	122	5.33	1.6	99	5.65	1.8	1.39
SUBJECTIVE ANXIETY	127	3.81	1.4	102	4.11	1.5	1.54
Tense-Relaxed	125	5.00	1.8	101	5.46	2.0	1.78
Fear evoking-Not fear evoking	127	3.50	2.1	101	3.79	2.2	.30
Threatening-Non-Threatening	125	2.93	1.9	101	3.11	2.1	.68
UNDERSTANDABILITY	127	4.79	1.1	102	4.85	1.3	.41
Easy-Difficult	126	5.10	1.5	99	5.03	1.7	-.34
Simple-Complex	126	3.32	2.1	100	3.75	2.3	1.50
Clear-Unclear	126	5.94	1.6	102	5.72	1.9	-1.01

When groups were contrasted on each of the five individual factor scores[6] i.e., *evaluation, potency, activity, subjective anxiety and understandability*) by way of univariate t-tests for independent groups, a significant group difference (p< .05) emerged on the activity factor alone, with l.c. students experiencing the psychometric test as slightly more active (x = 5.22) than m.c. students (x = 4.91). The social groups were particularly differentiated (p< .05) on the "fast-slow" scale, with l.c. children (x = 5.55) rating the psychometric test as faster than m.c. children (x = 4.97).
No reliable group differences were found along the remaining four dimensions. While groups did not differ significantly in their evaluative ratings of the present concepts, l.c. students did evidence a slightly more favorable disposition than m.c. students, viewing the psychometric test as both "good" (p< .01) and more "pleasant" (p< .05).
On the whole, the psychometric test was evaluated by students of both social groups in a relatively positive light, being perceived as quite "fair", "valuable", "good", "important" and "pretty".

Semantic Profile of the "Classroom Test"

o students of varying social backgrounds differ in their perception of the "classroom test" along the dimensions assessed by the semantic-differential scale? A multivariate test (Hotelling's T_2) testing for between social group differences on all 5 semantic-differential factor score means assessing the stimulus "classroom test" was found to be highly significant (F = 4.36, d.f. = 5.221; p < .001). Social class explained about 9% (g = .91; R_2 = .91; R^2 = .09) of the shared variance among the factor scores included in the analysis.

A post-hoc insection of the individual factor score means by social group revealed that the social groups were mainly differentaited along 3 major dimensions, namely: *evaluation* (p < .01), *potency* (p< .01) and *subjective anxiety* (p < .001) (see Table 3).

---

6   Semantic-differential factor scores are italicized whereas single scale scores are enclosed in quotation marks.

Table 3

Social Group Differences in Perceiving the "Classroom Test"
- Semantic Differential Mean Ratings, S.D.s and t-Values

Dimensions and Scales	Middle-Class			Lower-Class			t values
	N	x̄	S.D.	N	x̄	S.D.	
EVALUATION	126	5.07	1.02	101	5.57	1.1	3.28**
Pleasant-Unpleasant	126	4.48	2.1	101	5.53	1.8	3.27**
Pretty-Ugly	126	4.75	1.8	101	5.42	1.9	2.69**
Good-Bad	125	5.14	1.8	101	5.97	1.5	3.75***
Fair-Unfair	124	5.44	1.9	99	5.54	1.9	0.36
Valuable-Worthless	125	6.12	1.5	100	6.00	1.7	0.58
Sweet-Sour	125	4.50	1.7	100	5.22	1.9	2.90**
POTENCY	126	4.28	1.1	101	3.78	1.4	−2.90
Strong-Weak	124	5.12	1.6	98	5.04	1.9	− .34
Heavy-Light	124	3.84	1.8	99	3.03	1.9	−2.20
Hard-Soft	124	4.13	1.9	100	3.28	2.2	−3.08**
ACTIVITY	126	4.21	1.2	101	4.42	1.2	.84*
Fast-Slow	126	3.88	2.1	99	3.46	2.2	−1.49
Hot-Cold	124	4.22	1.7	101	4.26	2.1	.43
Active-Passive	122	5.18	1.8	100	5.73	1.8	2.27*
SUBJECTIVE ANXIETY	126	4.26	1.6	101	3.39	1.7	−3.98***
Tense-Relaxed	126	4.85	2.7	101	4.19	2.4	−2.18*
Fear evoking-Not fear evoking	125	3.97	2.2	101	3.20	2.2	−2.59*
Threatening-Non-Threatening	124	3.98	2.2	98	2.79	2.1	−4.11***
UNDERSTANDABILITY	126	4.29	1.3	101	4.54	1.4	1.40
Easy-Difficult	126	3.83	1.7	101	4.25	2.1	1.69
Simple-Complex	123	3.59	2.0	101	3.82	2.3	0.79
Clear-Unclear	124	5.44	1.8	98	5.59	1.9	0.61

54

Interestingly enough, the classroom test was viewed more favorably, on the average, by l.c. (x = 5.57) than m.c. ($\overline{x}$ = 5.29) students. An inspection of the individual evaluative scales revealed that 1.c. children perceived the classroom test as markedly more "pleasant" (p < .01), "pretty" (p < .01), "good" (p < .001) and "sweet" (p < .01), than their m.c. counterparts did. At the same time, however classroom tests were perceived as significantly less *potent* on the average (p < .01) by l.c. (x = 3.78) than by m.c. (x = 4.28) students, with social class explaining 3% of factor score variance. In addition, 1.c. children (x = 3.39) rated the classroom test significantly lower (p < .001), on the average, in terms of *subjective anxiety* relative to their m.c. counterparts (x = 4.26) with social class explaining 6% of factor score variance. In specific, 1.c. students perceived the test as significantly less "tense" (p < .05), "fear provoking" (p < .05) and "threatening" (p < .001) compared with m.c. students.

Comparison of Group Perceptions of "Psychometric" vs. "Classroom" Test

In order to test for and pinpoint possible differences in group perceptions of the "psychometric" versus "classroom" test as stimulus objects, the group ratings of the two concepts on the semantic differential factor scores as well as individual scales were treated as repeated measures and group differences assessed by means of t-tests for correlated group (see Table 4).

Table 4

Social Group Perceptions of "Psychometric" vs. "Classroom"
Test - Semantic Differential Mean Ratings Scales and t-Values[1]

Dimensions	Middle-Class			Lower-Class		
and Scales	Psycho-metric Test	School Test	t values	Psycho-metric Test	School Test	t values
EVALUATION	5.53	5.07	4.29**	5.72	5.57	1.50
Pleasant-Unpleasant	5.25	4.48	4.05***	5.69	5.33	1.90
Pretty-Ugly	5.52	4.75	4.21***	5.84	5.42	2.22*
Good-Bad	5.68	5.14	3.46**	6.13	5.97	0.56
Fair-Unfair	5.84	5.44	2.07*	5.58	5.54	0.27
Valuable-Worthless	6.14	6.12	-.14	5.97	6.00	-.18
Sweet-Sour						
POTENCY	3.91	4.28	−3.00***	3.79	3.78	0.05
Strong-Weak	4.78	5.12	2.16	4.78	5.04	0.69
Heavy-Light	2.94	3.58	−3.37**	2.71	3.03	−1.69
Hard-Soft	3.91	4.13	-.95	3.85	3.28	1.99*
ACTIVITY	4.91	4.42	3.98***	5.22	4.40	5.48***
Fast-Slow	4.97	3.88	4.63***	5.55	3.46	7.60***
Hot-Cold	4.35	4.22	-.55	4.48	4.26	1.06
Active-Passive	5.33	5.18	0.96	5.65	5.73	-.51
SUBJECTIVE ANXIETY	3.81	4.26	−2.81**	4.11	3.39	3.78**
Tense-Relaxed	5.00	4.85	-.82	5.46	4.19	5.00***
Fear evoking-Not fear evoking	3.50	3.97	−2.42	3.79	3.20	2.21*
Threatening-Non-Threatening	2.93	3.98	−4.85***	3.11	2.79	1.23
UNDERSTANDANDABILITY	4.79	4.29	3.69**	4.85	4.54	1.63
Easy-Difficult	5.10	3.83	7.17***	5.03	4.25	3.07**
Simple-Complex	3.32	3.59	−1.06	3.75	3.82	0.23
Clear-Unclear	5.94	5.44	2.43*	5.72	5.59	0.37

1) The scale value of 4.00 represents the scale midpoint. Scores above 4 indicate a tendency in the direction of the polarized adjective on the right; scores below 4 indicate a tendency in the direction of the polarized adjective on the left

* = p ‹ .05 ** = p ‹ .01 *** p ‹ .001

The psychometric test was, on the average, rated more positively on the *evaluation* dimension (p < .001) than the classroom test. In specific, the former test was viewed as significantly more "pleasant" (p < .001), "good" (p & .01) and even "pretty" (p < .01) than the latter. Curiously enough, although both tests were perceived as comparable in terms of "value", the psychometric test was viewed somewhat "fairer" than the classroom test. It is particularly instructive that both the psychometric (x = 6.06) and school test (x = 6.06) and school test (x = 6.07) were assigned relatively high mean scores on the "value" scale, suggesting that both tests were regarded by students as quite valuable or important.

In addition, a comparison of the mean *activity* factor scores for the two tests indicates that the psychometric test (x = 5.05) was viewed as significantly more *active* (p < .001) than the school test (x = 4.44). In particular, the "fast-slow" scale seemed to be mainly responsible for group differentiation, with the psychometric test (x = 5.22) being viewed as considerable "faster" (p < .001) on the average than the classroom test (x = 3.69). The preceding datum is not particularly surprising in view of the relatively speeded administration of the psychometric compared with the classroom test in general.

Also, the psychometric test (x = 4.82) was rated significantly higher (p < .001), on the average, than the classroom test (x = 4.42) on the *understandability* factor, being perceived as much "easier" (p < .001) and slightly "clearer" and less "complex".

Although the two respective tests did not differ significantly with respect to *subjective anxiety*, a comparison of the test ratings on individual scales revealed that while the classroom test was regarded as significantly (p < .05) more "threatening" (x = 3.46) than the psychometric test (x = 3.00), the latter was viewed as significantly more "tense" (x = 5.21 > x = 4.56; p < .01).

In addition, separate comparisons between the semantic profiles of the two tests were made by social group (see Table 4). In contrast to m.c. students who appear to evaluate the psychometric test more positively, on the average, than the classroom test, l.c. students appear to evaluate the

two tests in a homogeneous manner. Accordingly, m.c. children, in direct contrast to 1.c. children, accorded the psychometric test significantly higher ratings than the classroom test on the *evaluation* factor (x =
5.53 › x = 5.07; p ‹ .001), as reflected on the following four semantic differential scales: "pleasant" (p ‹ .001), "pretty" (p ‹ .001), "good" (p
‹ .01) and "fair" (p ‹ .05). Similarly, the linear distance Dij^2 [Σdij^2]$^{1/2}$ between the evaluative scale means for the two concepts under consideration was more than twice the size among m.c. children (Dij = 1.31) than
among 1.c. children (Dij = .59). It therefore appears that the two tests
are perceived as considerably more disparate and differentiated on the
evaluation scales by the former group.
Moreover, unlike their 1.c. counterparts, m.c. students viewed the classroom test as significantly (p ‹ .001) more potent than the psychometric
test (x = 4.28 › x = 3.91), appraising the former test as both "stronger" (p
‹ .01) as well as "heavier" (p ‹ .01) than the latter.
Furthermore, m.c. children rated the psychometric test as significantly
(p ‹ .001) more *understandable* than the school test (x = 4.79 › x = 4.29),
viewing the former as "clearer" (p ‹ .05) and particularly "easier" (p
‹ .001).
Whereas both m.c. and 1.c. children perceived the psychometric test as
significantly more active, on the average, than the school test, the magnitude of the differences appears to be slightly greater for the 1.c. group. In
fact, the linear distance between the tests on the *activity* loaded scales
was greater for 1.c. (Dij = 2.10) than for m.c. (Dij = 1.10) children.

It is particularly interesting to note that while m.c. students view the
school test as characterized by a higher average degree of *subjective
anxiety* relative to the psychometric test, the opposite pattern holds true
for 1.c. students. In other words, m.c. children rate the classroom test significantly higher on the average (p ‹ .01) than the psychometric test (x =
4.26 › x = 3.81) with respect to the *subjective anxiety* dimension, viewing
the former as significantly more "threatening" (p ‹ .001) and "fear-evoking" (p ‹ .01). In contradistinction, 1.c. children rated the psychometric
test significantly higher, on the average (p ‹ .001), on the *subjective
anxiety* factor (x = 4.11 › x = 3.39), viewing the former test as more
"tense" (p ‹ .001) and "fear-evoking" (p ‹ .01).

58

Self-Estimates of Performance

As may be recalled, students were asked to evaluate their overall level of psychometric test performance on a 10-point scale (1 = very low 10 = very high).

An analysis of variance of the anticipated level of performance with social class as an independent variable revealed that the mean differences between m.c. (x = 7.71) and l.c. (x = 7.90) pupils were not statistically reliable (F = 1.28, d.f. = 1.221., p > .05).

The Relationship between Test Attitudes and Test Scores

The multiple regression of psychometric test scores[7] on the five factor scores gauging the concept "Psychometric test" (as predictors) performed separately by social group, pointed to a low and statistically nonsignificant multiple correlation coefficient for both m.c. (R = .14) and l.c. (R = .36) groups.

In addition, when psychometric test scores were regressed on the semantic differential factor scores assessing the concept "school test" (as predictors), the multiple correlation was low and nonsignificant for the l.c. group. However, for the m.c. group, a significant multiple correlation of R = .34 was evidenced, indicating that about 12% of the ability test score variance may be accounted for by attitudes towards the "school test". In particular, the evaluative factor (F = 7.65, d.f. = 89, p < .001) appears to be the most prominent dimension contributing to the significant correlation.

The above datum suggests that among m.c. students the ability test performance may be more related to general attitudes towards the school context, including attitudes towards school tests, rather than to specific dispositions towards the given psychometric test.

It is noteworthy that while the correlation between the ability test scores and the estimated level of test performance was nonsignificant among l.c. students (r = .13), the two variables correlated slightly but signifi-

---

7   Only verbal test scores (=Milta Intelligence Scale) were included in this analysis, which was based on the available test scores of n=49 l.c. and n=94 m.c. students.

cantly among m.c. students ($r = .28$, $p < .05$). Thus, m.c. students may be somewhat more capable of objectively assessing their cognitive perform-ance than their l.c. counterparts.

Discussion

The affective dispositions of different social groups towards the stan-dardized psychometric test context were found, on the whole, to be highly comparable. Middle class and lower-class children were observed to be largely alike in their perceptions, attitudes and reported motiva-tions towards conventional psychometric testing, responding to measures gauging test attitudes much as if they were two random samples drawn from the same population. Our data, therefore, lend little support to the notion that poor test attitudes and motivational dispositions charac-terize the test orientation of lower-class children. Indeed, in a number of instances, lower-class students revealed slightly more favorable attitudes towards testing than middle-class groups.

In addition, our data provide little support for the commonly held belief that test attitudes and test scores covary; the data supported the contrary. Most of the observed correlations between the test attitudes and test scores were typically of unusually low magnitude and mainly statistically unreliable.

A number of methodological considerations ought to be kept in mind while evaluating the attitudinal data elicited during the present research.

First and foremost, a number of factors may be at play in limiting the generalizability of our findings.

For one, the student sample as an incidental one and may not have been representative of the target populations, namely middle-class and lower-class students respectively. Furthermore, due to the descriptive and ex-post-facto design employed, a number of situation specific parameters (tester, climate, etc.) may have varied from one test situation to the other, introducing considerable static and error variance in the data. Moreover, the particular test context may interact with the specific test-ing tradition or climate of the schools included in our survey of test atti-tudes. Evidently, additional research is in order to substantiate the exter-nal validity of our findings.

Secondly, in spite of the claimed virtues of the associative group tech-nique in providing richer and perhaps more penetrating data than conventional paper and pencil measures, the tool is known to suffer from inherently low reliability (Szalay and Deese, 1978). In addition, the inherent ambiguity of single associative responses and resultant difficulty in figuring out - with limited syntactical cues - what a given response means, makes the interpretation of associative data a delicate and most intricate task.

Notwithstanding the foregoing shortcomings, the associative group technique was employed, since it was thought to provide attitudinal data relatively untarnished by social desirability factors possibly invalidating more conventional scales. Also, students are not coerced in using specific dimensions provided by the researcher in their attitudinal response, but may instead use their own subjective criteria in assessing the stimulus object. This may explain why the associative data do not respond more closely to such traditional measures as the semantic-differential (cf. Szalay and Deese, 1978), as evidenced in our study. In a related manner, one of the main problems encountered in using the semantic differential in our present study was its apparent susceptibility to various response sets (e.g., social desirability, tendency towards extreme responses, acquiescence, etc.). For lower-class students in particular, the evaluative ratings of the stimuli tended to be directed upward, perhaps on account of the deep involvement and vested interests students had in the topic. If, as suspected, a meaningful proportion of response variance is due to social desirability factors, we may actually be detecting ideas and beliefs about what students of varying social groups perceive as socially acceptable rather than their actual affective dispositions towards psychometric (or school) tests.

However, even if one chooses to attribute the favorable test dispositions of lower-class groups evidenced in the present study to "social desirability" or other response sets, it is nevertheless informative and interesting to note thay they are fully aware of normative attitudes and school expectations with respect to standardized testing - and respond accordingly.

In addition, it is possible that group differences in test attitudes exist, but the instruments used herein were too crude and insensitive to detect subtle differences in group attitudes. Indeed, it may very well be that lower-class children are just as unmotivated to reliably respond to noncognitive scales as they are allegedly unmotivated in responding to the very cognitive measures the attitudinal scales are directed at. Thus the very scales utilized to tap differential attitudes may show differential validity for lower-class groups.

Obviously, additional work is called for in assessing test attitudes and motivational disposition pretested and validated in both middle and lower-class groups. Upon the availability of such scales, research could proceed to establish more accurate and reliable estimates of the proportion of test variance attributable to attitudinal factors. Furthermore, future research need not be confined to paper and pencil measures, but may preferably adopt a "multimethod approach", including observation of students during the testing process, in situation assessment of student affectivity and perceptions as well as in depth interviews of students upon completion of the testing session.

A number of research problems centering on group differences in test attitudes and dispositions deserve the attention of investigators. For instance: Are there social or ethnic group differences in the perceived facility, importance, interest and degree of enjoyability associated with varying test modes (e.g., verbal versus nonverbal) or item formats (e.g., analogy, completion, odd man out)? Are there group differentials in perception of varying dimensions of the test situation (e.g., examiner, climate, rapport)? What would students of differing social-cultural backgrounds like to see changed in the standardized test situation and for what reasons? And so on.

Overall, bearing the methodological limitations in mind, our findings are consistent with a number of studies reported in the literature indicating that minority or lower-class groups may be not less motivated or cooperative in taking standardized tests than majority or middle-class groups (cf. Brim et al., 1969; Jensen, 1980).

Interestingly enough, research among elementary schoolchildren in Israel suggests a tendency towards conformity with school norms and expectations among oriental subgroups even more so than among western groups (cf. Minkowitch et al., 1982); this conformity may generalize to positive attitudes towards the standardized test and test situation as well. In addition, the relatively tenuous relationship between test attitudes and test performance found in our research are analogous to the findings of the Minkowitch report (1982) revealing consistently low correlations between scholastic achievement and a variety of scholastic attitudes (e.g., academic self-image, perceived importance of success, etc.).

Conclusion

The many lines of evidence in the present research tend to converge towards the conclusion that the prevalent standardized psychometric tests used among elementary schoochildren, in Israel do not appear to be perceived as "biased" from the examinees' perspective, at least with respect to the dimensions explored in the framework of this study. Overall, our data do not lend support to the commonly held assumption of situational bias in conventional psychometric testing.

By and large, our findings are consistent with the bulk of published research suggesting that when specific tests are conducted to test the validity of the situational bias hypothesis (or most other types of bias for that matter), the results generally tend to be negative. It is truly instructive that the findings with respect to situational bias based on the examinees' viewpoint concur with the results of studies employing more conventional research strategies, thus lending additional support or "convergent validity", so to speak, to the observed data.

It is hoped that the present research has contributed to the understanding of some of the contextual and motivational factors underlying the academic test performance of students in general and of disadvantaged students in particular, casting doubt on one of the commonly claimed extrinsic sources of measurement error said to contribute to social group disparities in the mean level of test performance.

References

Anastasi, A. (1976). *Psychological Testing*. (4th ed.) New York: Mcmillan.

Barnes, E.T. (1972). Cultural Retardation or Shortcomings of Assessment Techniques. In: Jones, R.L. (Ed.) *Black Psychology*. New York: Harper & Row.

Berk, R.A. (Ed.) (1982). *Handbook of Methods for Detecting Test Bias*. Baltimore: John Hopkins Press.

Brim, O.G.M., Neulinger, J. & Glass, D.C. (1969). *American Beliefs and Attitudes Towards Intelligence*. New York: Russell Sage Foundation.

Cole, M. & Bruner, J.S. (1971). Cultural Differences and Inferences About Psychological Processes, *American Psychologist*, 26, 867-876.

Deutch, M. et al. (1967). Guidelines for Testing Minority Group Children. In: Passow, A.H. (Ed.), *Education of the Disadvantaged*. N.Y.: Holt, Rinehart Winston, Inc.

Eckberg, D.L. (1979). *Intelligence and Race: The Origins and Dimensions of the I.Q. Controversy*. Praeger Publishers.

Eells, K. et al. (1951). *Intelligence and Cultural Differences*. Chicago: University of Chicago Press.

Epps, E.G. (1974). Situational Effects in Testing. In: Miller, L.P. (Ed.), *The Testing of Black Students*. New York: Prentice-Hall.

Evans, R.A. (1974). Psychology's White Face. In: Gartner, A. et al. (Eds.) *The New Assault on Equality*. New York: Harper & Row.

Feuerstein R. & Shalom, H. (1967). Learning Potential Assessment of Culturally and Socially Disadvantaged Children, *Megamot*, 15, 174-187.

Feuerstein, R. et al. (1979). *The Dynamic Assessment of Retarded Performers*. Baltimore: University Park Press.

Flaugher, R.L. (1978). The Many Definitions of Test Bias, *American Psychologist*, 33, 671-679.

Ginsburg, H. (1972). *The Myth of the Deprived Child*. New York: Prentice-Hall.

Havighurst, R.J. (1970). Minority Subculture and the Law of Effect, *American Psychologist*, 25, 313-322.

Hertzig, M.E. et al. (1968). Ethnic Differences in the Responsiveness of Pre-School Children to Cognitive Demands, *Monographs of the Society for Research Child Development*, 33, pp. 117.

Jensen, A.R. (1980). *Bias in Mental Testing*. New York: Free Press.

Katz, I. (1967). The Socialization of Academic Motivation in Minority Group Children. In: Levine, D. (Ed.), *Nebraska Symposium on Motivation*, 133-192.

Labov, W. (1970). The Logic of Non-Standard English. In: Williams, F. (Ed.), *Language and Poverty* 153-187. Chicago: Markham Publ. Co.

Minkowitch, A. et al. (1982). *Success and Failure in Israeli Elementary Education*. New York: New-Brunswick.

Nunnally, J.C. (1978), *Psychometric Theory*. New York: McGraw-Hill.

Osgood, Ch.E. & Tannenbaum, P. (1957). *The Measurement of Meaning*. Chicago: University of Illinois Press.

Riessman, F. (1974). The Hidden IQ. In: Gartner et al. (Eds.),*The New Assault on Equality: IQ and Social Stratification*. New York: Harper & Row.

Samuda, R.J. (1975). *Psychological Testing of American Minorities*. New York: Harper & Row.

Sattler, J.M. (1982). *Assessment of Children's Intelligence and Special Abilities*. Boston: Allyn & Bacon, Inc.

Scarr, S. (1981). *Race, Social Class and Individual Differences in IQ*. New York: Lawrence Erlbaum Associates.

Schmeiser, C.B. (1982). Use of Experimental Design in Statical Item Bias Studies. In: Berk, R.A. (Ed.), *Handbook of Methods for Detecting Test Bias*. London: John Hopkins Press Ltd.

Severson, R.A. & Guest, K.E. (1970). Toward the Standardized Assesment of the Language of Disadvantaged Children. In: Williams, F. (Ed.), *Language and Poverty*. Chicago: Markham Publ. Co.

Stahl, A. (1977). Language and Thought of Culturally Deprived Children in Israel. *Otsar HaMorch*, (in Hebrew).

Szalay, L.B. & Deese, J. (1978). *Subjective Meaning and Culture: An Assessment through Word Association*. New York: Lawrence Erlbaum Associates.

Tatsuoka, M.M. (1971). *Multivariate Analysis: Techniques for Educational and Psychological Research*. New York: John Wiley & Sons.

Vernon, Ph.E. (1979). *Intelligence: Heredity and Environment*. San Francisco: W.J. Freeman & Co.

Williams, R.L. (1972). Abuses and Misuses in Testing Black Children. In: Jones, R.L. (Ed.), *Black Psychology*. New York: Harper & Row.

Zeidner, M. (1983). *Some Situational Determinants of Group Performance on Standardized Tests of Scholastic Ability*. Unpublished doctoral dissertation. Jerusalem: Hebrew University.

5

Essay Versus Multiple-Choice Type Classroom Exams: The Student's Perspective

Moshe Zeidner

Abstract

The major aim of the present research, based on two independent field studies, was to compare students' attitudes and dispositions towards teacher-made "essay" versus "multiple-choice" type exams. The primary study was conducted on a sample of 174 junior high school students, who were administered a test attitude inventory specifically designed to assess students' attitudes towards essay vs. multiple-choice type formats on a variety of critical dimensions (e.g., perceived difficulty, complexity, fairness, success expectancies, evoked anxiety, etc.). The study was partially replicated on a sample of 101 7th and 8th grade students, who were administered a modified version of the test attitude inventory used in the first study. Overall, the data from both studies were remarkably consistent, pointing to more favorable student attitudes towards multiple-choice compared to essay type formats on most dimensions assessed. The practical significance of the results for classroom test construction are discussed and some suggestions are made about potential future applications of test attitude inventories in the classroom setting.

Introduction

Planning and developing a classroom test typically entails, among other things, the specification of the particular format that the test exercises are to take. As classroom testing experts have pointed out (e.g., Gronlund, 1976; Thorndike & Hagen, 1969) the choice of a particular item format should normally be determined by theoretical and practical considerations such as the relative ease with which various test objectives are measured; the degree of difficulty in constructing or scoring items; freedom from irrelevant sources of variation in test results; the degree of precision required in reporting results, and so on.

The item formats used most often in the construction of classroom tests may be conveniently classified into two broad categories (Gronlund, 1976): (a) the more objective and structured "selection" type formats (e.g., multiple choice, true/false, matching, etc.), that require the examinee to select the correct answer among a number of given alternatives; (b) the more subjective "construction " type format (e.g., essay, short answer), that permits the examinee to organize, construct and present the answer in written form. Over the past three decades or so, the multiple-choice and essay type formats have become two of the most popular formats employed in the construction of classroom achievement tests (cf. Thorndike, 1982).

The diverse considerations delineated and discussed in the measurement literature for choosing one item format over another in planning a classroom test generally revolve around three major factors that are of concern to the test enterprise: (a) the subject-matter domain being assessed (e.g., adequacy and ease of measuring specific course objectives); (b) the test constructor or user (e.g., ease of test preparation, ease of scoring test, etc.); and (c) the test's reliability (e.g., freedom from extraneous influences such as guessing, copying, bluffing, etc.) and validity (e.g., adequacy of covering test content and behavioral objectives, etc.). However, one major factor which has been generally ignored by educational measurement specialists, and which probably should be given serious attention and due consideration when planning a classroom test is the perspective of the very student examinee who is taking the test.

Unfortunately, apart from a sprinkling of studies focusing on student's perceptions of various facets of the standardized psychometric ability test situation, (e.g., Zeidner, 1985; Zeidner, in press) very little is presently known about student attitudes, dispositions and preferences with respect to varying tests in particular (e.g., achievement, personality, etc.) in general or test formats (e.g., essay vs. multiple-choice). Which particular format do students perceive to be more convenient, interesting, motivating, anxiety evoking, eliciting greater success expectancies, and so on? These and other questions have not been sufficiently addressed in school based evaluation research, and classroom testing experts have generally payed little attention to the examinee's perspective - one of the most potentially useful sources of information about the subjective qualities of a test or its constituent components.

Given the assumption that (a) examinees who experience the test first hand are among the best sources of information about the subjective qualities of a test (or its constituent components), and (b) the examinee's test attitudes and dispositions should be taken into consideration by test constructors and users when deciding upon test construction and administration policy (Nevo, 1985; 1986; Zeidner, 1985; Zeidner, in press), it is truly surprising that so little research has been devoted to assessing examinees' attitudes toward varying facets of classroom testing. Furthermore, very little work has been devoted to the development and implementation of specific feedback systems designed to study examinee's reactions toward various facets of the classroom test.

In view of the gaps in classroom testing and evaluation literature, the major aim of the present study is twofold: (a) To compare and contrast systematically the preferences, attitudes and perceptions of student examinees with respect to two of the most popular test formats currently in use for constructing teacher made tests - namely, essay versus multiple-choice type formats; and (b) to delineate the construction, characteristics and potential use and application of a test attitude inventory specifically designed to gather data on examinee's attitudes toward various item formats. The research is based on two independent field studies conducted among junior high school student groups, with the second study designed to serve as a partial replication of the first.

Study 1

Method

Subjects

The sample consisted of 174 junior high school students drawn from two middle-class neighborhood schools situated in Northern Israel. The entire sample was distributed about equally by sex (males, 49%; females, 51%), but unevenly by grade level (7th grade, 33%; 8th grade, 51%; 9th grade, 16 %).

Instruments and Procedure

A test attitude inventory was specifically constructed and pretested for the purpose of gathering data on student's perceptions and attitudes toward varying test formats (i.e., multiple-choice versus essay type). Students were provided with several examples of essay and multiple-choice type items on the blackboard before responding to the attitude inventory. The inventory consisted of two main instruments briefly described below:

1) *Likert-type rating scale*, composed of 10 Likert-type items on a five point continuum. Examinees were asked to rate each stimuli (i.e., Multiple-Choice Type Classroom Test and Essay Type Classroom Test) separately along the following ten different dimensions: (a) perceived facility (5=very easy, 1=very difficult); (b) perceived complexity (5=not at all complex, 1=very complex); (c) perceived clarity (5=very clear, 1=very unclear); (d) perceived interest (5=very interesting, 1=not at all interesting); (e) judged trickiness (5=not at all tricky, 1=very tricky); (f) perceived fairness (5=very fair, 1=not at all fair); (g) perceived value (5=very valuable, 1=not at all valuable); (h) success expectancy (5=very high, 1=very low); (i) degree of anxiety evoked (5=minimal degree of anxiety evoked; 1=high degree of anxiety evoked); and (j) feeling at ease with format (5=feeling very much at ease, 1=feeling very ill at ease). The stimuli appeared on the inventory in counterbalanced order.

The alpha reliability estimates calculated separately for scale ratings of essay and multiple choice exams were about .85 in each case, which is considered to be quite satisfactory for group comparison purposes. Individual scales were linearly combined and averaged, using equal weights, to form a composite attitude scale, with higher scores indicating more favorable dispositions toward the test format under consideration.

2) *Relative ratings scales*. The second part of the inventory consisted of a series of relative rating scales, asking students directly to compare essay and multiple-choice exams along the following relevant dimensions, and to indicate their preference in each case: (a) relative ease of preparing for exam; (b) reflection of student's actual knowledge; (c) technical ease or convenience of usage ; (d) perceived expectancy of success; (e) perceived degree of fairness; (f) degree of anxiety evoked by particular test format;

and (g) overall preference for format. Also, students were asked to explain their choice in each case. The reasons given by students for their choices on each dimension were categorized into predetermined categories by two independent coders, who reached an agreement level of about 88 percent.

Students were told that school authorities were directing efforts at improving classroom testing and were therefore interested in student's reactions toward various aspects of the classroom test, including item formats. The inventory was administered with no set time limit, and responded to anonymously by students.

Results

Likert-type rating scales. Table 1 shows the sample means and standard deviations for the composite score and individual ratings of essay versus multiple-choice exams. On the whole, multiple-choice type exams (M= 3.48) were rated significantly higher on average than essay type exams, (M= 3.02) t(172)=8.55, p< .001. Furthermore, multiple-choice exams were judged more favorably than essay typ exams by males [(3.54> 3.42),t (87)=4.14, p< .0001] as well as females [3.42> 2.97), t(83)=5.16, p< .001].

72

Table 1

Attitude Scale Ratings of Essay vs. Multiple Choice Type Exams:
Means and Standard Deviations ($N = 174$)

Scale	Essay		Multiple Choice		t values
	M	SD	M	SD	
Difficulty	2.63	.85	3.37	1.02	7.09***
Complexity	2.39	1.00	2.97	1.19	5.03***
Clarity	3.47	.86	3.92	.85	5.27***
Interest	3.20	.99	3.62	.95	3.84***
Trickiness	3.07	.88	3.32	1.02	2.37***
Fairness	3.44	.95	3.87	.80	4.47***
Value	3.81	.90	3.62	.95	-2.20***
Success	2.86	.84	3.47	.98	5.93***
Anxiety	2.83	1.04	3.39	1.00	5.11***
At ease	2.30	.96	3.23	1.14	7.67***
Composite Scale	3.48	.65	3.02	.60	6.53***

Note: All scales appearing in Table 1 range from 1 to 5 and were scored so that higher scores are indicative of more favorable test attitudes than lower scores.

t tests for correlated measures were conducted with 173 degrees of freedom.
$*p < .05, **p < .01, ***p < .001$.

Consistently higher mean ratings were observed for the multiple-choice type exam for nine out of the ten individual scales appearing on the inventory. Specifically, the multiple-choice type format is viewed as being significantly "easier" than the essay type (3.37> 2.63), with about half (51%) of the students judging multiple-choice exams to be "very easy" or "easy", in contrast to only about 12% similarly perceiving the essay exam. Furthermore, the multiple-choice exam is judged to be "less complex" (2.97> 2.39) and "clearer" (3.92> 3.47) than the essay type exam.

Additionally, students tend to view the multiple-choice exam, in comparison to the essay exam, as relatively more "interesting" (3.62> 3.20), less "tricky" (3.32> 3.07), and "fairer" (3.87> 3.44). Inspection of the category response distribution for the foregoing scales shows that about 60% of the sample perceived multiple-choice exams to be "interesting" or "very interesting", in comparison to only about 39% who similarly perceived the essay exam. Moreover, whereas about 47% of the sample judged the multiple-choice type exam as being "not tricky" or "not at all tricky", only about 28% felt similarly about essay type items. Further, multiple-choice and essay type exams were viewed as "fair" or "very fair" by about 73% and 53% of the sample, respectively.

With respect to the assessed motivational variables, the multiple-choice exam was viewed, in comparison to the essay exam as eliciting higher "success expectancies" (3.47> 2.86) and to be less "anxiety evoking" (3.39> 2.83), and made respondents feel more "at ease" while taking the exam (3.23> 2.30). The scale response distributions show that about 53% of the sample expected to receive "high" or "very high" scores on multiple-choice type exams, compared to only about 19% for essay type exams. A meaningfully higher percentage of the sample (51%) reported that essay exams were "anxiety evoking" (or "very anxiety evoking"), as compared to only about 18% who felt the same about multiple-choice exams. Similarly, about twice the percentage of students (about 56%) reported feeling "ill at ease" with essay type formats as compared to students having the same attitude to multiple-choice type formats (about 25%).

Relative rating scales. As mentioned, students were also asked to compare directly and state their preference for one of the two item types with respect to a selected number of criteria, and to provide reasons for their choice in each case. The following are some of the salient results, organized according to the major criteria for comparison among the formats.

1) *Ease of preparation.* The majority of the sample (67%) found it easier to prepare for multiple-choice than for essay type exams, for two main reasons: (a) preparing for multiple-choice-exams normally requires less rote memorization of factual material than preparing for essay type exam ($f=45$); and (b) multiple-choice exams also typically require somewhat less time and effort for adequate preparation ($f=36$). The minority of students who found it easier to prepare for essay type exams believed that the latter (a) required a more superficial and less profound mastery of the subject matter than did multiple-choice exams ($f=18$); that (b) students can more easily identify the key topics likely to appear on essay exams ($f=5$); and that (c) as a last resort, students can try to bluff their way through an essay exam ($f=5$).

2) *Reflection of student's knowledge.* About 70% of the students in the sample believed that grades on essay exams were more reflective indicators of student's knowledge of the exam material compared to grades on multiple-choice type exams. The major reason offered was that essay exams provided students with the opportunity of accurately and optimally expressing their knowledge and ideas in writing ($f=105$). The remainder of the students believed that multiple-choice exam scores are a more sensitive index of knowledge, mainly because they normally cover a broader range of topics and sample a greater range of facts, concepts and principles than do essay exams ($f=18$).

3) *Convenience of format usage.* The majority (81%) of the students in the sample felt that the multiple-choice format is more convenient than the essay format, mainly because (a) there is no need to express answers in written form ($f=75$); (b) it is possible to guess the correct answer with some probability of success ($f=26$); and (c) a minimal amount of preparation is required for success ($f=12$). On the other hand, students who found the essay type format more convenient attributed this primarily to the possibility of freely and accurately expressing ideas in writing ($f=7$).

4) *Success expectancy.* About three-quarters of the students in the sample believed that students actually had a better chance of succeeding on multiple-choice than on essay type exams for the following reasons: (a) multiple-choice exams are as a rule relatively easier than essay type

exams ($f=79$); (b) the availability of options on multiple-choice type exams provide examinees with a sense of security and increased confidence while taking the test ($f=26$); (c) examinees can guess (or copy!) the correct answer ($f=13$); (d) multiple-choice exams preclude the possibility that examince's scores will be unfairly lowered by grader on account of student's spelling mistakes or poor writing ability ($f=6$); and (e) such exams require less preparation and effort in order to succeed ($f=3$). The remainder of the students, who believe that they have a higher probability of succeeding on essay type exams, attribute their expectancies mainly to the fact that (a) essay exams in principle allow students to give expression to a maximum degree of their knowledge of the topic ($f=26$); and (b) the tendency for the teacher's subjective grading of essay papers to work to the advantage of students, thereby increasing their grades and probability of success on the exams ($f=8$).

5) *Perceived fairness.* About half of the sample (51%), perceived essay type exams to be more fair than multiple-choice exams for two main reasons: (a) the nil probability of guessing the correct answer assures that the examinee's score reflects actual knowledge rather than pure luck or error ($f=25$); (b) students are offered the possibility of accurately expressing and elaborating ideas, thereby maximizing their chances for success ($f=17$). The remainder of the sample believe that multiple-choice type exams are fairer than essay type exams mainly because of (a) the partial information provided to students by the availability of options ($f=36$); and (b) freedom from having to construct and present the answer in written form ($f=12$).

6) *Degree of anxiety aroused.* The vast majority of the students (89%) reported that taking an essay type exam is more anxiety arousing than taking a multiple-choice type exam, for the following reasons: (a) the additional effort expended by students and emotional energy demanded of them in having to select, organize and express ideas in essay form ($f=52$); (b) the total absence of information or clues leading to the correct answer ($f=33$); (c) the marked degree of overlearning required to succeed on essay type exams ($f=27$); and (d) the relatively greater length and complexity of responses required in construction type items ($f=26$). The minority of the students, who report that multiple-choice type exams are relatively more anxiety arousing, attributed this mainly to (a) the difficulty and stress involved in choosing among given options ($f=10$); (b) the relatively large number of items that students normally have to respond

to on multiple-choice exams (f=6); and (c) the increased probability of error (f=4).

7) *Overall preference.* About three quarters of the sample (77%) reported a clear overall preference for multiple-choice over essay type exams for four main reasons: (a) the availability of options to choose from (f=66); (b) the convenient item format (f=62); (c) the freedom from having to organize and write the answer (f=12); and (d) the possibility of guessing or copying the correct answer (f=7). The minority (23%) of the students reported a preference for essay over multiple-choice type exams, and attributed their choice mainly to (a) the possibility of accurately communicating ideas in written form (f=19); (b) simplicity of the item format (f=10); and (c) the possibility of obtaining some credit for a partially correct response (f=2).

In sum, the data presented in Study 1 point to a more positive attitudinal disposition of students toward multiple-choice relative to essay type exams with respect to the majority of dimensions assessed.

Study 2

Method

Sample

The present study, designed as a partial replication of Study 1, was conducted on a sample of 101 7th and 8th grade students studying in two neighborhood schools (i.e., middle-class, n=62; lower-class, n=39) in Northern Israel. The sample was about evenly divided by sex (male, 47%; female, 53%) and grade level (7th grade, 54%; 8th grade, 46%).

Instruments and Procedure

1) *Semantic differential rating scale.* First, students were asked to evaluate multiple-choice versus essay type classroom exams along essentially the same ten dimensions used in Study 1 (see Methods section, Study 1). However, for convergent validity purposes, the items in the present study were presented in the format of a 7-step Semantic differential scale conti-

nuum (Osgood & Tannenbaum, 1957), anchored by the following adjective pairs: difficult/easy, complicated/simple, unclear/clear, boring/interesting; tricky/straightforward; unfair/fair; worthless/valuable; low expectancy of success/high expectancy of success; maximally anxiety arousing/minimally anxiety arousing;feeling uncomfortable with exam/feeling at ease with exam.

2) *Comparative rating scale.* Furthermore, as in Study 1, students were asked to compare and choose between essay and multiple-choice exam types with respect to the following seven criteria: (a) ease of exam preparation, (b) accuracy in reflecting student's knowledge, (c) convenience of usage, (d) success expectancies, (e) perceived fairness, (f) degree of anxiety aroused, and (g) overall preference. In contrast to Study 1, students were not required to explain their choice.

In addition, students filled out a personal data inventory and rated themselves with respect to scholastic achievement along a five-point scale (5=very much above average, 1=very much below average).

Results

Semantic differential scale ratings. Table 2 presents the means and standard deviations for the semantic differential scale ratings of essay versus multiple-choice type exams. Overall, the mean composite attitude score (average linear combination of semantic differential scale ratings) was significantly higher for multiple-choice than for essay type exams (5.44> 4.11), $t(99)=8.55$, $p< .001$. With respect to specific scales, as shown in Table 2, multiple-choice, relative to essay type exams, were viewed as significantly "easier" (5.70> 3.30), "less complicated" (4.48> 2.91), "clearer" (6.01> 4.94), "more interesting" (6.01> 5.01), less "tricky" (4.82> 4.00), "fairer" (5.79> 5.40), "eliciting higher success expectancies" (5.23> 3.35), "less anxiety arousing" (5.25> 2.78) and making students feel more "at ease" (5.28> 3.65) during the exam. Thus, with the exception of "perceived value", multiple-choice exam formats were evaluated more favorably than essay type exams on 9 out of the 10 scales included on the inventory.

78

Table 2

Attitude Scale Ratings of Essay vs. Multiple Choice Type Exams:
Means and Standard Deviations ($N = 101$)

Items	Open		Closed		
	M	SD	M	SD	t values
Difficulty	3.30	1.60	5.70	1.77	9.27***
Complexity	2.91	1.84	4.48	2.22	5.05***
Clarity	4.94	1.98	6.01	1.51	3.75***
Interest	5.01	1.95	6.01	1.76	3.90***
Trickiness	4.00	1.85	4.82	2.06	2.62*
Fairness	5.40	1.97	5.79	1.71	1.59
Value	5.73	1.79	5.82	1.70	.27
Success	3.35	1.74	5.23	1.70	8.36***
Anxiety	2.78	1.71	5.25	1.99	9.14***
At ease	3.65	2.19	5.28	1.93	5.45***
Composite Scale	5.44	1.07	4.11	.96	8.55***

Note: All scales (ranging from 1-7) appearing in Table 2 were scored so that higher scores are indicative of more favorable test attitudes than lower scores.

t tests for correlated measures were conducted with 100 degrees of freedom.
*$p < .05$, **$p < .01$, ***$p < .001$.

An Anova for the effects of sex, social background (disadvantaged vs. advantaged, as assessed by official criteria used by the Ministry of Education in classifying school populations) and the sex x social background interaction effect all prove to be nonsignificant. Thus, both disadvantaged [(5.64﹥ 3.94), t(38)=6.94, p﹤.001] and middle-class students [(5.32﹥ 4.21), t(59)=5.49, p﹤.0001] favored the multiple-choice over essay type exams. By the same token, both males [(5.31﹥ 4.15), t(43)=6.10 p﹤.001)] and females [(5.53﹥ 4.13), t(50)=5.81, p﹤.001] preferred the multiple-choice to the essay type exam. In addition, the ratings of students who perceived themselves to be above average and those who perceived themselves to be below average were virtually identical. Thus student's attitudes toward varying test formats are unaffected by gender, social background and perceived classroom achievement.

Direct Comparison of multiple-choice and essay exams. Multiple-choice type exams were judged by 80% of the respondents to be "easier" than essay type exams, and also believed to elicit higher success expectancies by about three-quarters of the sample as well. In addition, 83% of the students in the sample reported that multiple-choice type exams aroused less anxiety than essay type exams. About 83% of the respondents reported an overall preference for the multiple-choice type exam. However, the essay type exam was judged to be a more valid and suitable measure of subject matter content by the majority (66%), with a slight majority (56%) also viewing the essay type test as a slightly fairer measure as well.
In sum, the data this study attest to more favorable student attitudes toward the multiple-choice relative to essay type exams by most criteria under consideration, with the exception of perceived value, fairness, and validity in assessing student's knowledge.

General Discussion

Overall, the data presented for the two independent field studies constituting this research were highly consistent, with the various lines of evidence indicating that multiple-choice type exams are generally perceived more favorably than essay type items along most dimensions assessed. The observed preference for multiple-choice type exams is observed to hold true for students of differing gender and social background. In both studies, multiple-choice and essay formats were perceived to be most differentiated in favor of the multiple-choice test, along the dimensions of perceived difficulty, anxiety, success expectancy, complexity and feeling at ease with format. Also, in both studies the smallest differences between the formats were evidenced on the dimensions of trickiness, perceived interest, and perceived value. Furthermore, students perceived essay exams to be somewhat more valid than multiple-choice exams for the purpose of reflecting one's knowledge in the subject matter being tested.

From a methodological point of view, it should be kept in mind that the student samples were not drawn at random, and that the research was conducted among junior high school students only. It may very well be that different results would have been obtained for other age groups or students in different educational or cultural settings. Therefore future research is needed in order to extend the validity of the findings beyond the specific age groups studied and the specific educational and cultural setting in which this study is embedded.

Bearing the methodological caveats in mind, the data clearly indicate that students perceive multiple-choice items more favorably than essay type items. Curiously, over the past few years multiple-choice type tests have been the target of severe public and professional attack on various grounds (e.g., failure to measure higher cognitive or psychological processes, penalizing the creative examinee, placing too much emphasis on speed and rote memory, etc; cf. Allen & Yen, 1979). Indeed, the attitude and semantic profile of multiple-choice exams emerging from the examinee's perspective is largely at variance with the unfavorable and negative profile of multiple-choice exams often emerging from some of the anti-test literature.

From a practical point of view, teachers may profit from the routine administration of test-attitude inventories designed to gauge student's attitudes and dispositions toward varying facets of the classroom test (e.g., format, time limits, instruction, wording, etc.). Student's attitudes and opinions with respect to the classroom test should be given due consideration and weight, and should be taken into consideration by teachers during the initial test-planning and item-construction phase.

The use of test attitude inventories on a large-scale and routine basis in the classroom may serve to fill the needed gap for a judgmental approach to the face validity of classroom tests and their constituent components, providing teachers and educational researchers with useful information about key dimensions in the test situation from the examinee's point of view. Furthermore, information elicited via test attitude inventories might help teachers identify specific problem arcas of classroom testing and use this information for modifying or remedying certain testing conditions perceived to be problematic from the examinee's point of view. In sum, then, examinee feedback appears to be one of the most valuable yet neglected sources of information about the subjective qualities of a classroom test or its components.[1]

References

Allen, M. J. & Yen, W. M. (1979). *An introduction to measurement theory.* Monterey, CA: Brooks/Cole.

Grondlund, N. E. (1976). *Measurement and evaluation in teaching. (3rd Ed.).* New York: Macmillan.

Nevo, B. (1985). Face validity revisited. *Journal of Educational Measurement, 22,* 287-293.

Nevo, B. (1986, July). *The practical value of examinee's feedback questionnaires.* Paper presented at the 21st Congress of the International Association of Applied Psychology, Jerusalem, Israel.

Osgood, C. S. & Tannenbaum, P. (1957). *The measurement of meaning.* Urbana, IL: University of Illinois Press.

Thorndike, R.L. (1982). *Applied psychometrics.* Boston: Houghton Mifflin. Thorndike, R.L. & Hagen, E. (1969) (3rd Ed.). *Measurement and evaluation in psychology and education.* New York: John Wiley

Zeidner, M. (Chair). (1985, February). *Psychological testing: The examinee's perspective.* Symposium conducted at the annual meeting of the Israeli Psychological Association.

---

1   Requests for additional information should be sent to Moshe Zeidner, Ph.D., School of Education, University of Haifa, Mt. Carmel, 31999, Israel.

Zeidner, M. (in press). Situational bias: The examinee's perspective. In B. Nevo (Ed.). *Psychometric testing: the Examinee's perspective.* Toronto: Dr. C.J. Hogrefe.

Part 3:

University and College Admission Tests

6

The Practical and Theoretical Value of Examinee Feedback Questionnaires (EFcQ)

Baruch Nevo

Abstract

Test taking can be a meaningful experience for the examinee, and can often arouse very intense reactions. Experts in the field are in agreement that the feelings and attitudes of examinees toward tests have to be taken into account by test designers and users. However only very limited work has been done to date to develop feedback mechanisms for the systematic study of examinee reactions. The Examinee Feedback Questionnaire (EFeQ) described here, has been devised to fill the gap. The need for examinee feedback is considered in the first section of this article. The second section offers a historical review of the EFeQ. The third section describes the basic structure of the EFeQ. In the fourth section, ten examples of EFeQ items are presented; each of these consists of an actual item, the statistical data related to it, and a consideration of the implications of the data. The fifth section sets out information regarding reliability indices. In the last section some of the difficulties associated with the EFeQ are described, along with plans for its future application.

Introduction

The Need for an Examinee Feedback Mechanism[1]

Every day untold numbers of people throughout the world undergo psychological or educational testing of one type or another - students, job applicants, persons seeking for counseling, patients and so on. Being in a

---

1   This article is based on earlier studies by the author and his colleagues (Nevo 1985, 1986; Nevo & Sfez, 1985; Nevo & Jäger, 1986) and on new input from EFeQ reports at the National Institute for Testing and Evaluation (Lifshitz, 1986, 1987).

test situation arouses a variety of emotions, thoughts, and attitudes in examinees. Some of these can have a negative influence on test performance. In order to reduce these negative influences as to a minimum, experts in the field have recommended that those who design and administrate tests should take into account the nonpsychometric features of tests.

The value of learning about examinees' reactions has been recognized among testologists. Thus Moiser observed in 1947: "The term 'face validity' implies that a test which is to be used in a practical situation should, in addition to having pragmatic or statistical validity, appear practical, pertinent and related to the purpose of the test as well; i.e. it should not only be valid, but it should also appear valid." Eighteen years later, Fiske (1965) wrote: "... Such examinees' perceptions and reactions to tests are important insofar as they can affect responses to tests and thus contribute variance to scores. There appear to be few publications on subjects' perceptions and reactions to tests. Neither the immoderate critiques of testing written by laymen nor the moderate discussions by test experts offer systematic information on the topic" (p.287). The test users' guide of the American Psychological Association (1974) emphasizes the importance of a non-hostile environment, respect and politeness in the test situation (p.65). In their influential textbooks on psychological testing, Anastasi (1982) and Cronbach (1984) discuss the importance of the face validity of the test and of examiners' behavior.

These, as well as other authors, explicitly or implicitly assume that the conditions under which tests are administered, the behavior of the examiners, the face validity of the test, and the clarity of the test instructions are all nonpsychometric factors of major importance to testing. Moreover, it seems reasonable to expect that if test designers and administrators were able to take these factors into account, benefits would be reaped in a number of spheres, namely: (a) curtailment of measurement errors; (b) attraction of potential test users; (c) reduction of dissatisfaction and resentment on the part of examinees who perform poorly; and (d) improved public relations.

Tests are generally designed and adjusted on the basis of "hard" statistical data obtained from the analysis of the responses of examinees to test items, either taken alone or in relation to test takers' performance of measurable tasks. What we seek to show here is that there are additional methods of obtaining information for the purpose of improving tests. What is of concern to us in particular in this regard is the acquisition of feedback from the examinees themselves. Although such information is subjective, the examinee perspective of tests is both important and relevant, and can be used to improve tests and the testing process. It is the examinees alone who actually submit to test procedures. Only they experience tests in a personal and direct way. It is more than likely, therefore, that they should notice things which have escaped the attention of test designers and administrators.

We believe that the effort to develop examinee feedback mechanisms is justified on three grounds - moral, practical, and theoretical: examinees should be given the opportunity to express their reactions; it is useful to listen to what examinees have to say; and it is interesting to learn about examinees' reactions. Here we shall be dealing with the practical and theoretical aspects of the issue. It is important to stress, however, that any effort to investigate examinee feedback must be systematic, and should be undertaken in conjunction with methodologically sound techniques which have been determined in advance. In this article we are not concerned with spontaneous and randomly collected reports.

The Development of EFeQ

Although test experts would agree on the importance of knowing about the reactions of examinees to tests, relatively little work has been done so far to develop feedback systems for obtaining the responses of test takers (some exceptions are Fiske, 1967; Davis, 1987; Zeiner, 1988). The Examinee Feedback Questionnaire (EFeQ) described in the pages that follow is a device which was constructed in order to meet this need. This device was designed for a specific test battery - namely the Inter-University Psychometric Entrance Examination, which is one of two test-requirements for admission to all six universities in Israel (the other is the high school GPA which will not be discussed here). This college entrance examination is designed and administered by the National Institute for Testing and Evaluation (NITE), an organization established by Israeli universities for this specific purpose. The examination consists of a psychometric battery comprising five tests: General Knowledge, Figural Reasoning, Comprehension, Mathematical Reasoning, and English. All of the tests are of a multiple-choice type. The time allotted to the whole battery is about three and a half hours. The EFeQ is administered immediately following the conclusion of the psychometric battery to either a sample or all of the examinees.

The EFeQ was first administered by NITE to 1,800 examinees at the end of the first Inter-University Psychometric Entrance Test Examination in December 1983. Since then, different versions of the questionnaire have been administered to thousands of examinees, at various sessions of the psychometric examination. Currently it is routinely administered each time the college entrance exams are held which is six or seven times a year. Initially, those involved in working with the EFeQ were primarily motivated by ethical considerations; that is to say we were concerned with giving examinees a chance to express their feelings and attitudes about the test, and with sharing their test experiences with them. Gradually, however, the practical value of the questionnaire came to be recognized as an indirect means of monitoring the quality of an exam, the conditions under which it is given, and the procedures by which it is administered. The EFeQ became a major tool in our efforts to obtain a perceptive understanding of the observations and suggestions of examinees. This continues to be the function of the EFeQ as far as NITE is concerned, and is likely to remain so in the future. However, in addition to its practical utility, the EFeQ has the potential of becoming a rich source of information for researchers in the areas of social psychology, test anxiety, and cross-cultural psychology.

It should be noted that the Israeli questionnaire which we shall describe below does not have to be adhered to in its details, but is presented merely as a model or paradigm from which a great variety of examinee feedback questionnaires can be developed by testing organizations in other countries. EFeQ users are free to modify the questionnaire, say by adding or deleting items, as their specific needs may dictate. The version set out here should then be regarded as a suggestive framework rather than an established device, and readers are encouraged to design their own questionnaires.

The Instrument

Most versions of EFeQ consist of three sections:

Section A consists of two sets of questions which are fixed across all versions of the questionnaire - namely (1) a set of items concerning the examiners' behavior, and (2) a set of items inquiring about the test conditions.

Section B consists of items which are changed from time to time. Items in this section in any particular version of the EFeQ may be classified as pertaining to one of three categories, depending on whether they focus on (1) the test situation, (2) the test itself, or (3) the individual examinee. Items in the first category deal with topics such as clarity of test instructions, convenience in using the answer sheet, and the specific physical conditions under which the test is administered. Items in the second category are devoted to such issues as the face validity of the test i.e., its suitability as a selection device, the perceived cultural fairness of the test, the attractiveness of the test to examinees, the sufficiency of the time allotted to examinees to complete the test, and the subjective difficulty of the test. The third category of items is addressed to topics such as preparation for the test, self-assessment of success in test performance, emotional responses to the test, and previous experience with tests.

This last category is neither inclusive nor exclusive (some of the questions, together with our findings, are presented on pages 15-28). Section C consists of only one item that is an open question in which respondents are given about half a page to comment on any topic of their choosing concerning the test. The issue of the open question in this section of the questionnaire is treated in detail below, and which includes examples of some of the responses of examinees to this item.

Ordinarily, the EFeQ is administered anonymously in order to encourage examinees to answer freely and without fear that this might prejudice their psychometric test scores. However the disadvantage of this procedure is that it involves a loss of information concerning the relationship between the responses of examinees to the EFeQ and data bearing on the background of examinees and their performance on the psychometric test. From time to time, therefore, several hundred examinees are sampled and asked to write their names voluntarily on the questionnaire.

A typical EFeQ consists of 7-8 items. The time required to complete the questionnaire is 5-10 minutes. It should be noted that examinees are generally very receptive to the EFeQ, and most of them are cooperative in filling out the questionnaire. Normally, the response rate for each item of the EFeQ is 80% or higher.

Examples of EFeQ Items

Below, ten EFeQ items are presented, along with the statistical data that pertains to them. The items are quoted in their original phrasing. Translated into English from the Hebrew. Each item is followed by the relevant findings and conclusions. We have selected ten items from among a total of 52 that have appeared in EFeQs drawn up by NITE between 1985 and 1986. These were selected on the basis of their being representative of the great variety of items in the questionnaire.

Example No. 1: Physical Conditions

How do you rate the physical conditions in which the examination was conducted?

Choose a number 1 to 5 in accordance with the ratings defined below:

  5 Excellent

  4 Good

  3 Satisfactory

  2 Unsatisfactory

  1 Poor

☐	☐	☐	☐	☐
Seating	Temperature	Quiet	Lighting	Crowding

Findings:

Means and Standard Deviations for the Rating of Physical Conditions
(5 = Excellent conditions ‹----› Poor conditions = 1)

	No. respondents	Mean	SD
Seating	3,419	2.66	1.14
Temperature	3,339	3.73	0.94
Quiet	3,341	4.16	0.89
Lighting	3,333	4.24	0.80
Crowding	3,326	4.25	0.83

Conclusions

On the average the examinees would appear to have been satisfied with the test conditions. The one exception was seating, which were evidently, inadequate. To improve seating, the worst examination rooms in the country have to be identified by means of the EFeQ and new ones found to replace them.

Example No. 2: Behavior of Examiners

How do you rate the behavior of the examiners during the test?
Choose a number from 1 to 5 in accordance with the ratings defined below:

    5 Excellent

    4 Good

    3 Satisfactory

    2 Unsatisfactory

    1 Poor

☐	☐	☐	☐	☐
Familiarity with test instructions	Permitting questions from examinees	Attention given to requests of examinees	Strictness in enforcing silence	Silence maintained among examiners

Findings:

Means and Standard Deviations for Rating Behavior of Examiners
(5 = Excellent ‹ ..... › Poor = 1)

	No. respondents	Mean	SD
Permitting questions from examinees	3,272	4.29	0.81
Familiarity with test instructions	3,317	4.17	0.89
Attention given to the requests of examinees	3,295	4.35	0.77
Strictness in enforcing silence in the test room	3,348	4.35	0.83
Silence maintained among examiners	3,348	4.10	1.00

Conclusions

The overall rating given to examiners was good. The lowest mean was found for silence maintained among the examiners. This would seem to indicate that examiners have to be made aware of their failings in this regard and urged to improve their conduct accordingly. In any case, examiners whose total is found to be under a given cut-off score are not invited to return to work in that capacity.

Example No. 3: Time (a)

Which of the following tests, if any, did you fail to complete because of insufficient time? You may mark more than one item.

Findings:

Frequency and Reported Percentage of Failure to Complete Subtests

$(N = 2,305)$

Test	Number of respondents	Percentage respondents
General Knowledge	201	8.7
Figural Reasoning	886	38.4
Comprehension	530	23.0
Mathematical Reasoning	871	37.8
English	1,541	66.8

Conclusions

In a situation in which guessing is encouraged and examinees tend to mark all items on the answer sheet during the very last seconds of every subtest, an item of this sort is the only method by which we can learn about the time required to complete the test. The classic formulas, based on the number of items omitted, do not apply here. It is clear that the time allotted to the fifth test, English as a foreign language, was regarded by the examinees as being too short. A few extra minutes may improve the situation.

Example No. 4: Time (b)

How do you rate the amount of time alloted for each test?

Choose a number from 1 to 5 in accordance with the ratings defined below:

    5 Far too much time

    4 Too much time

    3 Sufficient time

    2 Too little time

    1 Far too little time

☐	☐	☐	☐
General Knowledge	Figural Reasoning	Comprehension	Mathematical Reasoning

☐	☐
English	Entire exam

Findings:

Means and Standard Deviations for Rating the Time Allotted for

Tests

(5 = Far too much time ‹----› Far too little time = 1)

	No. respondents	Mean	SD
General Knowledge	1,661	3.10	0.66
Figural Reasoning	1,658	2.49	0.70
Comprehension	1,647	2.61	0.68
Mathematical Reasoning	1,649	2.54	0.79
English	1,656	2.11	0.87
Entire battery	1,586	2.61	0.67

Conclusions

Here, too, although the findings were obtained from an examination which was different from that in which the preceding findings were derived, and although a different wording was used for this item than for the earlier one, the English test was once again found to be the most problematic as regards the time required for completion.

Example No. 5: Face validity of selection methods

Apart from the psychometric exam, there are other methods for selecting applicants for admission to university. For each method choose a number from 1 to 5 in accordance with the ratings defined below:

5   Very suitable

4   Suitable

3   Quite suitable

2   Unsuitable

1   Very unsuitable

□	□	□	□	□
Psychometric exam	Personal interview	Matriculation GPA	Achievement tests	Letters recommendation

□	□	□	□	□
High school GPA	Personality test	Graphology	Palmistry	Astrology

Much the same item appeared in three versions of the EFeQ (Dec. 1983, Dec. 1985). The last three methods (graphology, palmistry, and astrology) were included in the 1985 version only.

Findings:

Means for Ratings of Different Applicant Selection Methods

Selection Method / Year	Psycho-metric Test	Personal interview	Person-ality Test	Achieve-ment Test	Matric-ulation GPA	High School GPA	Letter of Recom-mendation	Graphology	Palmistry	Astrology
1983 (N = 1,096)	3.79	3.66	3.15	3.03	3.07	2.40	2.26	–	–	–
1984 (N = 475)	3.79	3.73	3.29	3.18	3.07	2.50	2.36	–	–	–
1985 (N = 1,764)	3.79	3.38	3.18	2.92	3.14	2.51	2.13	2.21	1.45	1.23

Conclusions

The rankings obtained for this item can serve as indices of face validity. The selection method which received the highest rating at all three successive years exam administrations was the psychometric examination (3.79). The personal interview ranked second on each occasion. The literature on personnel selection is highly critical of the personal interview, a circumstance of which examinees are obviously unaware. They seem to believe that personal contact is a necessary element in the selection process. The reason for this can be investigated further by adding another item to the EFeQ or by interviewing a sample of examinees. The findings in this regard may be of some interest to social psychologists, especially to those working in the field of attribution theory.

Example No. 6: Exam Preparation (two items)

How did you prepare for the psychometric tests? More than one answer may be given.

6   No preparation

5   By reading the information brochure

4   By solving sample questions and discussing them with friends

3   By reading books that prepare for the test

2   Received tutoring for the test

1   Other (specify) _____

What advice would you give a friend who is about to take a psychometric test? You may give more than one answer.

6   Not to prepare

5   To read the instruction brochure

4   To solve sample questions and discuss them with friends

3   To read books that prepare for the test

2   To receive tutoring for the test

1   Other (specify) _____

Findings:

Frequency of Methods of Test Preparation at Various Sessions During
1983-1984 (in percentage, to nearest whole number)*

	Average	5 Sept. '84	4 June '84	3 April '84	2 Feb. '84	1 Dec. '84
No preparation	14 4	16 4	17 5	20 7	9 4	10 1
Reading instruction brochure	35 28	39 30	37 28	29 23	29 21	40 36
Solving sample quest− ions & discussion with friends	10 14	10 13	10 14	7 11	8 12	14 19
Reading books	39 46	33 41	35 42	41 50	51 57	34 39
Tutoring	1 7	0 12	1 9	1 6	1 6	2 4

How did you prepare?
Advice to a friend

Conclusions

Speaking generally, the respondents would advise their friends to work harder when preparing for psychometric tests than they themselves had done. Fourteen percent of the respondents did not prepare for the test at all, but only 4% will advise their friends to do so. Only 1% received private tutoring prior to the test. However after completion of the test, 7% recommended that this should be done (a circumstance that creates other problems). The two methods preferred most by respondents were preparing from a book and reading the instruction brochure. This item will be reviewed every two or three years to determine if there is any change in examinee behavior in this regard, and what effect this might have on test

---

Example No. 7: Exam information

How did you first find out about the psychometric test?

1 Information brochure for applicants to the institute to which you applied or intend to apply (university registration guide)
2 Newspaper advertisement
3 Radio announcements
4 Wall poster
5 Friends or acquaintances
6 Other (specify) _____

Findings:

Sources of Information about the Existence of the Examination
(Percentage of those answering the question) $\underline{N}$ = 1,747

Source	Percentage of respondents
Information booklet of institution (university registration guide)	29.9
Newspaper advertisement	14.9
Radio announcement	0.7
Wall poster	0.9
Friends or acquaintancees	51.2
The university (by direct inquiry)	0.6
Israel Defence Forces bulletins	1.6
Prior knowledge	0.2
Total	100 %

Conclusions

The results indicate that NITE can abandon two of the most expensive methods of advertisement, namely radio announcements and wall posters, thereby saving itself considerable expense every year.

Example No. 8: Newspaper readership

Which daily newspaper do you usually read?

1 Ma'ariv

2 Yediot Aharonot

3 Ha'aretz

4 Davar

5 Hadashot

6 Other (specify) _____

7 I do not read any newspaper regularly

Findings:

Division of Newspaper Readers (Percentage of those who answered the question)

$N = 1,819$

Newspaper	Percentage of respondents
Ma'ariv	31.6
Yediot Aharanot	41.1
Ha'aretz	5.9
Hadashot	1.0
Davar	1.3
Jerusalem Post	0.9
Al Hamishmar	0.7
La'isha	0.1
Read more than one newspaper	7.9
I do not read any newspaper regularly	9.5
Total	100 %

Conclusions

Most examinees read Ma'ariv and Yediot Aharonot (72,7 % combined). By concentrating its advertisement on these newspapers, NITE can economize here as well.

Example No. 9: Guessing

There are two policies regarding guessing on tests. One is to encourage examinees to guess at the right answer, even if their guess is completely wild. The other is to discourage wild guessing by announcing and implementing a procedure of reducing test scores by a given amount for each wrong answer.

We are interested in knowing which of the two systems you prefer. Before indicating your preference, you ought to consider the fact that although the policy of encouraging guessing may enable you to achieve a higher score (since no deductions are made for wrong answers), the same rule applies to the other examinees as well, so that there is no guarantee that you will benefit by it. Try, therefore, to consider the other aspects of the issue.

Findings:

Psychometric EFeQ-April 1985 ($N = 2,141$)

1	I definitely prefer being encouraged to guess	28 %
2	I prefer being encouraged to guess.	26 %
3	I have no preference: both systems are equally acceptable to me.	27 %
4	I prefer that "blind" guessing be discouraged (by deducting points).	13 %
5	I definitely prefer that "wild" guessing be discouraged (by deducting points).	6 %
6	Total	100 % ($N = 2,141$)

Conclusions

Most of the respondents obviously preferred that guessing should be encouraged (54%) rather than discouraged (19%). Since psychometricians have been debating this issue for half a century without having been able to establish any clear statistical advantage to either of these approaches to scoring, we might do well to leave the decision to our examinees.

The Open Question

Every EFeQ contains an open question which is placed at the end of the questionnaire and takes the following form:

> We are interested in any remarks or suggestions you may have for improving registration procedures for the test, our information brochure; the exam itself and so on. In the space allotted below you may write about any aspect of the test that you feel requires improvement or, for that matter, that you regard as being praiseworthy.

The open question provides a wealth of feedback. Some examinees used the space provided in order to explain their answers to the preceding multiple-choice questions. Others made evaluative judgments about the exam which were either favorable ("This was a brilliant test"; "You, test people, ought to be praised for what you have done"), or unfavorable ("It was a frustrating experience"; The university should be ashamed of putting people through all of this"). Another group of respondents raised a number of issues that had not been anticipated by EFeQ designers.

The issues raised most frequently in reply to the open question were as follows: criticism of the seating arrangements which (confirming the data obtained from answers to the closed questions); requests for a recess between parts of the examination; opinions and suggestions concerning registration procedures; and general opinions, most of them favorable, concerning test battery and the related procedures.

In principle there is no reason that data obtained from the open question shoud not be amenable to quantitative analysis. On the other hand, since the main part of the EFeQ is handled quantitatively, we might do well to leave some room for subjective and interpretative processes to come into play.

Reliability Indices

It is important to establish the reliability of EFeQ, since one of its purposes is to serve as a bridge between the reactions of examinees to the test and the practical procedures implemented by the questionnaires users. The EFeQ consists of a set of items, each dealing with a different topic. Therefore its reliability cannot be measured by the customary procedures but requires a somewhat different approach.

The results concerning reliability which are presented below are based on a sample of 1,385 examinees tested in 1982 who responded to a specific pilot EFeQ (Nevo & Sfez, 1985, 1986; Nevo, 1986). Three measures of reliability were used:

a) *Correlation between examinees' rankings for two similar items:*
In 1982, the rating of the face validity of the battery generally appeared twice in the EFeQ, in somewhat different wording and contexts, at the beginning and end of the questionnaire. The correlations between the two ratings across 1,385 respondents was .65.

b) *Comparison of data from the open question and from the multiple-choice section:*
The open question provided an opportunity for checking intra-individual consistency in still another way. Two hundred questionnaires were sampled at random, and responses to the open question were then examined for each of them. In 125 cases the responses were directly related to various items in the multiple-choice section of the questionnaire. An independent evaluator compared each of these statements with the responses to the relevant multiple-choice item. A score of (+) was given if the two corresponded, of (-) if they were not in agreement, and of (0) in cases of uncertainty. Out of the total of 125, a score of (+) was given to 79 pairs; a score of (0) to 32 pairs; and only 9 pairs were marked as inconsistant (-).

c) *Test-retest reliability:*
Three weeks following the examination, letters were sent to 100 examinees who had filled in the EFeQ immediately after the examination. In these letters, the examinees were asked to respond once

again to the same questionnaire. Only 54 examinees replied. Stability (test-retest) correlations were calculated for all items. The lowest was .46, the highest was .88, and the median was .72.

Effects of the Actual Test Experience on the Ratings

In 1982 a small sample of 154 subjects was given the EFeQ before they had actually taken the entrance examination. They filled out the questionnaire while sitting in the examination rooms waiting for the examination. Like most candidates, the respondents in this sample had become acquainted with the entrance examination through special introductory brochures which were sent to them several weeks in advance of the test, and which described the test and contained a number of sample items. This sample, albeit small, appeared to be representative of a substantial population that had information about a specific test without actually having taken it.

The comparison of the "before" sample with the principal "after" sample revealed interesting differences that possibly resulted from the test-taking experience. For instance, the average rating for "Preparation for the entrance examination" dropped from 2.13 before the test to 1.65 after the test. This represented a drop of half a standard deviation - a result which would indicate that many examinees realized only after having taken the test that their preparation was inadequate. The face validity average for the battery as a whole fell from 3.74 to 3.43 (about one-third of a standard deviation), as a result of the test-taking experience. A similar decrease was observed as regards the "attractiveness" of all tests. The scale of these changes is certainly sufficient cause for concern, although the reasons for them is as yet unclear. Many other statistically significant changes were observed as well, but of a smaller magnitude.

Discussion

Since the first year of its application in 1983, the EFeQ has contributed substantially to improving our understanding of examinee attitude regarding the Inter-University Examination. Some of the more important findings were considered in the foregoing. A few of these have already led to concrete changes in the administrations of future tests, and some have stimulated new research; others are still under consideration. Since the ratings of EFeQ items have no "natural" or "absolute" anchors, part of the questionnaire's value depends on the possibility of carrying out meaningful comparisons. It is, therefore recommended, that a continuous rather than "one-shot" design should be employed wherever possible. The cost of undertaking an EFeQ survey for a particular examining institution need not be excessive. As we have noted, examinees tend to be very receptive to the EFeQ. Most of them are cooperative, and regard it as a token of the goodwill of those responsible for the examination program. Whether the outcome justifies the investment is a question which can only be answered by the users themselves. With appropriate changes, similar questionnaires could be used to gauge the responses of examinees to almost any kind of test.

Since the EFeQ is subjective by its very nature, we must ask ourselves whether the questionnaire might not be a biased source of information. If examinees think that they might be able to raise their psychometric scores factitiously by responding to the EFeQ in a manner which they believe corresponds to the desires of the examiner, this could be a serious biasing factor. Therefore the probability of obtaining sincere answers from respondent is greatly increased if the questionnaire is administered anonymously. Even then, the EFeQ cannot be regarded as entirely bias-free. So, for example, examinees who are angry because they feel that they did not perform well on the test, may wish to punish the system by assigning low ratings to EFeQ items and being critical of the test. However we have nothing to lose in such cases if we accept the feedback as is, since it may nevertheless indicate that more effort has to be made by the examining body.

More often than not, the complaints of the examinees cannot be dealt with in any practical way. But even when the criticism of examinees turns out to be unjustified, the very fact of their having been invited to express their opinion can help to assuage their ill feelings over what may appear to them as unfair treatment - if only for the reason that they have been given the sense that someone cares and is prepared to listen to them. This not only applies to university entrance examinations, but also to the ordinary run of tests which are given at school and university, and to professional and vocational proficiency tests. In all these cases, feedback questionnaires can serve to reduce postexamination stress, in addition to fulfilling their primary task of helping test designers to improve tests as well as testing procedures.

It is recommended that all test designers should employ the EFeQ developing their own tests, and that reports of examinees' reactions should be included in the test manual. We recommend, as well, that all test users employ the EFeQ and take its findings into account in their decisions concerning the continuation of a testing program. Guidelines for the development of the EFeQ are provided in Appendix A.

References

American Psychological Association, (1974) *Standards for Educational and Psychological Tests.* Washington, DC:

Anastasi, A. (1982). *Psychological testing (5th ed.)* New York: MacMillan.

Cronbach, L.J. (1984). *Essentials of psychological testing (4th ed.).* New York: Harper Institute.

Davis, R. (1987, June). *When applicants rate the examinations: Feedback from 2,000 people.* Paper presented at the 10th Conference of International Personnel Management Associations, San Francisco.

Fiske, D.W. (1967). The subjects react to tests. *American Psychologist, 22,*287-296.

Lifshitz, H. (1987). *Reports of EFeQ Findings* (Report Nos. 36, 40, 41). Jerusalem: National Institute for Testing and Evaluation.

Mosier, C.I. (1947). A critical examination of the concepts of face validity. *Educational and Psychological Measurement, 7,* 191-206.

Nevo, B. (1985). Face validity revisited. *Journal of Educational Measurement, 22,* 287-293.

Nevo, B. (1986, July). *The practical value of Examinees Feedback Questionnaires.* Paper presented at the International Congress of Applied Psychology, Jerusalem.

Nevo, B., & Jäger, R. (Eds.). (1986). *Psychological testing: The examinee perspective.* Toronto: Hogrefe.

Nevo, B., & Sfez, J. (1985). Examinees' Feedback Questionnaires. *Assessment and Evaluation in Higher Education, 10,* 235-243.

Zeidner, M. (in press). Sociocultural differences in examinees' attitudes towards scholastic ability exams. *Journal of Educational Measurement.*

Appendix A:

Guidelines for the Development and Application of Examinee Feedback Questionnaires

This appendix is in the form of a manual intended for the development, administration, analysis and application of the EFeQ by interested organizations. The term "interested organization" is used here to refer to any institution (or even individual) that is involved in a large-scale testing program and has undertaken to learn systematically about the reactions of examinees to the tests being administered under that program. The following are the steps required in carrying out such an enterprise:

1. A Survey of the Literature
   A review should be carried of articles and reports dealing with examinees' attitudes toward tests; public attitudes toward tests; existing feedback devices; examinees' self-reports of behavior before, during and after tests.

2. Determining the Feedback Needs of the Organization
   The major issues of concern can be defined by means of interviews with organization officials and test takers, and by an analysis of newspaper articles, and radio and TV interviews. The topics covered in the EFeQ can be subsumed under three broad issues to which the self-report of examinees would be addressed: (a) the behaviors, attitudes, and feelings of respondents to (b) the test, tester, and test situation in (c) the time before, during, and after the test.

3. Designing a Number of Examinee Feedback Questionnaires
   On completion of stages 1 and 2, several versions of the EFeQ should

be prepared. Each version would consist of 10-15 questions, most of them multiple choice. No version of the questionnaire should take more than 10 minutes to fill out.

4. Administering the EFeQ

Samples of examinees should be defined in accordance with the priorities of the testing organization. The EFeQ should be administered to the respondents immediately after they have completed the test (this will add 10-15 minutes to the testing procedure).

5. Data Analysis

The data collected in stage 4 is quantitatively analyzed and the application of the results are then considered.

6. Evaluation and Reformulation

The project is evaluated and decisions are made regarding its future course. If necessary, some of the items, and possibly all of them, will need to be reformulated.

7

Supporting Peak Performance
Standardizing and Humanizing the Testing Environment[1]

Educational Testing Service

Abstract

Educational Testing Service (ETS) is committed to creating optimum test-taking conditions that will not only insure score validity but give each examinee the opportunity to do his or her best work. While this means „standardizing" test administration, it also means tempering a stressful environment by helping test supervisors become more sensitive to the pressures felt by examinees. Supervisors and staff play a key role in both standardizing and „humanizing" the test-taking environment. ETS selects qualified supervisors, then provides them with training through several different media. Feedback about the quality of the test experience is solicited from a number of sources, including a test-taker's questionnaire, a supervisor's comment sheet, and discrepancy reports.

Introduction

ETS has been called „the testing giant," and with good reason: In 1987, for example, ETS administered tests to 4.1 million examinees in more than 43,000 testing sessions at 10,000 sites in 170 countries and territories around the world. The sheer volume of work is staggering.

But in addition to being known for the number of tests given, ETS also has gained a reputation for its parallel commitment to the quality of the testing experience: that each and every test, no matter where it is given, be administered fairly, objectively, and efficiently in a convenient, com-

---

1   This chapter was written by several E.T.S. staff members headed by R. Noeth.

fortable, and distraction-free environment. ETS invests considerable time and energy making sure that in every test center examinees are afforded the same opportunities to do their best work and are treated with the same respect.

A Commitment to Quality and Fairness

ETS's commitment to a positive testing environment is an integral part of the ETS Standard for Quality and Fairness, a 30-page document of principles, policies and procedures developed by the ETS Board of Trustees in 1981. That charter commits ETS to „high standards of quality and fairness in constructing, administering, reporting, and evaluating"[2] tests. These comprehensive guidelines are at the forefront of the testing and measurement field, reflecting joint American Educational Research Association, American Psychological Association, and National Council on Measurement in Education standards as well as principles enumerated in the Code of Fair Testing Practices in Education, recently adopted by ETS and five major testing companies in the United States.[3]

The Standards are not high-minded declarations of purpose that are ignored in daily life; they are a concrete set of guidelines against which ETS regularly measures itself. A Visiting Committee (composed of distinguished educational leaders, experts in testing, and representatives of organizations that have been critical of ETS) annually reviews ETS's adherence to the Standards. In addition, adherence to the standards is regularly assessed through a rigorous carefully-structured audit program and subsequent management review.

Creating the Optimum Testing Environment

According to the Standards, ETS must establish „standard processes for test administration that minimize variations in test performance due to circumstances or conditions not relevant to the attributes being

---

2   Educational Testing Service, ETS Standards for Quality and Fairness. Princeton, N.J. 1981, 1987 (revised).

3   Those testing companies are: American College Testing Program, The College Board, CTB/McGraw-Hill, Educational Testing Service, The Psychological Corporation, and Riverside Publishing Company.

measured."[4] Put another way, ETS is expected to provide a „standardized" testing environment free of distractions and unnecessary stress. Over the years, ETS has developed a series of policies and procedures, carried out by testing staff, that help create that optimum testing environment.

The Supervisor's Role

The 60-80,000 test supervisors, associate supervisors and proctors who administer ETS tests are central to assuring the establishment of the „optimum testing environment." Without their cooperation and commitment, ETS's guidelines for test administration would be mere words on paper.

The testing staff's responsibilities begin with seemingly routine chores that are, in actuality, the first critical steps towards assuring ETS's ultimate goal of *guaranteeing score validity*. Supervisors are expected to select appropriate support staff and find comfortable testing sites that feature good lighting and ventilation, ample writing surfaces, and a minimum of outside noise. Supervisors are charged with securing testing materials throughout the test administration process. Directional signs are to be posted for easy location of the testing site. The entire testing team must be familiar with standardized procedures.

On test day, admission documents and accompanying forms of identification are scrutinized before examinees are admitted for testing; examinees are then seated randomly in well-separated rows. Once the room is secure, supervisors read a carefully prepared script (written by ETS and found in the *Supervisor's Manual* that is provided for each testing room) that describes the test process and regulations.

Once the test has begun, room supervisors and proctors are expected to remain vigilant and prepared to handle any problems with a minimum of distraction to the examinees. Following the examination, supervisors record any testing irregularities or test-taker complaints, then prepare test materials for swift dispach to ETS.

---

4   Educational Testing Service, ETS Standards for Quality and Fairness, Princeton, N.J., 1981, 1987 (revised).

118

Humanizing the Test Administration

ETS believes, however, that standardizing the test administration process is not enough. Test supervisors and staff have „a very special responsibility to conduct every examination in an empathetic way."[5] A list of tips designed to help supervisors better „humanize" the test-taking atmosphere accompanies all training material provided to test center supervisors. Taken individually, many of those suggestions are no more than good common sense; taken together, they go a long way toward reducing the anxiety that inevitably accompanies any kind of testing.

Supervisors and staff are encouraged to be *visible* as well as *accessible*. Name tags are provided by many testing programs, and supervisors are reminded that simple, warm greetings and farewells can mean a lot to nervous test-takers. Noting that „most people under stress tend to relieve their tensions through talk and movement,"[6] the guidelines urge supervisors to be tolerant of nervous noise and commotion before testing. Questions should be dealt with patiently, promptly, and with sensitivity.

Above all, the guidelines urge, supervisors should make an effort to be *inclusive*. „Treat all examinees equally," the guidelines say. „Knowing that examinees can be affected by the psycholigical atmosphere of the testing center, you will want to make certain that none of your procedures make minorities feel different from other examinees. When appropriate and feasible, have minority staff, female as well as male, read test directions to examinees."

To be sure, ETS's long standing practice of stndardizing the testing evirqfnment has proven effective and important. But equally important is people-to-people contact offered by those supervisors who believe that a little warmth can go a long way.

That point was brought home in a letter received by ETS: "I am writing to comment the proctor of the exam I took recently," the examinee wrote.

---

5   Educational Testing Service. ETS Guide to Administering Tests, 1985-86. Princeton, N.J. 1985.

6   Educational Testing Service. ETS Guide to Administering Tests, 1985-86. Princeton, N.J. 1985. .

"His relaxed approach (toward) the test-takers and his clear instructions regarding the exam were helpful, particulary for the one test-taker who had gotten a speeding ticket and another who had a flad tire on the way to the exam. With an unfeeling proctor, the whole tone could have been different. "

Training Test Center Staff

Clearly, then, the selection and training of test center staff is crucial to achieving ETS's goal of creating a testing environment that is both comfortable and fair.

ETS seeks supervisors who are experienced in test administration, astute in hiring support staff (associate supervisors and proctors), sensitive to the needs of test-takers, and committed to the concepts of standardized and fair testing. On the basis of those criteria alone, ETS has been able to attract a core of dedicated personnel.

One supervisor in Vancouver staffed a center with „water bearers" after a flood polluted the city's water supply. In Spokane, Washington, a supervisor and staff camped overnight in their test center after a snowstorm threatened to postpone the exam; and in Huntsville, Alabama, another supervisor managed to administer a test on schedule at a different site when an early morning fire on test day burned the original center to the ground. (Not surprisingly, throughout ETS test supervisors have earned a justifiable reputation for tenacity.)

Selecting dedicated personnel is only half the task, however. Comprehensive training is the second important step in bringing the attitudes and actions of all supervisors in line with ETS policy. But the logistics are overwhelming: How do you offer comprehensive and effective training to 60-80,000 people stationed worldwide?

ETS's primary tool is the *Supervisor's Manual*, a slim but thorough volume that accompanies every ETS test and details the responsibilities of both supervisors and staff regarding test security and administration. Included in the Manual are the standard instructional „script" (to be read aloud before, during and after the examination), directions for securing and returning answer sheets and test booklets, forms to report discrepancies, and ETS telephone numbers to call in case of emergency. The vast majority of those who administer ETS tests use only these self-explanatory booklets to prepare for test administration.

Another form of „training" is afforded supervisors and staff who receive announced or unannounced *test center observations* by ETS officials. While the primary goal of these occasional visits is to ensure that the administration of the test meets ETS standards, observers can also suggest changes in routine or environment that could improve the quality of the test-taking experience.

In addition, each year ETS schedules a series of *supervisor workshops* where supervisors can discuss test administration procedures face-to-face with ETS officials. Workshop sites are selected not only on the basis of geography, but on concerns common to area test centers. In 1987-88, over 800 supervisors attended 40 workshops held both in the United States and abroad.

During the past three years, ETS has been using other approaches to training that are proving increasingly effective. *The Training Kit for ETS Test Administrators*, for example, includes not only a written instruction book, but video and audio tapes that feature staged re-enactments of actual test-taking situations. Since their development in 1986, more than 3,000 kits have been distributed worldwide.

Also, supervisors now receive Test Administration *Highlights*, a newsletter that offers test administration tips, news items, notes about maintaining test security, and short features on supervisors and test centers. Highlights also reports changes in ETS policy and procedures in detail.

How Are We Doing? Getting Feedback about Test Administration

All of ETS's efforts to assure optimum testing conditions are of little value without a mechanism to gauge their effectiveness. Over the years ETS has developed several methods to judge whether test centers and staff are meeting ETS's high standards.

The Test Taker Questionnaire

Perhaps the most valuable source of feedback is the Test Taker Questionnaire, a short (12 to 15 questions, depending on test) survey administered
at a select number of test sites each year (selection is carried out, so that
each center is surveyed once every three to five years; participation is
mandatory for the centers chosen). Following the test, examinees are
asked to respond to specific questions about the test's administration
(„Were you directed to your seat?" „Did you understand the instructions?" „Was there a clock in the room?") Answers are given by filling in
„yes/no/don't know" ovals. Space is also provided for written comments.

Responses are then tabulated by center, and each center participating in
the survey receives a report describing the results for that particular
center as well as all participating centers. If the percentage of positive responses to any question falls below a desired minimum response rate
(usually around 90 percent), that question and its responses are brought
to the attention of the test center supervisor. When reports indicate a
need for corrective action, followup surveys are administered.

Correspondence from supervisors indicate that they find such a review
helpful. „We greatly appreciate your vigilance," wrote one. „We're always open to improving the operation of our test center."

Since 1985, when the Test Taker Questionnaire became a regular part of
ETS's US testing program, almost 600,000 questionnaires have been administered at more than 5000 test centers.

The Supervisor's Comment Sheet

Likewise ETS solicits opinions about the test administration process
from test center supervisors. To encourage such critical observation, an
open-ended *supervisor's comment* sheet is supplied with every *Supervisor's Manual*. While most suggestions have, in fact, proven helpful, a few

have prompted significant changes in test administration policy and procedure. In 1986-87, over 1700 completed forms were returned.

The Supervisor's Irregularity Report

While such comments are important, reports of errors, omissions, or rule infractions are treated with greater concern. Even one such incident: a damaged test book, a delayed or mistimed testing, or an incident of improper conduct, has the potential to jeopardize both test administration and score validity and, by extention, ETS's commitment to quality and fairness.

To keep track of such discrepancies, ETS supplies a Supervisor's Irregularity Report (SIR) with every Supervisor's Manual. The simple, two-sided document provides space for reporting group irregularities (mistimings), individual irregularities (defective materials, mistimings, illnesses, canceled scores, cheating) and potentially ambiguous or erroneous test questions (as pointed out by examinees).

All irregularity reports are investigated by ETS. If action is warranted, it is usually swift and sure, but never at the expense of the test-taker's rights. Reports of improper conduct, for instance, must clear both the Test Security Office as well as a three-member ETS review panel before an examinee is contacted, by letter, regarding the incident. The examinee is then offered five non-punitive options: a free retest; the opportunity to submit information explaining the discrepancy; the release of the test file (including evidence) for summary review by an admissions officer from the examinee's school; score cancellation (with refund); or case review by the American Arbitration Association, with attendant costs absorbed by ETS.

Most importantly, every irregularity in test administration, no matter how large or small, is handled as sensitively as possible. A 1986 incident illustrates the point well. Because of a printing error, over 8000 students across the United States taking the Scholastic Aptitude Test (a key test for college admission) were suddenly confronted with two blank pages in their test booklets. The week after the test, ETS staff personally telephoned every affected examinee and offered a variety of options, including retesting or refund. Two weeks later, with the help of a nationwide network of test supervisors and guidance counselors, the test was re-administered at some 300 locations around the country. Many examinees later expressed amazement that such a large organization would use such a personal approach to solve a problem.

Examinee Complaints

In addition to the test taker questionnaire, examinees are encouraged to either write or telephone ETS if they have a complaint about the administration of the test, the test center, or the test itself. ETS's address and telephone number are clearly printed on all material sent to the examinee, beginning with the Bulletin of Information for the test. As is the case with other feedback sources, all complaints are investigated by ETS, and action is taken when required.

ETS staff have received a wide variety of complaints, from poor lighting to the noise created by a physics class dropping eggs from the roof of a test center. But no complaint is rejected as frivolous or insignificant. ETS believes that if the mere perception of distraction exists, then the quality of the test administration for the individual or group may have been compromised.

Conclusion

Both anecdotal and statistical evidence gathered at ETS suggest that efforts to standardize and humanize the testing environment have been successful. Nevertheless, new developments in test administration are forcing a wholesale re-examination of the test administration policies and procedures that have served ETS well in the past. For example, an experimental computer-based test being developed at ETS is expected to generate a whole new series of questions about test administration and security. Whatever the changes, ETS's fundamental commitment stands: To provide an optimum testing environment in which examinees can do their best work.

124

References

Educational Testing Service (1987). *ETS Standard for Quality and Fairness.* Princeton, New Jersey.

Educational Testing Service (1985). *ETS Guide to Administering Tests,* 1985-86. Princeton, New Jersey.

Appendix

Includes:

1. Test-Taker Questionnaire
2. Principles, Policies and Guidelines Relating to Test administration for the *Standards of Quality and Fairness*
3. Code of Fair Testing
4. Test Center Observer Questionnaire
5. Supervisor's Irregularity Report
6. Supervisor's Comment Sheet

126

1. Test-Taker Questionnaire*

Please take a few minutes to indicate your reactions to the test administration that has just been completed. Your responses will help us to improve the quality of services to test takers.

Yes No Don't
Know

	Yes	No	Don't Know
1. Were you permitted to enter the building by the published reporting time?	• •		• • •
2. Did you have to show your admission ticket or other form of authorization to a member of the testing staff?	• •		
3. Did you have to show identification **or, if not,** were you admitted by a member of the testing staff who knows you?	• •		
4. Were you directed to your seat?	• •		
5. Were you seated more than an arms length away from the person (s) sitting beside you?	• •		
6. Was the desk or table you used big enough to hold your answer sheet?	• •		
7. Did the testing begin within our hour of the rime printed on your admission ticket or other from of authorization?	• • •		
8. Did a member of the testing staff personnaly give you your test book and answer sheet?	• •		
9. Did you understand the person who read the instructions to you?	• •		
10. Was there a clock in the room big enough for you to see clearly **or, if not,** was the remaining testing time posted?	• •		
11. Was a member of the testing staff in the room at all times?	• • •		
12. Did a member of the testing staff personnaly collect your test book and answer sheet?	• •		
13. Did you feel that members of the testing staff were trying to be helpful?	• • •		
14. Was there anything about how the test that interfered with your ability to do your best? If yes, please comment below.	• •		

* © 1988 by Educational Testing Service, Princeton, New Jersey.

Please write any comments you would like to make about today's administration:

_____

_____

_____

_____

_____

Where was the test administrated?
Fill in the appropriate circle below.

- Auditorium
- Cafeteria
- Classroom
- Language Laboratory
- Lecture Hall
- Library
- Multipurpose Room
- Other _____

2. Principles, Policies and Guidelines Relating to Test Administration*

Procedural Guidelines: Test Administration

1. Before the test is administered provide prospective examinees (and, in some programs, parents or guardians as well) with information about the following as appropriate:
   * the test's intended purpose and what it is designed to measure, typical test items, clear directions for the test and the response method to be used, a description of how scores are derived including formation of composite scores, strategies for taking the test (e.g., guessing and pacing), whether the test contains items not intended to be scored, and the background and experience relevant to test performance;
   * the program procedures and requirements, including test dates, test fees, test center locations, special testing arrangements for handicapped persons or others, test registration, score reporting, score cancellation by examinees or by ETS, or the sponsor, and registering complaints; and
   * test administration procedures and requirements, including those related to identification and admission to the test center, materials permitted in or excluded from the testing room, and the consequences of misconduct.
2. Establish test centers that are convenient, nondiscriminating, comfortable, and accessible to all individuals, including those with disabilities. Locate test centers in both minority and majority communities to foster accessibility.
3. Advise test center staff of the need to minimize distractions and to make examinees comfortable in the testing situation. Instruct staff to be sensitive to the psychological as well as physical needs of examinees. Direct supervisors to consult with or include on the test center staff, when appropriate, subgroup members and persons knowledgeable about handicapping conditions.
4. Provide test center staff with a description of the program, the expected candidate population, the duties of staff, and the procedures for:
   * receiving, storing, and distributing test materials to examninees, and returning them to ETS;
   * admitting examinees to the test center, including ID requirements;
   * administering the test to examinees, including handicapped individuals;
   * using appropriate seating plans and assignments, and monitoring the testing room to reduce opportunities to obtain scores by questionable means;
   * handling of suspected cheating, misconduct, so emergencies; and
   * reporting irregularities (e.g., disturbances, mistimings, defecting test questions or materials, power failures, or misconduct) so that, after review, appropriate action can be taken.

5. Provide test center staff with directions (to be read aloud before the test begins) that cover the recording of answers on answer sheets or via other devices, timing of test sections and breaks, guessing strategies, and the consequences of using unauthorized aids or engaging in other forms of misconduct.
6. Utilize effective and equitable procedures for preventing, identifying, and resolving scores obtained by questionable means.
7. Encourage examinees to report any irregularities so that, after review, appropriate action can be taken.
8. Undertake quality control activities (e.g., test center observations, solicitation of suggestions from test administrators and examinees, training of test administors) to assure effective and, when necessary, secure test administrations.
9. Make tests available at no additional cost to individuals with handicapping conditions through special testing arrangements or special test editions.
10. Provide users of locally administered tests with instructions about standardized conditions for administering and scoring the tests.

---

* © 1987 by Educational Testing Service.

3. Code of Fair Testing

A. Developing/Selecting Appropriate Tests*

| Test developers should provide the information that test users need to select appropriate tests. | Test users should select tests that meet the purpose for which they are to be used and that are appropriate for the intended test-taking population. |

Test Developers Should

1. Define what each test measures and what the test should be used for. Describe the population (s) for which the test is appropriate.

2. Accuratley represent the characteristics, usefulness, and limitations of test for their intended purposes.

3. Explain relevant measurement concepts as necessary for clarity at the level of detail that is appropriate for the intended audience (s).

4. Describe the process of test development. Explain how the content and skills to be tested were selected.

5. Provide evidence that the test meets its intended purpose (s).

6. Provide either representative samples of complete copies or test questions, directions, answer sheets, manuals, and score reports to qualified users.

7. Indicate the nature of the evidence obtained concenring the appropriateness of each test for groups of different recial, ethnic, or linguistic backgrounds who are likely to be tested.

8. Select and use only those tests for which the skill needed to administer are available.

Test Users Should:

1. First define the purpose for testing and the population to be tested. Then, select a test for that purpose and that population based on a thorough revbiew of the available information.

2. Investigate potentially useful sources of information, in addition to test scores, to corroborate the information provided by tests.

3. Read the materials provided by test developers and avoid using tests for which unclear or incomplete information is provieded.

4. Become familiar with how and when the test was developed and tried out.

5. Read independent evaluations of a test and of possible alternative measures. Look for evidence required to support the claims of test developers.

6. Examine specimen sets, disclosed tests or samples of questions, directions, answer sheets, manuals and score reports before selecting a test.

7. Ascertain whether the test content and norms groups (s) or comparsion group (s) are appropriate for the intended test takers.

8. Identify and publish any specialized skills needed to administer each test and to interpret scores correctly.

---

*Many of the statements in the Code refer to the selection of existing tests. However, in customized testing programs test developers are engaged to construct new tests. In those situations, the test development process should be designed to help ensure that the completed tests will be in compliance with the Code.

B. Interpreting Scores

| Test developers Should help user interpret scores correctly. | Test users should interpret scores correctly. |

Test Developers Should:

9. Provide timely and easily understand score reports that describe test performance clearly and accurately. Also explain the meaning and limitations of reported scores.

10. Describe the population(s) represented by any norms or comparison group (s), the dates the data were gathered, and the process used to select the samplers of test takers.

11. Warn user to avoid specific, reasonably anticipated misuses of test scores.

12. Provide information that will help users follow reasonable procedures for setting passing scores when it is appropriate to use such scores with the test.

13. Provide information that will help users gather evidence to show that the test is meeting its intended purpose (s).

Test Users Should:

9. Obtain information about the scale used for reporting scores, the characteristics of any norms or comparison group(s), and the limitations of the scores.

10. Interpret scores taking into account any major differences between the norms or comparison groups and the actual test takers. Also take into account any differences in test administration practices or familiarity with the specific questions in the test.

11. Avoid using tests for purposes not specifically recommended by the test developer unless evidence is obtained to support the intended use.

12. Explain how any passing scores were set and gather evidence to support the appropriateness of the scores.

13. Obtain evidence to help show that the test is meeting its intended purpose (s).

C. Striving for Fairness

Test developers should strive to make tests that are as fair as possible for test takers of differnt races, gender, ethnic backgrounds, or handicapping conditions.

Test users should select tests that have been developed in ways that attempt to make them as faire as possible for the test takers of different races, gender, ethnic backgrounds, or handicapping conditions.

Test Developers Should:

14. Rewiev and revise test questions and related materials to avoide potentially insensitive content of language.

15. Investigate the performance of test takers of different races, gender, and ethnic backgrounds when samples of sufficient size are available. Enact procedures that help to ensure that differences in performance are related primarily to the skills under assessment rather than to irrelevant factors.

16. When feasible, make appropriately modified forms of tests or administration procedures available for test takers with handicapping conditions. Warn test users of potential problems in using standard norms with modified tests or administration procedures that result in non-comparable scores.

Test Users Should:

14. Evaluate the procedures used by test developers to avoid potentially insensitive concent or language.

15. Review the performance of test takers to different races, gender, and ethnic backgrounds when samples of sufficient size are available. Evaluate the extent to which performance differences may have been caused by inappropriate characteristics of the test.

16. When necessary and feasible, use appropriately modified forms of tests or administration procedures for test takers with handicapping conditions. Interpret standard norms with care in the light of the modifications that were made.

D. Informing Test Takers

Under some circumstances, test developers have direct communication with test takers. Under other circumstance, test users communicate directly with test takers. Whichever group communicates directly with test takers should provide the information described below.

Test Developers or Test Users Should

17. When a test is optional, provide test takers or their parents/guardians with information to help them judge whether the test should be taken, or if an available alternative to the test should be used.

18. Provide test takers the information they need to be familiar with the coverage of the test, the types of question formats, the directions, and appropriate test-taking strategies. Strive to make such information equally available to all test takers.

Under some circumstances, test developers have direct control of test scores Under other circumstances, test users have such control. Whichever group has direct control of test and test scores should take the steps described below.

Test Developers or Test Users Should

19. Provide test takers or their parents/guardians with information about rights test takers may have to obtain copies of tests and completed answer sheets, retake tests, have tests rescored, or cancel scores.

20. Tell test takers or their parents/guardians how long scores will be kept on file and indicate to whom and under what circumstance test scores will or will not be released.

21. Describe the procedures that test takerts or their parents/guardians may use to register complaints and have problems resolved.

Test Center Observer Questionnaire

Part I: Observation Information

Program _____ Center # _____ Test Date _____

ETS Representative: _____ Observation Announced: Yes ___ No ___

Arrival Time at Center: _____ Departure Time: _____

Supervisior's Name: _____

Center Reporting Address: _____

_____

If you need to contact ETS on the test day, please call collect to (609) _____

See attached TCMIS report for aditional information on supervisor including years of service, ETS programs served and center history.

A. Please pay particular attention to the problems listed below and report on each in section B.

_____
_____
_____
_____

B. Summation of problems (listed in A) discussed with supervisor. (Continue on back of page, if necessary).

_____
_____
_____
_____

C. Specify actions you recommend TCM take.

_____

Part II: Questions you Need to Ask the Supervisor

Detailed instructions for administering ETS testing programs are explained in the respective Supervisor's Manual. Please respond to the following questions. Describe any unsatisfactory procedures or concerns that you have. Indicate any corrective action taken by you or the test center supervisor.

Preadministration Procedures   Description/
                                    Comments Must be Provided

1. Where were the cartons of test materials delivered upon receipt at the institution?

   a. If materials were not delivered directly to the supervisor, where were the cartons stored before the supervisor received them?
   Was this location locked and secured?

   b. If the materials were delivered Directly to the supervisor, where did the supervisor store them?
   Was this location locked and secured?

2. When did the supervisor, or a member of the center staff, check the shipment against the Shipment Notice? Was this within 24 hours of receipt?

3. Were there any problems with the contents of the shipment?
   If yes, when were the problems reported to ETS?

4. Did the supervisor brief staff on security procedures before the test date?

5. If more than one testing room was used, did the supervisor keep a record of the serial numbers of the test books issued to each associate supervisor?

6. Was a seat chart prepared for each testing room? _____

7. FOR TOEFL ONLY - Was a copy of "Duties of Proctors" given to each proctor before the administration? _____

8. FOR TOEFL ONLY - How were seat numbers assigned? _____

Post Administration

9. Where were the test books stored after the administration? _____

10. Does the supervisor intend to mail the test books back to ETS within two working days of the test date? _____

11. Were all reports and forms (e.g., attendance rosters, Supervisors' Report Form) completed as required for return to ETS with the completed answer sheets? _____

Other Items

12. Is the supervisor able to recruit staff members with ease? _____

13. What does the supervisor think of the current honoraria schedule? _____

14. Is the supervisor satisfied with the Supervisors' Manual other ETS puplications? _____

15. Has the supervisor had any problems in communicating with ETS? _____

16. Supervisors' comment and suggestions:

_____
_____
_____

138

17. Please list any items that you discussed with the supervisor, including non-adherence
    to program procedures, seating arrangements, test center staff performance, etc.

_____

_____

_____

18. If the center history indicates the center has had a test taker questionnaire (TTQ),
    please ask the supervisor for reactions to the results of the TTQ. (Sample TTQ
    attached).

_____

_____

_____

Part III: Your Observations and Impressions about the Test Center

Preadministration Procedures

1. Were directional signs posed outside the test center to help examinees locate the reporting address?

2. Was a member of the testing staff present at the given reporting address when you arrived?

3. Was the reporting address, indicated on this report, the one used on the test day? If no, explain.

4. Were directional signs posted in the building to help examinees locate the testing rooms and rest rooms?

5. Were the examinees ádmission tickets examined by a member of the testing staff?

6. FOR TOEFL ONLY - Were the examinees Photo File Records checked and collected?

7. Were identification documents requested and examined according to program requirements?

8. In your opinion, did the staff member(s) responsible for checking the identification documents do a thorough job? If applicable, was the ID also checked in each test room?

9. If applicable, were standby/walk-in registration procedures adhered to?

10. If more than one testing room was used, how were the examinees assigned to their rooms?

140

Administration Procedures

In any testing rooms you were in:

11. How were the examinees assigned to seats in the testing rooms?

12. Was the attendance roster used to record the presence of each examinee?

13.a) Did a member of the testing staff personally hand each examince his/her test materials?

b) Were the test books distributed in serial number order in each testing room?

14. Were the Manual instructions read clearly and verbatim?

15. Did the associate supertvisor create a seating chart with serial numbers?

16. FOR TOEFL/NTE - Were the recorded answer sheet instructions used? If not, why?

17. Did you observe any examinees using unauthorized test aids during the administration? How was that handled by testing staff?

18. If applicable, were rest breaks given according to program requirements?

19. Did a member of the testing staff personally collect each examineé test book and answer sheet?

20. If applicable, were the test book collected in serial number order in each testing room?

21. FOR TOEFL/NTE - When
collecting the answer sheets, did
the staff members re-check each
examinees ID against the name
gridded on the answer sheet?

22. Were test materials collected,
counted, and placed in a secure
location before any examinees
were dismissed from the testing
room?

23. Did you observe anyone (any
center staff) read the contents of
a test book?

24. Was there adequate security of
test materials at all times during
the administration?

25. Was the test administration conducted on an entirely non-discriminatory basis? If
not, comments *must* be provided below.

26. By a visual observation, determine if the staff is in approximately the same ethnic and
sex ratio as the examinees. If not, comment *must* be provided below.

142

Facilities

27. Were the buildings, testing
rooms and rest rooms accessible
by wheelchair?

   _____
   _____

28.a) Please list the types of rooms and evaluate their overall suitability (e.g., lighting, temperature, ventilation, acoustics, etc.)

Type of Room (s)	# of Rooms Used	# of Examinees Per Room	Suitability* E.A.U

E - Exceptional

A - Adequate

U - Unsatisfactory

  b) ALL unsatisfactory rooms must be described here - please include room number, if possible.

29. Did the writing surfaces in each
room meet with our
requirement that they measures
at least 12" X 15" or hold the
test answer sheet?

   _____
   _____

30. If no, are there suitable testing
room available at this
institution that do have writing
surfaces that meet this
requirement? (Please discuss
with supervisor).

   _____
   _____

31. If full size writing surfaces or
left-handed table arm chairs
were not available for
left-handed examinees, how
were these examinees accommodated?

   _____
   _____

32. Were the examinees seated a minimum of five feet apart to the left and right?

_____

_____

33. If the testing room was on an incline (e.g, lecture hall, auditorium), was there also a five foot separation in front of and behind each examinee?

_____

_____

34. Were all examinees seated facing the same direction in each testing room?

_____

_____

35.a) Was each testing room equipped with a wall clock that was clearly visible to all examinees?

_____

_____

b) If no, did a member of the testing staff post the time remaining for each test/ section at regular intervals?

36. Besides the timepiece used by the administrator, was there at least one additional clock/watch in each room that could be used by the administrator as a check against mistiming?

_____

_____

37. Were the testing rooms free of charts, graphs, maps, or any other material that may have been related to the subject of the test?

_____

_____

Post Administration and Other Observations

38. Did you observe that the serial numers of used and unused test books were checked by the supervisor at the end of the administration?

_____

_____

39. Were any other ETS testing programs scheduled for administration at this institution on the day you observed? If yes, provide all details.

_____

_____

40. Did any irregularities occur during this administration? If yes, provide all details.

_____
_____

41. Did the supervisor use any special procedures that might be helpful to other test centers?

_____
_____

42. Were all examinees treated equally by the test center staff?

_____
_____

43. Were the testing rooms comfortable and free from distracting noise?

_____
_____

44. Were all staff members sufficiently trained?

_____
_____

45. Did the testing staff members remain alert and attentive during all phases of the test administration?

_____
_____

46. Were any of the testing rooms left unattended at any time during the administration?

_____
_____

47. Did testing staff circulate around the testing rooms regularly to make certain that the examinees were working on the correct sections of the test and to watch for misconduct?

_____
_____

48. a) If the supervisor of record did not
         supervise this administration,
         who was the acting supervisor?
_____

_____

    b) In your opinion, did the acting
         supervisor have experience in
         administering standardized
         tests?

49. Was there adequate security of the
test materials at all times during this
administration?
_____

_____

50. Identify areas of this administration where the supervisor and staff were
effective/efficient.

_____
_____
_____
_____
_____
_____

51. What is your overall impression of this administration?

_____
_____
_____
_____
_____
_____
_____

146

Observers Recommendation for Additional Staff

If you as an observer suggest that the supervisor recruit additional staff, the staff must be authorized by a TCM manager. This form must be completed by the Observer and signed by the TCM Supervisor in the space designated below. This information must be returned with your Observation Report within four (4) working days of the Test Administration.

Program _____ Date: _____

Center Code # _____ Observer: _____

Center Name _____

City/State _____

Admin. Date: Oct. _____   March/Apr. _____

           Nov. _____   May _____

           Dec. _____   June _____

           Jan. _____   All _____

Additional Staff Requested:

      Proctors # _____

Associate Supervisors _____

Comments/Reasons:

_____

_____

_____

TCM approval:

_____

_____

Addendum for Programms Using Audio Equipment

1. Acoustical characteristics of the testing rooms

 _____ POOR _____ SATISFACTORY _____ EXCELLENT

2. Were examinees in all areas of the room(s) able to hear the recordings clearly?

 _____

 _____

3. Quality of recordings

 _____ POOR _____ SATISFACTORY _____ EXCELLENT

 • If poor,explain in what way (weak volume, too much bass, muffled sound, echos etc.)

 _____

4. Type of recording and equipment used

 Cassette _____ Type _____

 Reel to Reel _____ Size _____

5. Was an internal loudspeaker (not part of unit itself)used?

 _____ YES _____ NO

 • If not, and more than 15 examinees were in the room, did this present a problem?

 _____

 _____

6. If any examinee(s) asked the administrator to make adjustments during the introductory section of the recording, did the administrator oblige?

 _____

 _____

7. Additional Comments:

 _____

 _____

148

5. Supervisor's Irregularity Report

Sign and return this form even if no irregularities occur and check the box at the bottom of the page. See the *Manual* for directions. Please print or type all information clearly and check the appropriate box(es).

City/State/Province   Postal Code

_____

Date _____   Center Number _____

Group Irregularities

List examinees affected on the reverse side.

Group Mistimings Only

_____ overtiming (number of minutes) _____
section

_____ undertiming (number of minutes) _____
section

Other Group Irregularities

_____
section

_____
Possible Test Question Errors

Individual Examinee Irregularities

1	2	3	4	Examinee's Name	Registration Number	Test Section	Time by Reset Watch

Remarks

Remarks

Remarks

Remarks

1 = defective materials
2 = illness   3 = inadequate identification   4 = other

150

If you are submitting more than one Supervisor's Irregularity Report for this session, indicate total number _____

Please attach all irregular answer sheets and test books to this report

• No irregularities at this administration: _____

Supervisor's Signature: _____

(Supervisor must countersign if report has been completed by someone else).

6. Supervisor's Comment Sheet

We could appreciate your suggestions for improving our procedures and making the testing program more effective. Test supervisor's have given us many helpful ideas that we have incorporated in our publications and procedures. We review all comments and answer specific questions.

If you have suggestions or questions, please write them in the space below and fill in the information requested at the bottom of the page. Return the page with your used answer sheets. Do not use this comment sheet to report any irregularities, such as defective materials, loss of time, or test question errors. Irregularities should be reported on the Supervisor's Irregularity Report in order to ensure prompt and appropriate action by the TOEFL office.

Name (please print)   Administration date

Institution   Center number

City   State/province   Country
Zip/postal code

8

Self-Evaluation of Success in Psychological Testing[1]

David V. Budescu

Abstract

The present study examines the ability of a large group of applicants to an academic institution, to evaluate accurately their own performance on a battery of six ability tests which was administered as part of the admission requirements. It was hypothesized that the subjective evaluations would be more valid if elicited after the testing session, and that examinees of higher intelligence and with a history of high achievement status would provide more valid assessments of their performance. The validities of the self evaluations were high (with the exception of the Verbal Analytical Thinking Test) and quite uniform across the six tests. The hypothesized pattern was obtained, but the achievement status factor was not significant in the analysis. A novel feature of the present study was the analysis of the similarity of shape of the profiles of the actual scores and of their subjective evaluations. The agreement between the two profiles was quite high, and statistically associated with the three individual and situational variables mentioned above. The validity of the evaluations was higher when there was a close match between the ability assessed and the nature of the self evaluation. Finally, it was shown that the examinees' assessments of success were correlated with the perceived difficulty and face validity of the tests and with the test-taker's previous experience and their attitudes towards the specific subject.

---

1   This is an updated version of chapter by the same name previously published in Nevo, B. and Jager, R.S.(eds.) Psychological Testing: The Examinee Perspective. (Verlag für Psychologie, Göttingen, 1986, pp. 69-91)

154

Introduction

Introspective reports[2] have played a major role in psychological research
from its earliest days and they still are an important data-collection tool in
such domains as opinion and attitudes measurement, sensory psycho-
physics, personality assessment, etc. The present chapter focuses on the
use of introspective reports in the area of ability measurement. More specifically, this study represents the results of an attempt to (i) evaluate
whether people can accurately assess and report the level of their performances on a battery of objective multiple choice ability tests, (ii) assess
the degree to which several selected characteristics of the examinees and
of the test situation affect the accuracy of these reports, and (iii) identify
test characteristics which are correlated with self assessment of success.
Mabe & West (1982) have recently reviewed 55 studies that addressed
these and several closely related issues. Their review appears to cover all
the work published in this area of research between the years 1942 and
1978. The total number of individuals involved in these studies was
14,811. The large majority of these individuals were college and high
school students, and they were typically required to report a subjective
evaluation of their performances and/or abilities. The studies covered a
large range of abilities; the actual measurement of the performance and
of its evaluations was achieved by an even wider variety of instruments.
In most cases the measure of accuracy of the self evaluations was some
form of correlation between the "objective" performance/ability and its
"subjective" counterpart. The 267 correlation examined ranged from
-0.26 to 0.80 with a mean of 0.29 and a standard deviation of 0.25. These
values are rather disappointing, but not too surprising, given the fact that
they were obtained from such a vast variety of abilities and by means of so
many different methods. Also, as Mabe & West correctly point out, many
of these studies suffered from serious methodological flaws (e.g., unrelia-
bility of measurements, restriction of range, etc.) which are typically associated with underestimation of correlations.
Mabe & West (1982) distinguish between two classes of factors which
tend to influence the validity of the subjective evaluations: chracteristics
of the individual examinees ("person variables" according to their termi-

---

2   The term self-evaluation, self-reports, introspective report, subjective evaluation and
     self-appraisal are used interchangeably.

nology), and measurement conditions (under this umbrella term they include characteristics of the test situation and of the measurement tools). In the former class three variables have been repeatedly and consistently associated with accurate and valid self reports: higher intelligence (e.g, Bailey & Bailey, 1971; Kooker, 1974), high achievement status (e.g., Bailey & Lazar, 1976, Kirk & Sereda, 1969, Kooker, 1974), and internal locus of control (e.g., Gilmor & Reid, 1978). In the latter category, Mabe & West considered nine different factors: the match between the self-evaluation and the criterion measure, the type of self evaluation elicited (performance vs. ability), the timing of the evaluation (before and after actual testing), emphasis on the relative aspect of the evaluation, reference to a certain well defined reference group, the range and distribution of the ability (or performance) reported, anonymity of reports, expectation of validation of the evaluations against a criterion, and prior experience in self-evaluations. Mabe & West's analysis of the data revealed that these nine factors combined for accounted about 37% of the total variation in the validity of the self-evaluations, and that the best subset of predictors in this context included the expectation of validation, the emphasis on the relative aspects of the evaluations (by means of social comparison terms such as "better than the average"), prior experience in self-evaluations, and guarantee of anonymity. Finally, a breakdown of the results by the type of ability (performance) judged indicated that athletic and clerical skills are the most predictable (validity coefficients of 0.48 and 0.45 respectively) followed closely by scholastic ability ($r=0.38$) and intelligence ($r=0.34$).

This conceptual organization developed by Mabe & West (1982) and the results of their meta-analysis provide us with a convenient theoretical framework and with reliable standards of comparison for the analysis of our own data. The present study allows us to replicate and generalize some of the relationships between the validity of self-reports and charachteristics of the individual test-takers, which were discovered by this meta analysis. We also propose to investigate one facet of the question of self-evaluation which was neglected in the past, namely ipsative validity. This term, which was introduced to the psychometric jargon by Cattell (1944), refers to relationships between different scores of an individual rather than normative comparisons of individuals. In this study all the respondents were administered a battery consisting of six tests measuring different abilities and were asked to report their subjective assessment of success on each of these six tests (Nevo & Sfez, 1986). Thus, each individual's scores can be described by two different profiles - one representing his/her actual scores, and the second representing his/her subjectively reported counterparts. The degree of similarity of these two profiles will be regarded as a measure of the ipsative validity of the self-evaluations, and will be analyzed by the same methods applied to the more conventional measures of validity.

Finally we will try to identify other perceived properties of the test which affect one's assessment of success.

The Samples and the Variables

Most of the results reported in this chapter are based on a sample of 1,219 individuals who took the 1981 Haifa University Entrance Examination. This sample consists of two random subsamples which will be handled separately in most cases: a sample of 921 candidates who completed the Examinees' Feedback Questionnaire (EFeQ) after completing the examination (the post-test sample), and a second group of 298 people who provided their evaluations prior to the testing (the pre-test sample). Members of this second sample reported their expectations regarding the tests, the testing situation, and their performances. These expectations were based on their previous experience in similar test situations (high school, the military, or other college entrance examinations). The references to the specific tests were based on the descriptions and examples provided in the explanatory brochures which were supposedly read by all candidates prior to the test session. All 1219 members of our sample completed the questionnaire and the six tests in the battery, so information regarding actual performance and self-evaluation could be matched for every one of them. Our main interest was in the actual scores of the six tests (General Knowledge Information (I), Figural Reasoning (FR), Mathematical Reasoning (MR), Vocabulary (V), Verbal Analytical Thinking (VA), and English as a Foreign Language (E) and the corresponding self-appraisals of performance. The test scores were defined by the total number of items answered correctly (no correction for guessing was applied since the instructions to the examinees encouraged them to guess when the correct answer was not known) and were re-expressed in standard form (i.e. zero mean and unit variance for the total number of candidates to Haifa University). The self-appraisals were obtained from the rating provided in response to Question 6 of the EFeQ (Nevo & Sfez,

1986). The wording of this item was slightly altered for the pre-test sample: "Try to evaluate on the basis of your abilities your chance to succeed in each of the tests", and the verbal labels of the five response categories were rephrased in terms of chances of success (e.g., "I feel that I have high chances of success in this test" for category 5).

In addition to these twelve basic measurements, several other variables will be used frequently in the course of our analysis:

1) General Psychometric Score (GP) - A simple (unweighted) average of the six test scores (in standardized form for the total number of candidates). In some of the analyses, examinees were classified into four categories corresponding to the four quartiles of GP.

2) Average Matriculation Grade (AM) - All high school graduates in Israel complete several achievement tests in their major areas of study during their last year of school. These examinations are planned, administered, and graded at the national level, and passing grades on all tests are a necessary condition for admission to any academic institution. AM is the simple average of these grades calculated on a scale ranging from 0 to 10. In some analyses, examinees were classified into four categories corresponding to the four quartiles of AM. It should be mentioned that AM values were not available for all the sample members so that some results are based on smaller sample sizes because of these missing values.

3) Ipsative Validity (IV) - A measure of similarity of shapes of the two profiles of scores of each individual described earlier. The measure selected for this purpose is Kendall's coefficient of rank correlation (Tb) between the two sets of six scores. This correlation ranges from -1 (the two orderings of the six scores are exactly opposite) to 1 (the two orders are identical), and any intermediate value can be given a straightforward probabilistic interpretation. For any pair of scores sampled in random fashion from the profiles:

Tb = Pr (the two scores are in the same order in both profiles)

Pr (the two scores are in opposite order in the two profiles).

In our cases (six scores) there are (6x5/2=)15 pairs of scores, and the relationship between Tb and the actual number of concording pairs can be easily spelled out. For example, 12 concording pairs yield a Tb value of (12-3)/15 =0.6, and 10 concording pairs yield Tb=(10-5)/15=0.333.

Table 1 displays a breakdown of the two samples by the sex of the examinees and descriptive statistics of the two auxiliary variables (AM and GP) in each subgroup.

4) The respondents answers to other items of the EFeQ related to the same tests. These items describe the examinees' reactions to the test, the testing environment, their attitude towards testing, and their previous experience with similar tests.

Table 1

Means and Standard Deviations of GP and AM by Sex

of Examinees in the Two Samples.

Sample	Variable		Sex		
			Male	Female	Combined
		n	347	574	921
Post-test	GP	M	0.230	-0.118	0.013
		S	0.936	0.943	0.965
	AM	M	7.090	7.220	7.170
		S	0.707	0.705	0.708
		n	122	176	298
Pre-test	GP	M	-0.041	-0.336	-0.233
		S	1.042	0.936	0.992
	AM	M	7.403	7.298	7.341
		S	0.925	0.847	0.880
		n	469	750	1.219
	GP	M	0.159	-0.176	-0.047
		S	0.990	0.947	0.977
Combined	GP	M	7.168	7.237	7.210
		S	0.777	0.739	0.754

Outline of the Analysis and Research Hypotheses

We start by analyzing the regular measures of validity of self-evaluations - their correlation with the respective criteria. Beyond the direct calcula- tion of these statistics and the comparison of their magnitude across the six tests in the battery, we will focus on the comparison of these validities in different subgroups of the total sample. We define three independent variables in our analysis (i) the timing of the evaluation (pre- or post-test), (ii) intelligence of the examinee as defined by his/her quartile membership according to the GP and (iii) achievement status as described by the testee's quartile membership according to the AM. In accordance with Mabe and West's meta-analysis (1982), we expect to observe higher validities in the post-test sample, and we hypothesize that the validity of the self-reports increases monotonicaly with GP and AM. In addition, we will be able to test for the existence of any interaction effects among these three factors.

One of the most surprising results in Mabe and West's analysis (1982) was their failure to confirm the hypothesis that validities of self-reports are related to the match between the self-evaluation measure and the criterion measure. The authors attributed this failure to the difficulties involved in identifying various levels of agreement between the two measures and to the small variance of this degree of agreement. In the present study we have a perfect setting for re-examining this hypothesis, since we can compare the validities of the self evaluations with the correlations between these reports with performance on other tests, and with intercorrelations between the tests and the EFeQ items. We expect the validities of the self-reports to be superior to all other correlations between the variables involved.

In addition, we will analyze the measure of ipsative validity defined in the previous section. Our expectations are that the same variables affecting the test's specific validities will also influence this measure of overall goodness of evaluation. Thus, we hypothesize that ipsative validities will be higher in the post-test sample and for examinees of higher intelligence and higher achievement status.

Finally, we will examine the degree to which one's perception of success can be predicted by his/her perception of the test and his disposition towards it. This is, essentially a preliminary and exploratory analysis, so we don't formulate specific hypothesis. However, we speculate that the best predictors of perceived success will be factors under the test taker control, such as the extent of his/her preparation for the test.

Results

Table 2 presents the validities of the self-assessments for each of the six tests, the total battery (GP), and the mean validity across the six tests (F). These measures (product moment correlations) are reported for the total sample and separately for the pre- and post- test samples, and are further broken down by general intelligence (GP) and previous achievement status (AM) of the examinee. As predicted, the mean validity, as well as most test specific validities, are higher in the post-test sample and increase with intelligence and achievement status. This observation is partially substantiated by results of a three-factor ANOVA of these validities. In this analysis the timing of the evaluation (2 levels), the intelligence (4 levels) and the status of achievement (4 levels) are the independent variables, and Fisher's Z transformations of the test-specific validities are the dependent variable. Thus we have 32 conditions and n=6 replications in each condition. None of the second or third order interactions is significant, but the main effects for time (F$_{1,191}$=8.32, p< 0.05) and intelligence (F$_{3,191}$=4.19, p< 0.05) are. Interestingly, we did not find a significant main effect for achievement status (F$_{3,191}$ =0.66, p> 0.05). A comparison of the columns in any given row of Table 2 reveals an interesting and consistent pattern of results regarding the differential validity of the six self-assessments. The consistent superiority of r over the GP column indicates that the validity of self-reports is much higher at the test level than at the battery level, i.e., specificity helps people to assess and predict the level of their performance. In the post-test sample the validities of the subjective assessments are quite uniform, the only exception being the Verbal Analytical Thinking test which is consistently and markedly the most difficult to assess from the examinee point of view. In light of this fact, a new ANOVA of the validities was performed without the Verbal Analytical Test. It was hoped that in this restricted and more homogeneous set of data, Achievement Status will be significant. We did not confirm the hypothesis - only the time and the intelligence factors were significant at the 0.05 level.

Table 2

Validities of Self-Assessments for the Various Tests

| Subsample | n | Test | | | | | | | r̄ |
		I	FR	MR	V	VA	E	GP	
Total	1.219	.41	.49	.45	.46	.22	.47	.17	.42
Post-test	921	.46	.58	.49	.48	.23	.47	.18	.45
Intelligence									
Lowest Quartile	207	.24	.49	.38	.34	.02	.40	.00	.30
Second Quartile	224	.45	.55	.56	.41	.26	.47	.04	.42
Third Quartile	241	.49	.64	.62	.51	.22	.57	-.03	.47
Highest Quartile	249	.62	.67	.69	.60	.21	.59	.30	.54
Achievement Status									
Lowest Quartile	206	.48	.58	.47	.42	.09	.42	.19	.38
Second Quartile	216	.47	.48	.50	.40	.27	.46	.18	.40
Third Quartile	201	.36	.62	.59	.51	.22	.38	.18	.42
Highest Quartile	175	.57	.58	.54	.65	.32	.50	.27	.46
Pre-test	298	.26	.17	.36	.38	.12	.54	.15	.31
Intelligence									
Lowest Quartile	98	.25	.08	.32	.43	-.06	.55	-.03	.26
Second Quartile	81	.35	.24	.30	.43	.17	.44	.22	.32
Third Quartile	63	.31	.32	.44	.28	.14	.48	.02	.33
Highest Quratile	56	.37	.08	.55	.59	.16	.62	.18	.40
Achievement Status									
Lowest Quartile	55	.11	.09	.32	.46	.03	.50	-.07	.25
Second Quartile	56	.34	.27	.45	.41	.00	.35	.21	.30
Third Quartile	52	.27	.13	.39	.42	.20	.59	.22	.33
Highest Quartile	78	.38	.15	.34	.34	.14	.60	.10	.32

Although the validities of the remaining five evaluations are very similar, it appears that the Figural and Mathematical Reasoning scores are somewhat more predictable than the others. A similar pattern was reported also by Arsenian (1942) and Denisi & Shaw (1977).

The validities of the pre-test assessments display a slightly different pattern. First, note that there are larger differences among the six tests. The tests for which relatively high validities are obtained are English, Vocabulary, and Mathematical Reasoning, while Figural Reasoning and Verbal Analytical Thinking seem to be the most difficult to predict. For a better evaluation of the relationships between test scores and subjective estimates, it is useful to go beyond analysis of the validities and to examine the pattern and magnitude of additional correlations. For example, it is interesting to see whether the validities reported earlier are higher than the intercorrelations between the test scores, the intercorrelations between the subjective ratings, and the correlations between the test scores and the subjective ratings of other tests. It is easy to see that all these relationships can be analyzed within the framework of the well known multitrait-multimethod matrix (Campbell & Fiske, 1959). We present in Table 3 the average correlation for each subset of the matrix as calculated for the total sample and the two subsamples.

Table 3

Summary of the Multitrait – Multimethod Matrix

Type of correlation	Number of correlations	Sample		
		Post-test (n = 839)	Pre-test (n = 272)	Combined (n = 1111)
Between methods Within tests	6	.453	.306	.418
Between tests Within methods	30	.221	.263	.224
Between tests Between methods	30	.025	.038	.027

Although a variety of statistical techniques have been developed to analyze such matrices (e.g., Schmitt, Coyle & Saary, 1977), it is sufficient in our case to examine the pattern of the correlations evident from Table 3. Clearly, required by the method, the within-trait correlations dominate the within-method correlations and the between trait and methods set. This pattern provides strong support for our hypothesis that higher validities are obtained when there is a close match between the criterion and the self-evaluation measure. To support this notion further, the average correlation between the assessment of success on the battery as a whole and performance on each individual subtest was calculated. This value turned out to be 0.115 (0.104 in the pre-test sample and 0.120 in the post test sample), which is clearly lower than the within trait values summarized in the table.

We now turn to the analysis of the ipsative validities. Table 4 displays the average rank correlation between the test and the evaluation profiles for the total sample, the pre-test sample and the post-test sample, broken down by the level of intelligence and previous achievement status. A quick examination of the entries in the table reveals that here, as in the case of group validities (Table 2), higher validities are obtained in the post-test situation, and are associated with higher levels of intelligence and achievement, although the pattern is not as perfect as the one obtained for the mean validity.

Table 4

Ipsative Validity of Self-Evaluations

Subgroup	Sample		
	Combined Sample (n = 1030)	Post-test Sample (n = 798)	Pre-test Sample (n = 241)
Total	38	40	32
Intelligence			
Lower quartile	25	25	25
Second quartile	40	41	38
Third quartile	44	48	29
Upper quartile	39	40	36
Achievement Status			
Lower quartile	31	32	26
Second quartile	39	41	30
Third quartile	40	42	34
Upper quartile	42	44	36

Note: Decimal point omitted

In order to compare these results with those obtained at the group level, an ANOVA of the ipsative validities like the one reported earlier was conducted. This analysis indicates that none of the interactions is significant, thus a simple additive model can best account for the variation of the ipsative validities. The identification of the components of this model is complicated to a certain degree by the fact that the samples in the different groups are not equal. Two tests were performed for each of the three factors, one "ignoring" the influence of the other two, and another "eliminating" the joint impact of the other two (Appelbaum & Cramer, 1974). It turns out that time and GP are significant by both methods at the 0.05 level, while for the achievement status factor, the "ignoring" test is significant ($F_{3,1007} = 5.75$, $p < 0.05$) and the "eliminating" test is not ($F_{3,1007} = 1.66$, $p > 0.05$). Thus, when considered by itself, achievement status is related to the level of ipsative validity, but the degree of this relationship is lower than that of the other variables, and AM is not a necessary term in the additive model accounting for the total variance of these validities. Thus, the results of this individualized ANOVA are very similar to the results of the group based validities.

Aside from the assessment of success on the various subtests the EFeQ included various other questions referring to the test takers' previous experiences with similar tests, their preparation for the test, and the testing session itself (rating of the physical environment, assessment of the testers' behavior, clarity of the instructions, etc.) Finally, the examinees rated the tests themselves according to their difficulty, their face validity, and expressed their overall attitude towards the testing experience. Each of these items was rated on a 5-point scale, for each subtest separately. For the post-test sample we analyzed the relationships between these ratings and the examinees'assessment of sucess on the respective subtests. A preliminary examination of the results indicated that four questions were consistently and significantly associated with the sucess evaluations. They are: Previous experience ("What is the extent of your previous experience with this psychometric test?"), Perceived difficulty ("To what extent did the test require an extensive and tiring intellectual effort?"), Face validity ("To what extent is this test suitable for assesssment of scholastic aptitude and student selection?") and Overall attitude towards the test ("To what extent did you enjoy taking the examination?"). Statistics describing the level of association with the measures of success are displayed in tables 5 and 6.

The former presents coefficients of contingency (nominal measures association based on X^2 values), and the latter presents rank order correlations (Kendall's Tb).

Table 5

Contingency Coefficients Between Assessment of Success
and Four Items of the EFeQ (Post-Test Sample Only)

Item	I	FR	MR	V	VA	E	GP
Previous Experience	18	15	16	15	16	13	11
Perceived Difficulty	44	41	50	51	32	51	24
Face Validity	37	32	36	41	31	25	23
Overall Attitude	55	56	51	54	43	54	33

Note: Decimal points omitted

Table 6
Rank Correlations (Kendall Tb) Between Assessment of
Success and Four Items of the EFeQ (Post-Test Sample Only)

Item	Test						
	I	FR	MR	V	VA	E	GP
Previous Experience	17	11	20	15	13	19	15
Perceived Difficulty	-32	-30	-42	-42	-23	-40	11
Face Validity	28	21	28	31	24	19	16
Overall Attitude	43	42	55	42	37	45	24

Note: Decimal points omitted

Both tables tell a very similar story. The best predictors of one's perceived success on a test are his/her overall attitude towards the test, and its perceived difficulty followed by the test's face validity (e.g. Nevo, 1985), and one's previous experience with similar tests. Based on the rank correlations we can conclude that people are most likely to report higher levels of success on tests they consider easy, familiar, appropriate for the selection task and enjoyable. For each of the tests in the battery, the assessed success was regressed on the various items of the EFeQ. In Table 7 we summarize results of three versions of the multiple regression. The success estimates are predicted by (i) all nine items in the questionnaire, (ii) the four predictors identified above, and (iii) only the two best predictors.

Table 7

Squared Multiple Correlations Between Self-Assessed
Success and Other Items on the EFeQ

	Predictors		
Test	All 9 items	4 items only	Overall attitude + Perceived difficulty
I	36	36	32
FR	34	32	30
MR	45	45	42
V	39	39	36
VA	26	25	22
E	39	38	34
GP	12	11	09

Note: Decimal points omitted

Obviously, the top four variables exhaust all the variance that can be re-producted from the questionnaire, and the other five items are either re-dundant or unrelated to perceived success. The two best predictors ac-count, roughly, for 85-90% of this variance. Finally, note that the success on the specific subtests is easier to predict than is the performance on the battery as a whole, and that succes on some tests (Mathematics, Vocabu-lary and English) is more predictable than on others (especially Verbal Analogies).

Summary and Discussion

This study has examined the ability of candidates for admission to an aca-demic institution to evaluate their own performance on a battery of tests used in the selection process. Before going into a detailed discussion of the results, we should emphasize several characteristics of this particular research-setting. We have drawn a very large sample from a finite and well-defined population with known characteristics. The results in Table 1 indicate that our sample is very similar in many important respects to the total population of interest, so we can generalize our conclusions and apply them to this large population.

The results of the test session are of crucial importance to all the candidates and to the university. For each examinee, the tests are a major component of the decision regarding his/her ability to pursue the career of his/her choice, and from the university's point of view, the screening based on the test results determines the level and characteristics of its student population, its reputation, etc. This fact assures us that all candidates are highly motivated when taking the tests, and that the tests are properly prepared, well written and highly reliable[3]. Thus, we can safely assume that we have reliable and accurate measures of the abilities of all the testees.

The instructions to the respondents of the EFeQ emphasized the fact that the questionnaire is not part of the examination and has no impact on the selection and admission procedures. Yet, it seems that this has not affected, in any negative sense, the respondents' attitudes to the quetionnaire. The response rate to most items is very high, the reliability of the instrument is satisfactory (Nevo and Sfez., 1986), and no member of the sample expressed any strong objection to the idea of filling out a feedback questionnaire. In fact, it seems that people were pleased that they were given a chance to react and comment on the test and the test situation. These facts indicate that the self-evaluations are also of high quality.

Finally, we should mention that in sampling candidates during the test session rather than those students accepted to the university, we have almost completely eliminated the problem of restriction of range which has affected so many studies in this domain (Mabe and West, 1982). Our analysis was centered around some of the hypotheses derived from the meta-analytical study of Mabe and West; therefore, we can also compare our results to theirs. To summarize the results pertaining to the "regular" measures of validity, we can state:

---

3   The reliabilities of the six tests in the battery vary from 0.81 (Verbal Analytical Thinking) to 0.88 (English, and Mathematical Reasoning)

1) The validity of the self-evaluations in our study is higher than the average validity of self-reports of intelligence and scholastic ability.
2) Individuals of higher intelligence are capable of providing more valid self-evaluations.
3) Individuals with a history of higher achievement status do not necessarily provide more valid self-reports.
4) Evaluations of post performances are superior to evaluations (projections) of future performances.
5) Validity of self-evaluations is enhanced by specifity and by the degree of match between the criterion and the evaluation measure.

The mean validity in our sample is 0.42 (0.45 in the post test sample). This value is to be compared to 0.34, the mean validity for self-evaluations of intelligence in Mabe and West's review. Although a significance test is not possible, a direct comparison of the coefficients of determination (r^2) reveals a relative improvement of almost 60%, which is quite impressive. This difference can be attributed to the improved methodological features of the present study (large sample, reliable instruments, highly motivated test-takers, etc.), and to the specificity of the abilities assessed.

To better appreciate the magnitude of this mean validity, we must emphasize what was missing in our design. The questionnaire did not use any relative comparative terms in the wording of the items, and the instructions neither defined a specific reference group, nor gave information regarding the range and/or distribution of the abilities tested. Finally, the candidates in our sample had no special or unusual experience of past self-evaluations and were never led to expect that their reports would be validated against their true performances, nor that their evaluation would be kept anonymous. All these missing features have been shown by Mabe and West to be associated with higher levels of validity. The fact that we have achieved a relatively high validity in their absence indicates that even higher validities can be obtained by means of an appropriate design.

Typically, intelligence and achievement status are considered factors enhancing validities. It is assumed that more intelligent and capable subjects can exercise better perception of their ability-related performance and make more accurate judgements concerning the measuring of their performance (Mabe and West, 1982, p.288). Although the mean validities support this hypothesis (see Table 2), only intelligence was found to have a significant effect in the ANOVA. Also, some of the validities of the test specific evaluations in the four groups of achievement do not confirm the hypothesized pattern. The failure to replicate the achievement status-effect can be attributed to problems of restriction of range. While the intelligence measure used here was based on items developed for this particular population of candidates for admission, the matriculation grades are defined for the much larger and the more heterogeneous population of high school graduates. Only a restricted and selected segment of this population is represented in our sample, and apparently the differences between the four quartiles of this self-selected group are not large enough to show a significant impact on the validities, although the pattern of the results is in the predicted direction.

As expected, the self-reports in the post-test situation were more valid. Mabe and West (1982, p.289) argue that in the pre-test situation the evaluation involves assessments of past performances projected into expected performance conditions and, therefore, it will lack accuracy unless these conditions exactly match the conditions encountered in the past. Such a coincidence is very unlikely, and our case is no exception to this rule. Our results show that the post-test validities are not only higher but are also more homogeneous across abilities. If we ignore for a moment the Verbal Analytic test, it appears that the actual performance has the effect of increasing (or decreasing, as is the case for the English test) the pre-test evaluations to an almost uniform level which seems to be independent of the nature of the ability being evaluated. This results deserves further investigation, preferably by a within subject design. The summary of the multitrait-multimethod matrix contains some interesting results: First, note that the six tests and the six self-evaluations are positively intercorrelated, i.e. we have significant intra-method relations. This finding of consistent positive correlations between items of different ability tests is well documented and known as "the first law of inteligence" (Guttman and Levy, 1980). Apparently, the law holds for self-evaluations of ability as well. The intra-trait correlations, i.e. the validities of the ability specific evaluations, are, however, much higher than the intra-method correlations, particularly in the post-test sample. Finally, one can safely conclude that the between-methods correlations are O. These correlations are essentially validities of mismatched evaluations. The fact that these correlations vannish in a situatin with high intra-method correlations is remarkable and clearly indicates the ability of our subjects to make fine distinctions between performances on related tasks completed within a very short period of time. It can be argued that it is inappropriate to compare a test-specific evaluation with performance on another test, no matter how related the two tests are, and that a better standard of comparison for the validities of interest would be the validity of a general measure of self evaluation. When the self-evaluation measures of the general performance (for the total battery) is correlated with the six test scores, we obtain positive correlations but of much lower magnitude than the intra-trait ones. Thus, it is obvious that a close match between the ability and the self-evaluation measures yields higher validities. However, a good match between the two variables is not a sufficient condition for high validity as evident by the disappointingly lower validity of the self reported General Psychometric score. In order for self-reports of abilities to be valid, they must be elicited by a measurement procedure which closely matches a specific ability.

One of the purposes of our study was to obtain self-reports for all the tests composing the admission battery. This is not the first attempt to collect such data (see Arsenian, 1942; Berdie, 1971; Denisi and Shaw, 1977); but it is the first serious effort to quantify an analyze the differential pattern of validities, and the ipsative validity of the evaluations.

We have already mentioned the fact that post-test validities tend to be more homogeneous than their pre-test counterparts. The examination of the pattern of pre-test validities offers one possible explanation for this phenomenon. The highest validities were recorded for the tests of English, Vocabulary, and Mathematical Reasoning. All these tests measure abilities well known and understood by the examinees by using items of format well known to them. Thus, from the test-taker's perspective these tests are "familiar". On the other hand tests like Figural Reasoning and Verbal Analytical Thinking attempt to quantify abilities which by the nature of their definition are more abstract, complex and less familiar to the subjects. Furthermore, the items used in these tests are highly specialized and of unusual format. Thus, we suggest that it is the level of performance on the tests of the less familiar abilities which is difficult to predict in the pre-test situation. Obviously, following the experience of the test itself, the degree of familiarity with the different tests becomes more uniform, and this is reflected in the magnitude of the respective validities. The test of Verbal Analytical Thinking is a puzzling exception. Its validity is higher in the post-test situation, but clearly inferior to that of the other five tests. This fact is even more difficult to explain in light of the fact that the test is relatively easy (the average item difficulty is 0.606 compared to 0.517 in the other five tests combined), and has relatively low variance. The only explanation we can offer at the present time is that the item format and the operations required in order to solve the analogies are so unfamiliar to the subjects that they find it very difficult to assess their performance. This interpretation is also supported by the fact that the self-evaluation for this test has the lowest reponse-rate (0.92 as compared to 0.96 for the other five tests), and the lowest variance (0.588 as compared to 0.852 for the other tests) in the post-test sample. Finally, this explanation is supported by the examinees' reports. When asked to rate their previous experience with the various tests, the average rating for this test was 2.18, and for the other five tests was 2.71. In any case, the unusual results for this Verbal Analytical test call for additional and more specific investigation.

The average ipsative validity is 0.38. This value indicates that of the 15 pairs of tests, on the average 10.35 (i.e. 69%) are concordant in the two profiles compared, and the remaining 4.65 pairs (31%) are discordant. This value is not very impressive, although it represents a 38% improvement over the chance level performance of 7.5 pairs. This mean value is somewhat misleading since it is heavily influenced by a small group of examinees (12% of the sample) with negative indices, and an even smaller group (6%) with zero validities. The median ipsative validity is 0.43.

The analysis of variance of these indices shows that the same factors affecting the group validity play a major role at the individual level as well. A test-taker can better evaluate the profile of his/her performance after the actual test, and the process of evaluation is more accurately performed by test takers of high intelligence, and with a history of high achievements. The explanation of this fact is the same one offered in the section dealing with the regular measures of validity.

References

Applebaum, M.I. & Cramer, E.M. (1974). Some problems in the nonorthogonal analysis of variance. *Psychological Bulletin, 81,* 335-343.

Arsenian, A. (1942). Own estimate and objective measurement. *Journal of Educational Psychology, 33,* 291-302.

Bailey, R.C. & Bailey, K.G. (1971). Perceived ability in rlation to actual ability and academic achievement. *Journal of Clinical Psychology, 27,* 461-463.

Bailey, K.G. & Lazar, J. (1976). Accuracy of self-ratings of intelligence as a function of sex and level of ability in college students. *Journal of Genetic Psychology, 129,* 273-290.

Berdie, R.F. (1971). Self-claimed and tested knowledge. *Educational and Psychological Measurement, 31,* 629-636.

Campbell, D.T. & Fiske, D.W. (1959). Convergent and discriminant validation by the multitrait-multimethod matrix. *Psychological Bulletin, 56,* 81-105.

Cattell, R.B. (1944). Psychological measurement: Normative, ipsative, interactive. *Psychological Review, 51,* 292-303.

Denisi, A.S. & Shaw, J.B. (1977). Investigation of the uses of self-reports of abilities. *Journal of Applied Psychology, 62,* 641-644.

Gilmor, T.M. & Reid, D.W. (1978). Locus of control, prediction, and performance on university examinations. *Journal of Consulting and Clinical Psychology, 46,* 565-566.

Guttman, L. & Levy, S. (1980). Two structural laws for intelligence. *Megamot, 25,* 421-438 (in Hebrew with English abstract).

Kirk, B.A. & Sereda, L. (1969). Accuracy of self-reported college grade averages and characteristics of non and discrepant reporters. *Educational Psychology Measurement, 29,* 147-155.

Kooker, E.W. (1974). Changes in ability of graduate students in education to assess own test performance as related to their miller analogies scores. *Psychological Reports, 35,* 97-98.

Mabe, P.A. & West, S.G. (1982). Validity of self-evaluation of ability: A review and meta-analysis. *Journal of Applied Psychology, 67,* 280-296.

Nevo, B. & Szef, J. (1986). Examinees' feedback questionnaire (EFeQ). In Nevo, B., and Jäger, R.S. (Eds.) *Psychological Testing: The Examinee Perspective.* Verlag für Psychologie, Göttingen, pp. 21-30.

Schmitt, N. Coyle, B.W. & Saary, B.B. (1977). A review and critique of analysis of multitrait-multimethod matrices. *Multivariate Behavioral Research, 12,* 447-478.

9

Attitudes and Reactions of West German Students with Respect to Scholastic Aptitude Tests in Selection and Counseling Programs

Günter Trost

Abstract

In the context of the evaluation of the Test for Medical Studies (TMS) as part of a new selection procedure for admission to West German schools of medicine, dentistry and veterinary science, the candidates' attitudes towards aptitude tests in general and towards the TMS in particular, their ways of preparing for the test and their ratings of the utility of these preparations were explored by means of a questionnaire. The relations between the applicants' responses to all questionnaire items and their performance in the test were analyzed.

As part of the evaluation of a new aptitude test battery for counseling senior secondary students in their choice of academic career, the testees were asked to judge various aspects of the test program such as information on the tests, test administration, feedback of results and the overall usefulness of participation in this program. Again the correlations between the testees' ratings and their test results were determined.

The author suggests that studies on the testees' reactions to psychological tests ought to be carried out as a regular part of the pretesting whenever large-scale assessment programs are to be established or new tests are to be published.

Introduction

Among all the standard textbooks on psychological testing issued in the last three decades I have found only one that devoted a chapter to the topic of "The Layman's View of Testing" (Fiske, 1971, pp. 204-206). It is true that the subjects' reactions to the diagnostic situation in general and their attitudes towards certain aspects of personality tests in particular have been investigated in a fairly large number of studies since the mid-sixties (see e.g., Spitznagel, 1982, pp. 260-267). However, with the exception of the aspect of face validity, very little research has been carried out to study the test-takers' reactions to ability and achievement tests. (e.g. Brim, Goslin, Glass & Goldberg, 1964; Brim, Neulinger & Glass, 1965; Haase, 1978).

Since the mid-eighties the testees' perceptions of aptitude tests and their reactions to the testing situation have attracted increased attention, not least due to the appearance of the first monograph on this topic edited in 1985 by Nevo and Jäger. In the same year Schuler and Stehle called for the "investigation of the (examinees') attitudes towards the various methods and their ways of experiencing the diagnostic situations" (1985, p. 135; translated by G.T.) as one of several measures to meet the increasing criticism of psychological testing.

On the following pages, I report on West German test-takers' attitudes and reactions with respect to scholastic aptitude tests. The data were obtained in two very different settings:

a) In the context of the evaluation of a new aptitude test as part of the selection procedure for admission to medical studies the candidates were asked about their opinions and judgments shortly before taking the test.

b) In the context of the evaluation of a new test battery which had been developed to give students graduating from upper secondary school some orientation for their choice of subject areas at university, the testees were asked for their comments on the tests and the counseling program after they had taken the tests and received the feedback.

Applicants' Attitudes Towards an Admission Test for Medical Studies and Some Other Elements of Selection

Before and after the nationwide introduction of an aptitude test as an obligatory part of the selection program for admission to West German schools of medicine, dentistry, and veterinary science, it was possible to ask large numbers of applicants about their attitudes towards the test - and also to compare these attitudes with those towards other instruments of selection - as well as about their preparation for the test.

In the Federal Republic of Germany, all but one of the schools of medicine, dentistry and veterinary science, are state institutions, and the admission regulations are equally valid for all of them. In the seventies and early eighties, five to eight times as many students applied for these schools every year as there were study places available (only in recent years has the selection ratio become less unfavorable). Until 1980 the necessary selection for admission was mainly based on two criteria: the average mark in the secondary school leaving certificate (Abitur) and the length of time the candidate had had to wait for admission. As a consequence of this system, with the number of applicants increasing from year to year, only candidates with top marks could be offered immediate access, whereas the rest had to wait up to eight years. This situation led to strong public criticism and to a ruling by the Federal Constitutional Court that the system had to be replaced.

In 1980, a new selection procedure was introduced for a transition period of six years. For the first time in German history, an aptitude test became part of a selection program for admission to university. The transition period was basically intended to be a "time of probation" for the new test. The main features of the selection procedure during that period were (cf. Trost, 1988, p. 216):

- Participation in the test was not compulsory; yet taking the test did improve chances of admission. The test was administered twice a year to a maximum of 6000 applicants each. About one fourth of the places were awarded according to a combined score of Abitur average mark and test result, the Abitur mark having a weight of 55 percent and the test score 45 percent. Another 2 percent of the places were reserved for those who did best in the test, no matter what school marks they had earned. 10 percent of the places were awarded to applicants with the best school marks.

- About 20 percent of the places were reserved for special groups of applicants, e.g., "hardship cases" and foreigners.

- All candidates who could not be admitted by the procedures mentioned above took part in a so-called "achievement-controlled drawing of lots" (the better average marks in the Abitur, the more lots could be drawn). 35 to 40 percent of the places were awarded by this procedure.

- All rejected candidates could apply repeatedly without restriction.

The "Test for Medical Studies" (TMS) which was used during the transition period consisted of 13 subtests with a total of 280 multiple-choice items; it lasted over five hours. The test was designed to measure the particular skills and aptitudes needed to meet the theoretical and practical requirements of courses in medical studies. Factual knowledge does not play an important part in the test; however, in the science comprehension section, familiarity with typical problems and terminology in biology, chemistry and physics does enhance the test results. Personality, motivation or interest scales are not included in the examination. Each time the TMS was administered a new test version was used.

Results of the Transition Period

During the trial period an extensive evaluation of the selection program was carried out. Part of the evaluation studies were focused on the applicants' attitudes towards the test and their preparation for the test session. All candidates who were registered for participation in the test were sent a questionnaire. They were asked to answer it and to bring the answer sheet to the test locality. Of course, responding to the questionnaire was not obligatory and the candidates' answers did not have any influence on the results of their application. Anonymity in the data processing was assured.

The questionnaire, which covered many more areas such as biographical data and interests, had been devised by the research psychologists of the Institute for Test Development and Talent Research in close cooperation with a scientific Board of Evaluation appointed by the government. No attempt was made to construct scales to measure psychological constructs. The primary purpose of this investigation was a descriptive one. (However, some psychological hypotheses regarding the relationship between certain answers and the results in the TMS could be tested; they will be mentioned below.)

Each topic of interest was represented by one item in the questionnaire. The items had been pretested in 1980 on a small sample of students. Not all questions were used for the whole time span of the transition period. This contribution will focus on nine questions. Six of them were used in the first three test sessions (August 1980, February 1981 and August 1981), the remaining three in seven subsequent test sessions (August 1980 through August 1983).

The rates of responses to these questions range from 97 to 100 percent, i.e., practically all candidates who completed the test and reported their average Abitur marks answered them. However it could not be taken for granted that the testees were representative for the total population of applicants for admission to medicine, dentistry, and veterinary science in the years in question because the number of participants in the TMS was restricted to a maximum of 6000 while the total number of applicants was 4.5-8 times higher. Nevertheless Bartussek, Raatz, Stapf and Schneider (1984, chap. 2), after a careful examination of this matter on the example of the first two test administrations, concluded that the testees were highly representative for all applicants of the respective years so that the results can be generalized.

These were the items and the responses offered:

a) "Have you taken an aptitude/intelligence test before?" (no, never/ yes, once/yes, more than once)

b) (To those who had taken such tests before:) "What were your experiences with aptitude/intelligence tests?" (positive/neither positive nor negative/negative)

c) "Do you think the information on the function of the test in the admission procedure is sufficient?" (yes/no)

d) "Do you think the information on the structure and content of the admission test is sufficient?" (yes/no)

e) "What is your general attitude towards achievement and aptitude tests?" (rather negative/neutral/rather positive)

f) "Do you think the admission test can measure the qualification for medical studies?" (yes/no)

g) "Do you think the average mark in the Abitur certificate tells more about the qualification for medical studies than the test does?" (yes/ no)

h) "Do you consider the introduction of the test an improvement of the admission procedure?" (yes/no)

i) "Do you consider it sensible to introduce an interview into the admission procedure?" (yes/no)

The frequencies of the responses, in some cases broken down by demographical data or by responses to other questions, as well as the average test results of the various subgroups of respondents were reported separately for each test session by Deter (1982a,b,c; 1983), Deter and Ebnet (1981), and Fay (1984). In order to allow for a synopsis of the results from different test sessions the data are presented here in an aggregated form. This proceeding is justified by the facts that

- the questionnaire items were always administered in the same wording and the same order,
- the structure of the population of applicants did not change markedly in the course of the years 1980-1983,
- the results of the questionnaire analyses on different test cohorts are

characterized by an extraordinary stability,
- for each test session the overall scores in the TMS were standardized on the basis of the distribution of scores of all testees of a given term,
- the test versions used on the different sessions can be considered as parallel forms (r_{tt} = .87).

Table 1 shows the proportion of responses to the different options for each of the questions presented above. The mean and standard deviation of the total test scores of those who had marked the respective options, the index h of the strength of effect between the responses and the test results,[1] the overall number of respondents and the period during which the questionnaire item was administered.

---

1   Like the product-moment correlation coefficient, the coefficient h ranges from .00 to 1.00 and indicates the degree of difference between two or more groups with regard to a continuous, normally distributed variable. According to Cohen (1987, pp. 283-288) h values of .10 can be interpreted as "small" size of effect of the grouping on the continuous variable, h >.24 as "medium" and h >.37 as "large" effect size.

183

Table 1

Percentage and Average Test Results of Applicants who Marked Different Answers on Questions a – i; Strength of Effect of the Grouping by Answers on Test Performance. (All η values above .03 are significant; p < .01)

questions	% of respondents	TSM score mean	stand. deviation	strenght of effect η median	range	total N of respondents	question asked on
a)	44	99,3	9,9				3 test sessions
	41	100,6	9,9	.08	.06-.09	16,114	(8/80-8/81)
	15	100,6	10,3				
b)	18	102,9	10,3				3 test sessions
	53	100,6	9,7	.13	.10-.15	9,036	(8/80-8/81)
	28	98,5	9,9				
c)	72	101,2	9,9				3 test sessions
				.14	.13-.15	15,653	(8/80-8/81)
	28	97,9	10,0				
d)	70	101,0	9,9				3 test sessions
				.14	.0	15,786	(8/80-8/81)
	30	97,9	9,9				
e)	47	99,3	9,7				7 test sessions
	35	100,3	9,6	.10	.08-.13	37,464	(8/80-8/83)
		102,0	0,9				
f)	36	101,9	9,9				3 test sessions
				.14	.12-.15	15,806	(8/80-8/81)
	64	99,9	9,9				
g)	9	101,9	9,8				3 test sessions
				.06	.05-.07	15,885	(8/80-8/81)
	91	99,8	10,0				
h)	67	100,6	9,8				7 test sessions
				.07	.03-.09	36,878	(8/80-8/83)
	33	99,0	9,9				
i)	63	99,3	9,7				7 test sessions
				.11	.10-.13	37,038	(8/80-8/83)
	37	101,5	9,8				

Only little more than half of the applicants-who were at least 19 years old-reported that they had taken an aptitude or intelligence test before (item a). A slight majority of those who had test experience judged this experience neither positively nor negatively; among the rest negative experiences were more frequent than positive ones (item b). Almost two out of three applicants considered the information on the function of the test in the transition procedure of admission sufficient (item c); about the same proportion judged the information on content and structure of the TMS sufficient (item d).

When asked about their general attitude towards achievement and aptitude tests almost half of the applicants expressed a "rather negative" attitude, about one third were neutral, only 18 percent indicated a "rather positive" attitude (item e). Two thirds doubted that the TMS could measure the qualification for medical studies (item f). Even more critical was the corresponding judgment regarding the Abitur average mark: Nine out of ten candidates do not think it tells more about the qualification for medical studies than the Abitur test does (item g).

Despite the majority's rather pessimistic view of the predictive value of the TMS, two-thirds of the applicants declared that they considered the introduction of the test an improvement of the admission procedure (item h). A somewhat lower proportion was in favor of the introduction of an interview (item i).

In a second step we tried to find out if those who differed in their answers to the questionnaire items also differed in their average performance in the test. The hypotheses were that those applicants who had had test experience before, who viewed this experience as a positive one, who felt better informed about the TMS and who had a positive attitude towards the test (and towards the average Abitur mark as another cognitive predictor of academic success), would on average earn somewhat higher overall test scores than the respective contrast groups. It was further expected that those who favored the interview would do less well in the TMS than the contrast group.

The data were generally in line with the hypotheses, as Table 1 shows. All differences in mean test scores tend in the expected directions. The effects are at best small: six out of the nine median h coefficients are equal to .10 or larger, but none is higher than .14. The comparatively largest differences were found in favor of those candidates who judged the information on the tests' function as well as its structure and content sufficient

(items c and d), those who believed that the TMS could measure the qualification for medical studies (item f), and those who had had positive experiences with aptitude or intelligence tests before (item b).

Interesting as this information may be, it was collected under the special
circumstances of the transition period when the Test for Medical Studies
was being tried out but was not yet established as an obligatory part of the
admission program. So it was necessary to replicate at least part of the
study at a later point of time, namely after the introduction of the new system of selection for admission to the schools of medicine, dentistry and veterinary science. A description of the new regulations and a report on
some results of an analysis on the total population of testees in the fall of
1986 is given in the next section.

Results of an Investigation after the Introduction of the New Admission Procedure

The analysis of the testees' attitudes towards the Test for Medical Studies
and other elements of the admission procedure was of course only one of
the numerous studies that were carried out to evaluate the new test during the probationary period. Other important areas of evaluation were
the predictive validity of the TMS with regard to medical courses, test fairness, the test's possible responsiveness to training and coaching, and the
correlation between test score and average mark in school (Bartussek et
al., 1984, 1985, 1986; Fay, 1986; Trost, 1985; Trost et al., 1980-1987).
On the whole the empirical data and the practical experience with test administration suggested that the introduction of the TMS as an obligatory
part of the selection procedure for admission to medical studies was justifiable from both the scientific and the political point of view. Therefore
the Ministers of Education and Cultural Affairs of the West German
states agreed upon a new admission procedure, which came into operation in 1986.
Each candidate-except those who have already completed another
course of study at university and foreigners - has to go through the test before applying for admission. The places are awarded in five different
quotas. In two of these quota the test result plays a part: 45 percent of the
places are awarded according to a combined criterion of average Abitur
mark (with a weight of 55 percent) and the test score (with a weight of 45
percent); another 10 percent of the places are reserved to those who do

best in the TMS. In the remaining three quotas, the criteria are the length of time the applicants have had to wait for admission (20 percent of the places), the result of an interview conducted by members of the faculty (15 percent) and special circumstances such as status of a foreigner, hardship cases, etc. (10 percent). (For further details see Kultusministerkonferenz, 1985.)

On the basis of the empirical data of the tryout period, the test was revised for its new function. Now it contains nine subtests with a total of 204 items. It is administered once a year.

When registering for the test, the candidates fill in a short questionnaire which, however, does not contain items related to their attitudes towards the TMS but only questions about their biographical and educational background.

To learn, among other things, about the applicants' preparation for the test and their opinions of the TMS and other aspects of the selection procedure, a separate questionnaire was devised and sent to all those who had registered for the test in the fall of 1986.[2] They were requested to fill it in on the day before the test and bring it to the test room; they were told that participation in this investigation was voluntary. In fact, 19,629 applicants (87 percent of the total number of 22,655 testees) responded to the inventory. In terms of performance in the TMS and average Abitur mark, the respondents do not differ from the total population of testees (Hensgen & Blum, 1988, p. 28, p. 77). One of the questions was: "How do you rate the usefulness of your personal method of preparing for the test?" The options to be rated separately were:

- Working through the sample items and explanations in the test brochure (abbreviation: "test brochure")
- Working through one or both of the published original versions of the TMS ("original versions")
- Working through one or several of the coaching books for the test ("coaching books") Participation in a coaching course/preparation seminar for the test ("coaching course")

---

2   This study was carried out by Thomas Kirchenkamp & Harald Mispelkamp; the complete results are reported in Kirchenkamp & Mispelkamp (1988).

Table 2

Number and Percentage of Applicants who Chose Various Ways of
Preparation for the Test for Medical Studies (TMS), their Rating of the
Chosen Methods of Preparation, their Average Test Results, and Strength
of Effect of the Grouping on Differences in Test Performance

method of preparation for the TMS	number of persons	% of all respondents	ratings of usefulness (1 = useless, 4 = very useful)	TMS score mean	stand. deviation	strength of effect η
test brochure	16,074	82	3.1	100.8	9.7	.07*
original versions	13,048	67	3.4	101.5	9.7	.06*
coaching books	2,077	11	3.0	102.6	9.9	.08*
coaching course	1,035	5	3.3	102.9	9.6	.03
other	325	2	-	101.1	9.0	-
no preparation	1,438	7	-	96.1	9.9	-
all respondents	19,629	100	-	100.3	9.8	-

The numbers of respondents to this question are 6-18 pereent lower than the numbers in column one.
*significant (p ‹ .01)

Table 2 shows the frequency of choice of each of the various methods of preparation, the average ratings of their usefulness, the average test scores of those who chose the respective options, and the index of the strength of effect. As can be seen in the table, before taking the TMS more than eight out of ten applicants had worked through the test brochure, which is distributed free of charge; and two out of three candidates had used the officially published original versions of the test which can be purchased at low price. Only one out of ten had used non-authorized coaching books, and one out of twenty applicants had taken a coaching course. Seven percent reported that they had not prepared themselves at all.

On average, the highest ratings in terms of usefulness were given to the original versions and the coaching courses; the test brochure and commercial coaching books obtained somewhat lower ratings but still were considered useful.

The differences in test scores of the various subpopulations grouped according to their ratings are very small. In general the values indicate a minor tendency for higher ratings to go along with higher test scores. Only in the case of "coaching books" did candidates with better test performance tend to judge the usefulness of this kind of preparation negatively.

Those who reported that they had attended a coaching course and those who reportedly had used coaching books achieved, on average, the highest test scores. However, more detailed analyses show that (a) both groups used the official material (test brochure and original versions) as well and that (b) especially the latter group are somewhat pre-selected with regard to abilities and motivation (Fay, 1985), i.e., there is a tendency for the abler and the more motivated ones to try and use as many possibilities as they can find to prepare themselves for the test.

For the effect of grouping the testees according to their various methods of preparation (including the most frequently chosen combinations) on performance in the test, the h coefficient amounts to .19 (Kirchenkamp & Mispelkamp, 1988, p. 257).

Another question was:

"Do you consider the introduction of the test an improvement of the admission procedure?"

For comparison, the testees were also asked:

"Do you consider the introduction of the interview an improvement of the admission procedure?" Table 3 shows the frequency of affirmative versus negative answers on both questions and the average test scores of those in favor or against the two diagnostic instruments in the given context.

Table 3

Number, Percentage and Average Test Results of Applicants
who Consider/dont't Consider the Introduction of the Test or the
Interview an Improvement of the Admission Procedure; Strength of the
Effect of the Grouping on Differences in Test Performance

question	response	% of respondents	TMS score mean / stand. deviation		strength of effect η	total N of respondents
Do you consider the introduction of the test an improvement of the admission procedure?	yes	54	101.1	9.7		
					.05*	15.923
	no	46	100.0	9.8		
Do you consider the introduction of the interview an improvement of the admission procedure?	yes	77	100.3	9.7		
					.05*	15.960
	no	23	101.5	9.7		

* significant (p ‹ .01)

Only a small majority of the testees consider the introduction of the test an improvement; in the years 1980-1983, when participation in the test was voluntary, the corresponding percentage had been 67. The similar question, now concerning the interview, was answered in the affirmative by 77 percent as compared with 63 percent in the years 1980-1983 when the interview was not employed at all and the question was formulated more hypothetically.

There are only slight differences in the average test scores of those who answered each of the questions differently, still they tend in the expected direction.
The last question of the inventory read as follows:
"In your opinion, which criteria or procedures ought to be applied for the selection in the context of the admission to medical studies?" (Mark one or several options.)

- average Abitur mark
- interview
- test result
- waiting-time

- practical work in a hospital
- lottery
- practical work in medical or
- social areas
- others: ....

In reply, 69 percent of the respondents marked "practical work in medical or social areas"; 67 percent chose the "interview", and 60 percent "practical work in a hospital." The criteria "Abitur average mark" and "waiting-time" were favored by 48 percent each, the "test result" by 44 percent. Only 18 percent felt that the study places should be awarded on the basis of a "lottery."

Examinees' Reactions to Aptitude Tests as Part of a Counseling Program

The Test Program

Since the mid-seventies the Institute for Test Development and Talent Research has been developing a test battery consisting of a general scholastic aptitude test and six "study-field oriented tests" (Studienfeldbezogene Tests) aiming at the assessment of the specific cognitive aptitudes which are relevant for success in the following university subject areas or "study fields":

- Business and Economics
- Engineering Sciences
- Law

- Mathematics
- Modern Languages
- Natural Sciences

Each test contains 4 to 10 subtests with 75 (Test for Mathematics) to 176 items (Test for Modern Languages) and lasts about 3 1/2 hours. (For a detailed description of the test battery including sample items and feedback forms see Blum, Hensgen & Trost, 1985.) The tests are intended to be used exclusively for counseling purposes. They are devised for students in upper secondary school who wish to obtain an orientation about their individual chances of succeeding at university in the particular study courses they are interested in. This information, along with the results of an interest questionnaire, are intended to help them in their decision about whether to go to university and if so in which courses to enrol. According to their preferences the counsellees can participate in one or several of the tests and are then given detailed feedback.

Several cross-sectional construct validity studies on almost 10,000 students were carried out in the late seventies and early eighties. At present, a long-term longitudinal study of the predictive validity of the tests is in its final stage. It is to be hoped that after the completion of this study and a revision of the tests based on its results the test program will be established on a nationwide scale. One of the cross-sectional studies was accompanied by an investigation of the testees reactions to the aptitude tests, the test situation, and the feedback they were given.

The Study

In 1983 and 1984 all secondary schools in a large circumscribed geographical area of one of the states of the Federal Republic (Lower Saxony) were asked to cooperate for the study; 79 out of the 82 schools complied with this request. All students of grades 12 and 13 were invited to take one or several of the tests. The total number of participants was 3717; 4428 individual test results were processed.

In the feedback letter sent to the private addresses of all testees with their individual test scores, reference data and a detailed interpretation of their results, a short questionnaire was enclosed inquiring about their judgments of the test program. 1691 students (45 percent of the testees) responded. A comparison of the group of respondents with the total group of testees revealed great similarity in terms of proportions of males and females as well as of grade 12 and grade 13 students, of educational aspirations, and of previous experience with tests; however, on average the respondents had achieved somewhat better test results than the total group. Therefore, at least with respect to academic aptitudes, the group of respondents is not totally representative for the population of testees.

Eight out of the 15 items in the inventory consisted of 5-point rating scales and were introduced by the question:
"How do you judge the following aspects of the trial administration of the test program?"

1) Information on the test program ("totally insufficient" -"totally sufficient")
2) Organization of test administration ("very poor" - "very good")
3) Degree of difficulty of the test(s) you took ("very easy" -"very difficult")
4) Layout and segmentation of the test(s) (e.g., sequence of items, timing of the break) ("very poor" - "very good")
5) Contents of the test(s) (e.g., supposed relation to requirements of the study courses, clearness of instructions) ("very poor" - "very good")
6) Intelligibility of the feedback of test results ("hardly intelligible" - "highly intelligible")
7) Value of information of the feedback ("not informative at all" - "very informative")
8) Usefulness of participation in tests of this kind ("not useful at all" - "very useful")

Each of these items except the last one also provided open space for free comments. Two further items were presented in multiple-choice format with optional answers to the questions:

9) "Would you also be willing to participate in tests of this kind if you were charged a fee of DM 20-30?"
10) "Which were the motive(s) for you to take the test(s)?"

The remaining five items were open questions asking for general remarks concerning the preparation and organization of the test administration, the structure and content of the test(s), the concrete meaning the test results had for the testee, and for suggestions as to the further development and use of the counseling tests.

Table 4

Frequency of Ratings on a 5-Point Scale and Median Ratings of Eight Aspects of the Counseling Test Program; Median, Minimum and Maximum Correlations with Total Scores in the Seven Tests (N = 1,691)

aspects of the test programm	frequency of ratings in per cent (poorest) 1 2 3 4 5 (best)	median rating	correlation with total test scores median	range
1) information on the test program	4 19 24 31 22	3.6	.07	.03 to .12
2) organization of test administration	1 5 13 39 42	4.3	.05	.02 to .16
3) degree of difficulty of test(s)	(very 0 10 36 42 12 (very easy) difficult)	3.6	-.31 *	-.18 to -.47 *
4) layout and segmentation of the test(s)	1 8 31 44 16	3.7	.25 *	.14 to .34 *
5) contents of the test(s)	3 11 33 40 13	3.6	.31 *	.24 * to .37 *
6) intelligibility of the feedback of test results	1 4 13 37 45	4.4	.24 *	.15 to .29 *
7) value of information of the feedback	2 17 38 34 19	3.3	.17 *	.06 to .28 *
8) usefulness of participation in tests of this kind	7 20 32 29 12	3.2	.33 *	.26 * to .39 *

* significant (p < .01)

Some Results

A detailed analysis and interpretation of the responses to all items of the questionnaire can be found in the book mentioned above (Blum et al., 1985, chap. 4.2). The data presented here are restricted to questions 1-8. Table 4 shows the percentage of ratings 1-5 and the median ratings given to the eight aspects of the test program. In all items except item 3 (test difficulty) higher ratings meant higher degrees of agreement or satisfaction with the aspects in question on the part of the testees. It can be seen at first glance that in all of the seven items the positive judgments prevail. In comparison, the two top points of the rating scale were marked most frequently with respect to the "intelligibility of the feedback of test results" (82 percent of the respondents) and to the "organization of test administration" (81 percent). In the rank order of the testees satisfaction the aspects "layout and segmentation of the test(s)", "information on the test program" and "contents of the test(s)" took a middle position (median ratings: 3.7, 3.6 and 3.6). Somewhat more reserved were the judgments on the "value of information of the feedback" and the general appraisal of the "usefulness of participation in tests of this kind" (median ratings: 3.3 and 3.2).

The numerous written comments in the questionnaires gave many useful hints as to the possibilities of improvement, especially with regard to the content and layout of the information or feed-back material and strategies of information. They also revealed, for instance, that a considerable proportion of respondents did not judge their personal participation in the test program very useful for the sole reason that they had already decided in which course of study to enrol before taking the test(s). The value of 3.6 for the median rating of the test difficulty means that on average the testees judged the tests as moderately difficult. A medium degree of difficulty had indeed been intended by the test constructors, and as the results of the test analyses indicate this was achieved: The p values for the difficulties of the total tests range from .41 to .56; the median p value over all seven tests is .49. Hence the testees judgment was quite realistic.

A separate inspection of the ratings given with respect to each of the seven counseling tests leads to the conclusion that the patterns of judgments are very similar for all of the "study-field oriented tests." Only the ratings for the general scholastic aptitude test are somewhat less favor-

able as far as its content and its usefulness are concerned for the obvious reason that it lacks specifity.
It was interesting to see if there was a relation between the ratings of the various aspects of the test program and the performance in the tests. The last columns in table 4 show the minimum, maximum and median correlation coefficients.
As expected, there is no significant relation between the testees' reactions to the information on the test program and organizational aspects of test administration on the one hand and their test performance on the other. Low but partly significant correlations can be found between test scores and the testees' satisfaction with the value of information as well as the intelligibility of the feedback and with formal aspects of the tests such as layout and segmentation. The correlations of test performance with judgments on the test contents, test difficulty (the better the score, the easier the testee rates the test), and the usefulness of participation in tests of this kind are moderate. Correlations were also separately calculated for the different tests; the coefficients not presented here show no marked differences for the individual tests.

Discussion

It is obvious that the information on the testees' attitudes and reactions gathered in the context of the two test programs only covers one sector of the examinees' total perspective on psychological testing. In both programs the construction and use of the questionnaire items were guided by specific motives. In the case of the counseling tests it was the primary interest of the test authors to learn about possibilities of improving the material and the strategies of information, test administration and modes of feedback; consequently the questionnaire items focused on these elements. In the case of the Test for Medical Studies there was a considerable political interest in knowing how acceptable the new test was to the applicants before the decision was made to introduce it into the selection system; therefore the questions aimed at more general aspects.
Although the questions and the testees' answers speak for themselves, in some instances a brief discussion of the results seems worthwhile.
The fact that almost half of the applicants for medical schools aged 19 and over have never taken an aptitude or intelligence test before going through the TMS may surprise readers in many other Western societies

(Table 1, question a). For comparison, note that as early as in the mid-six-ties Brim and his collaborators found that 76 percent of a representative sample of US adults who had attended school for 12 years have had experi-ence with intelligence or aptitude tests (Brim et al., 1965, p. 134); in a rep-resentative sample of senior students in public high schools, at least 88 percent had taken an intelligence test (Brim et al., 1964, p. 76). Yet the figure in Table 1 is typical for the situation in West Germany where apti-tude tests are not very common in education; however, they are widely used in personnel selection.

Also the fairly negative general attitude towards achievement an dapti-tude tests found in our study (question a) appears to be representative of the attitude in the total West German population. Against this back-ground it is rather surprising that two-thirds of the respondents of the early eighties considered the introduction of the Test for Medical Studies an improvement of the admission procedure (question h). At that time, however, participation in the TMS was voluntary, and only a random sample of those who had volunteered for the test were given the oppor-tunity to take it and also to answer the questionnaire. These special cir-cumstances may explain the difference between the pattern of answers to this question in the early eighties and the pattern found in 1986 (Table 3), when only 54 percent of all testees were in favor of the test; in 1986, how-ever, taking the test was obligatory for practically all applicants. Still it is fair to say that the TMS is accepted by a small majority of the candidates.

Brim et al. (1965, p. 130) reported a very similar percentage (56 percent) of US adults answering "yes" to the question "Given tests as they are now, do you think it is fair to use intelligence, IQ or aptitude tests to help decide who goes to college or who does not?" With respect to the use of a scholastic aptitude test for the same purpose, a more recent study re-vealed a considerably higher degree of acceptance: 79 percent of about 3000 students who participated in a survey in 1977 felt that the score in the Scholastic Aptitude Test should have a "great deal" or "fair amount" of in-fluence on the decisions on college admission (see Barbara Lerner in this book).

The finding that the interview is much more widely accepted as an instru-ment of selection for admission to medical studies than the test (Table 3), as well as the rank order of the criteria of selection according to the candi-dates' attitudes as presented in section 2, are very much in line with the outcome of a study by Fruhner and Schuler (1987) on 605 West German university students about their opinions concerning the various practices in personnel selection: the "interview" ranged on top, followed in decreasing esteem by "work sample," "practical work," "marks in school," "tests" and "lottery." It can be assumed that by and large these opinions are shared by the total population of this country. Obviously this rank order does not correspond to the actual predictive validity of the diagnostic instruments in question.

A high degree of acceptance of the interview as an instrument of selection in education was also found among American applicants for medical schools (Gee, 1957; Gellman & Stewart, 1975; Poorman, 1975) as well as among representative samples of adults in the USA (Fiske, 1971, p. 205) and in Australia (Linke, Chalmers & Ashton, 1981, p. 418).

The testees' judgments of the information about the tests and their functions are satisfactory in both studies reported here (Tables 1 and 4). It also seems that the applicants for medical courses make good use of the official information material on the TMS - more than seems to be the case in the US with regard to the SAT (cf. Lerner in this book) - and thus are familiar with the test when they arrive at the test room. This is probably the main reason why commercial coaching has no drastic effect on test performance (Table 2).

From the data presented in section 3 (Table 4) it may be concluded that offering aptitude tests for counseling purposes has met satisfactory acceptance among secondary students in grades 12 and 13. So far the feedback could only be based on a comparison of the individual's scores with those of a large sample of students with the same area of study interests who took the same test(s). Once the ongoing validity studies are completed and the feedback includes information on the probability of success in the study courses in question, the practical use of the test program for the participants will be enhanced and the degree of acceptance will presumably be even higher.

All in all the relation between the testees' responses to the questionnaire items concerning the tests and their individual test scores was markedly closer in the study on the counseling test battery (Table 4) than in the analyses with the Test for Medical Studies (Tables 1 and 3). Of course the findings are not directly comparable because the tests as well as the settings in which they were administered were different, and the questionnaire items were not identical. Yet the difference in the correlations can at least partly be explained by the fact that in the latter case the candidates were asked shortly before taking the TMS (which was already familiar to most of them by virtue of the information material they had studied) whereas

198

in the case of the counseling tests, the testees responded to the questionnaire after taking the tests and after learning about their results, which certainly had an effect on their judgment of the tests and the whole test system.

The two studies described in this article have one important feature in common: in both cases the testees' attitudes and reactions with regard to new tests and test systems were - to great extent examined before these tests were introduced as elements of regular educational programs.

It would mean considerable progress in psychological testing if the investigation of the examinees' judgments became a routine part of pretest studies for new large-scale test programs. These judgments can be biased or based on misconceptions, and other criteria of the usefulness of tests may be more relevant; furthermore, there may be situations where tests are needed even though they are not well accepted by the testees. But it is important to know how the testees feel, and if their attitudes are negative, which may in fact reduce the validity of the test, it is often possible to alter them by means of better information, better explanations, changes in the actual test situation and better feedback.

I would go one step further by suggesting that the psychological associations might appoint committees to collect the existing questionnaire items dealing with the testees' perceptions of psychological tests, form out of this pool a standard set of questions applicable to a variety of tests, and recommend that this questionnaire be used before new tests are published. Is it utopian to conceive of future test manuals and test descriptions in reference books that contain an additional standard criterion of test evaluation: "Acceptance by the testees"?

References

Bartussek, D., Raatz, U., Stapf, & K.H. Schneider, B. (1984), (1985), (1986). Die Evaluation des Tests für medizinische Studiengänge. 1. Zwischenbericht 1984, 2. Zwischenbericht 1985, 3. Zwischenbericht 1986, Abschlußbericht 1986. Bonn: Sekretariat der Kultusministerkonferenz.

Blum, F., Hensgen, A. & Trost, G. (1985). *Beratungstests für Oberstufenschüler und Abiturienten.* Bonn: Institut für Test- und Begabungsforschung.

Brim, O.G., Goslin, D.A., Glass, D.C. & Goldberg, I. (1964). *The use of standardized ability tests in American secondary schools and their impact on students, teachers, and administrators.* New York: Russell Sage Foundation.

Brim, O.G., Neulinger, & J. Glass, D.C. (1965). *Experiences and attitudes of American adults concerning standardized intelligence tests.* New York: Russell Sage Foundation.

Cohen, J. (1977). *Statistical power analysis for the behavioral sciences.* New York: Academic Press.

Deter, B. (1982a). Beziehungen zwischen Testleistungen und Merkmalen des außerschulischen Bildungsweges beim zweiten Einsatz des TMS. In G. Trost et al., *Modellversuch "Tests für medizinische Studiengänge".* Bonn: Institut für Test- und Begabungsforschung.

Deter, B. (1982b). Weitergehende Analysen der Beziehungen zwischen den Antworten auf den Fragebögen zur Begleituntersuchung und den durchschnittlichen TMS-Leistungen der Teilnehmergruppe vom August 1980. In G. Trost et al., *Modellversuch "Tests für medizinische Studiengänge."* Bonn: Institut für Test- und Begabungsforschung.

Deter, B. (1982c). Beziehungen zwischen Testleistungen und Merkmalen des außerschulischen Bildungsweges beim dritten Einsatz des TMS. In G. Trost et al., *Modellversuch "Tests für medizinische Studiengänge".* Bonn: Institut für Test- und Begabungsforschung.

Deter, B. (1983). Beziehungen zwischen Testleistungen und Merkmalen des außerschulischen Bildungsweges beim vierten und fünften Einsatz des TMS. In G. Trost et al., *Modellversuch "Tests für medizinische Studiengänge."* Bonn: Institut für Test- und Begabungsforschung.

Deter, B. & Ebnet, U. (1981). Beziehungen zwischen Testleistungen und Merkmalen des außerschulischen Bildungsweges. In G. Trost et al., Modellversuch *"Tests für medizinische Studiengänge".* Bonn: Institut für Test- und Begabungsforschung.

Fay, E. (1984). Beziehungen zwischen Leistungen im TMS und Merkmalen des außerschulischen Bildungsweges beim sechsten und siebten Testtermin. In G. Trost et al., *Modellversuch "Tests für medizinische Studiengänge."* Bonn: Institut für Test- und Begabungsforschung.

Fay, E. (1985). Vorbereitungsmöglichkeiten auf den "Test für medizinische Studiengänge": Was gibt es? Wie wird es genutzt? Nutzt es? In G. Trost et al., *Modellversuch "Tests für medizinische Studiengänge"*. Bonn: Institut für Test- und Begabungsforschung.

Fay, E. (1986). Die Rolle der Psychodiagnostik bei der Zulassung zum Studium der Human-, Tier- und Zahnmedizin. Psychologie und Praxis. *Zeitschrift für Arbeits- und Organisationspsychologie, 30, 68-76.*

Fiske, D.W. (1971). *Measuring the concepts of personality.* Chicago: Aldine.

Fruhner, R. & Schuler, H. (1987). *Bewertung eignungsdiagnostischer Verfahren zur Personalauswahl durch potentielle Stellenbewerber.* Vortrag, gehalten beim 14. Kongreß für Angewandte Psychologie des Berufsverbandes Deutscher Psychologen, 24.-27.9.1987 in Mainz.

Gee, H.H. (1957). The student view of the medical admissions process. *Journal of Medical Education, 32,* 140-152.

Gellman, E.P. & Stewart, J.P. (1975). Faculty and students as admission interviewers: Results of a questionnaire. *Journal of Medical Education, 50,* 626-628.

Haase, H. (1978). *Tests im Bildungswesen. Urteile und Vorurteile.* Göttingen: Hogrefe.

Hensgen A. & Blum, F. (1988). Vergleiche einzelner Teilnehmergruppen beim zweiten Termin des besonderen Auswahlverfahrens: zahlenmäßige Anteile, Test- und Schulleistungen. In G. Trost (Hrsg.), *Tests für medizinische Studiengänge (TMS): Studien zur Evaluation (S. 22-91).* Bonn: Institut für Test- und Begabungsforschung.

Kirchenkamp T. & Mispelkamp, H. (1988). Beziehungen zwischen Leistungen im Test für medizinische Studiengänge und verschiedenen Vorbereitungsmaßnahmen, Einstellungen zum Vergabeverfahren sowie links- bzw. rechtshändiger Schreibweise. In G. Trost (Hrsg.), *Test für medizinische Studiengänge (TMS): Studien zur Evaluation (S. 248-279).* Bonn: Institut für Test- und Begabungsforschung.

Kultusministerkonferenz. (Hrsg.) (1985). *Die Hochschulzulassung ab Wintersemester 1986/87, insbesondere zu den medizinischen Studiengängen. Informationsbroschüre.* Bonn: Sekretariat der Kultusministerkonferenz.

Linke, R., Chalmers, J. & Ashton, J. (1981). A survey of opinion among different occupational groups toward selection of medical students. *Medical Education, 15,* 414-421.

Nevo, B. & Jäger, R.S. (Eds.). (1986). *Psychological testing: The examinee perspective.* Göttingen: Hogrefe.

Poorman, D.H. (1975). Medical School applicant: A study of the admissions interview. *Journal of Kansas Medical Society, 76,* 298-301.

Schuler, H. & Stehle, W. (1985). Soziale Validität eignungsdiagnostischer Verfahren: Anforderungen für die Zukunft. In H. Schuler & W. Stehle (Hrsg.), *Organisationspsychologie und Unternehmenspraxis: Perspektiven der Kooperation (S. 133-138).* Stuttgart: Verlag für Angewandte Psychologie.

Spitznagel, A. (1982). Die diagnostische Situation. In K.-J. Groffmann & L. Michel (Hrsg.), *Grundlagen psychologischer Diagnostik. Enzyklopädie der Psychologie, Themenbereich B, Serie II, Bd. 1 (S. 248-294).* Göttingen: Hogrefe.

Trost, G. (1985). Pädagogische Diagnostik beim Hochschulzugang, dargestellt am Beispiel der Zulassung zu den medizinischen Studiengängen. In R.S. Jäger, R. Horn & K. Ingenkamp (Hrsg.), *Tests und Trends 4. Jahrbuch der Pädagogischen Diagnostik (S. 41-81).* Weinheim: Beltz.

Trost, G. (1988). Ein psychologischer Beitrag zur Regelung des Hochschulzugangs. In F. Losel & H. Skowronek (Hrsg.), *Beiträge der Psychologie zu politischen Planungs- und Entscheidungsprozessen (S. 213-224).* Weinheim: Deutscher Studien Verlag.

Trost, G., Blum, F., Deter, B., Ebnet, U., Fay, E., Hensgen, A., Maichle, U., Mausfeld, R., Mispelkamp, H., Nauels, H.-U. & Stumpf, H. (1980-1987). *Modellversuch "Tests für medizinische Studiengänge." 3. bis 11. Arbeitsbericht.* Bonn: Institut für Test- und Begabungsforschung.

10

Correlates of Students' Reactions to their Testing Environment

Oluf M. Davidsen and James Maxey

Abstract

The physical environment in which mental tests are administered can be an important factor in the veracity and reliability of the examination results. Using a 5 percent stratified sample drawn from a population of half a million students who took the American College Testing Program (ACT) college entrance examination in 1987, the authors summarize students' responses to a questionnaire about certain aspects of the physical conditions under which they took the tests: writing surface, lighting, spacing of examinees and noise level in the test room. Relationships between these responses and selected background characteristics of the students are explored and themes in these relationships are reported.

Introduction

The merit of test scores compared with teachers' marks or grades and other forms of evaluation of student progress and achievement has long been a source of debate in education circles. Most college admissions officers, academic advisers and other users of college entrance test results would agree that a primary advantage of test scores is that they are comparable for all test takers, given that the test has been "standardized" with respect to content, scoring scale, norming, and time allowed for responding to the test items.

To further promote comparability of results, care is taken to assure that the conditions under which the tests are administered are as uniform and as free from distractions as possible. The test room conditions, whether in terms of amount of light available, size of writing surface, or noise level, constitute a significant potential source of measurement error and, as such, have long been a topic of interest to the authors (Boggs, 1968; Igle, 1969; Traxler, 1942). The study reported here deals specifically with student test-takers' reactions to various aspects of the physical conditions under which they take the ACT Assessment Program (AAP) tests, a 3.1/2 hour examination used in the transition from secondary to higher education in the USA.

The AAP, popularly known as the ACT tests, is developed and administered by the American College Testing Program (ACT), a non-profit educational testing organization founded in 1959. Each year more than one million high school juniors and seniors take the ACT examination, which consists of four standardized tests in English, Mathematics, Social Studies and Natural Science. The tests are administered five times annually at approximately 3800 test centers (secondary schools and colleges) throughout the United States and overseas. Test results are used by students, parents, counselors, college and university personnel and scholarship agencies for a variety of purposes, including educational planning, admissions, academic advising, course placement and scholarship awards. The specific use made of the test results by colleges and universities is often a function of the type of institution involved, given that the nearly 3000 user institutions range from open admissions institutions to highly selective ones.

In addition to the four standardized tests, the AAP includes a comprehensive non-cognitive section - the Student Profile Section - made up of a vocational interest inventory, biographic and demographic items, and questions about the students' educational and career interests, aspirations and plans, secondary school courses taken and marks earned, and self-assessment of educational needs and strengths. In addition, students are asked to evaluate various aspects of their secondary school experience. The Student Profile Section is completed by students as part of the test registration process several weeks before the test date. Prior to the test date, students are invited to obtain from their high school a copy of an ACT publication, *Preparing for the ACT Assessment* , which provides a full-length sample of the examination as well as information about test administration procedures and advice to students designed to reduce anxiety.

On the test day, following completion of the four examinations, students respond to four questions about physical conditions of the room in which the tests were administered. The specific questions, each of which allows for a "Yes" or "No" response, are:

1. Did you have enough writing space on your desk or table to mark your answer sheet?
2. Were the seats spaced far enough apart so you were not crowded?
3. Was the lighting in your testing room adequate?
4. Was the testing area free from other than the usual classroom sounds?

These questions serve as one of several means by which ACT strives to maintain testing facilities and procedures that allow students to perform at their best when they take the ACT tests. Following the examination, students' responses to the four questions are tallied and reviewed. In cases where significant numbers of students in a given test center express dissatisfaction with the testing environment, an inquiry is initiated and steps are taken to correct the inadequacy. In severe cases of interference, students are given the opportunity to re-take the examination.

While in this way the Student Review items serve a useful operational function, it is of interest to examine the responses in more detail. Indeed, it is reasonable to assume that differences in students' perceptions of and reaction to the test-taking environment spring from two separate sources. The physical conditions, the actual amount of lighting or the size of the writing surface, is one obvious source. But even under identical physical conditions, one can expect to find differences in students' perceptions and reactions. These perceptual and affective differences are probably related to characteristics in students' background, and to the different circumstances and plans that bring students to register and take the examination.

The questions of interest in this study, then, include the following:
1) What is the overall level of satisfaction with test-room conditions and which conditions tend to elicit the fewest and greatest number of unfavorable ratings?

2) What differences exist among students in their opinion of testing conditions and how do these relate to differences in background characteristics?

3) Specifically, what is the relationship between academic performance, plans and aspirations and reactions to the testing environment? It is the hope and expectation of the authors that further examination of students' reactions will contribute to better understanding of them and, in turn, serve the purpose toward which all administrators of standardized tests strive, namely to reduce to the very minimum that amount of variance in test performance that is due to extraneous factors such as distractions in the test-taking environment.

Sampling and Reliability

Each year approximately one million students take the ACT tests on five annual test dates. On the April 1987 test date, 298,000 students sat for the examination. Of these, approximately 73 percent were juniors, i.e. attending the penultimate year in high school. In October 1987, some 255,000 students took the tests, nearly all of whom were seniors. In order to allow for inclusion of both juniors and seniors in the study, a 5 percent systematic sample was drawn from each of these two test dates. Because it soon became apparent that the reactions to test center conditions by the April and October test takers were very much alike, the two sub-samples were combined into a single sample of 27,631 records. Not only does this sample provide a representative mix of high school junior and seniors, but in other pertinent respects, e.g., academic aspiration and achievement, the April and October students tend to be representative of ACT-tested students in general. The number of students who express dissatisfaction with test-room conditions was found to be relatively small, and the number in various subgroups of this category is correspondingly smaller. Nevertheless, because of the large and carefully selected sample of students included in the study, the authors are quite content about the representativeness of the data and about the reliability of the findings.

A primary purpose of the study is to examine relationships between students' reactions to aspects of the physical conditions under which they took the ACT examination and variables in the students' background. For the most part, information about these background variables is self-reported by the students. This includes information about secondary school marks or grades and academic degree aspirations. The accuracy with which ACT examinees report these data is well documented. Recent studies by Valiga (1986), Laing and Sawyer, et al. (1987) describe a high degree of accuracy of such self-reported information.

Findings

The Student Review is included in the AAP as one of several measures designed and continuously employed to maintain testing conditions that are free of inconveniences and distractions. It is not surprising, therefore, that the large majority of students in this study found no fault with the test center conditions they reviewed. The figures in Table 1 bear this out. They show the percentage of students who gave a "No" response, i.e., unsatisfactory rating. The percentages are shown separately for male and female students. The latter group makes up 55 percent of the total study sample.

Table 1

Percentage of Students
Dissatisfied with Test Center Conditions, by Sex

Test Center Condition	Sex	
	Male	Female
C1 - Writing Space	11.0	9.5
C2 - Spacing Between Seats	5.4	3.8
C3 - Lighting	2.7	2.3
C4 - Sound Level, Noise	10.4	8.2

It is apparent that students' evaluations differ markedly as between the four circumstances included in the review. Twice as many students are concerned about the amount of space available for writing and about noise distractions as are those concerned about the other conditions evaluated.

It is evident as well that female test takers tend to be somewhat more tolerant of the conditions under which the tests are administered. The mix of male and female students is nearly the same for all test centers in this study.

Academic Aspirations

Students' reactions to the conditions under which they take the ACT tests may well be affected by the significance they attach to the testing experience and outcome. To test this assumption, we selected two variables from the Student Profile and examined students' evaluation of the test center conditions in the context of these. The two variables, highest academic degree sought, and type of college choice, may reasonably be assumed to reflect students' level of academic aspiration. Results are presented in Tables 2 and 3.

Table 2
Percentage of Students Dissatisfied with Test Center Coditions,
by Highest Academic Degree Planned

Test Center Condition	Voc-Tech Program	2-year College	BA/BS Degree	MA/MBA Degree	PhD/MD etc. Degree
C1 - Writing	8.0	8.1	9.5	11.2	11.3
C2 - Spacing Between Seats	3.5	3.6	4.2	4.8	4.9
C3 - Lighting	3.6	1.4	2.1	2.6	3.1
C4 - Sound, Noise	6.6	6.6	8.2	10.0	9.6

Table 3
Percentage of Students Dissatisfied with
Test Center Conditions, by Projected College of Enrolment

Test Center Condition	Voc-Tech Inst.	2-Year College	4-Year Public	4-Year Private
C1 -Writing Space	9.4	8.0	10.2	11.2
C2 - Spacing Between Seats	2.4	4.3	4.3	5.0
C3 - Lighting	2.3	2.1	2.5	2.7
C4 - Sound, Noise	5.2	6.8	8.6	10.3

Though the number of test takers who express dissatisfaction with test room conditions is relatively small, the trend in Table 2 is quite clear: the higher the academic degree aspiration, the more likely the student is to find fault with the testing conditions. A very similar trend is evident in Table 3, where student reactions are viewed in relation to type of institution of planned enrolment. For those less familiar with US higher education institutions, it should be noted that Vocational Technical Institutions usually offer programs of less than two years duration. Also, private 4-year institutions tend, on average, to be more selective than public 4-year Institutes.

Academic Achievement

It is of interest to examine the relationship between students' perception of test center conditions and their academic standing or achievement. In theory, one might advance two alternative hypotheses about this relationship. On the one hand, one might presume that the less able the student, the more important the outcome of the examination, and therefore the greater tenseness and sensitivity to adverse test-room conditions. Accordingly, one would anticipate that less able students would be more critical of test-room conditions. On the other hand, one might postulate that the abler the student, the higher the expectations of him or her and the greater the likelihood that the student is seeking entrance to a selective institution where the chances for admission are limited. Accordingly, much is at stake for this student, who is therefore more likely to be sensitive to distractions while taking the examination.

As Tables 4 and 5 indicate the latter hypothesis appears to be supported by the data, that is, the abler students tend to be more critical of distraction during the testing session.

Table 4
Percentage of Students Dissatisfied with Test Center Conditions,
by Rank in Secondary School Class

Test Center	Class Rank Quartile			
Condition	Highest	3rd	2nd	Lowest
C1 -Writing Space	11.0	9.8	9.2	9.2
C2 - Spacing Between Seats	4.7	4.0	4.5	6.1
C3 - Lighting	2.4	2.6	2.6	2.5
C4 - Sound, Noise	9.5	8.1	8.8	6.3

Table 5
Percentage of Students Dissatisfied with Test Conditions,
by Grade Point Average (GPA)

Test Center	Grade Average Range		
Condition	A-B	B-C	C-D
C1 -Writing Space	10.8	9.4	8.6
C2 - Spacing Between Seats	4.5	4.3	4.3
C3 - Lighting	2.4	2.6	2.2
C4 - Sound, Noise	9.4	8.0	7.4

The test itself affords an opportunity to examine the relationship between academic achievement and reactions to the testing environment. In Table 6, the ACT Composite Score, i.e., the average of the four scores in English, Mathematics, Social Studies and Natural Science, is shown respectively for students who found the testing conditions satisfactory ("Yes" response) and those who did not ("No" response). The ACT test score scale is 1-36 with a mean of 18.8.

Table 6
ACT Composite Test Score by
Level of Satisfaction with Test Center Conditions

Test Center	Satisfied with Test-Room Conditions?	
Condition	Yes	No
C1 -Writing Space	18.8	19.3
C2 - Spacing Between Seats	18.8	19.1
C3 - Lighting	18.8	19.1
C4 - Sound, Noise	18.8	19.4

As is evident from Table 6, students who score higher on the tests tend, by a small but consistent margin, also to be more critical of test-room conditions. One reason may be that these students find themselves in a more competitive world in terms of college admission or scholarship competition. The outcome of the testing experience is correspondingly more important to them.

General Critical Disposition

The date in Table 1 suggested that male students tend to be slightly more critical of what they perceive as flaws in test center conditions than females. This finding led the authors to search further for support of the hypothesis that part of the variance in students' reaction to their testing environment may be explained by an *a priori* difference in level of tolerance of inadequacies in one's environment in general, whereby some students may be more critical than others of a given same condition that impacts on them.

To explore this possibility, students' responses to test center conditions were examined in relation to their responses to questions in the Student Profile Section that ask them to evaluate certain aspects of their second-

213

ary school experience. Specifically, the relationship with opinions about classroom instruction and with the number and variety of courses or subjects offered was examined. The relationship is depicted in Table 7.

Table 7
Relationship between Satisfaction with Test Center
Conditions and Selected Secondary School Experiences
(Percent of Students Dissatisfied with Test Conditions)

Test Center Condition	Secondary School Experience			
	Instruction		Course Offering	
	Satisfied	Dissatisfied	Satisfied	Dissatisfied
C1 -Writing Space	9.5	12.8	9.3	12.1
C2 - Spacing Between Seats	4.2	5.5	4.3	4.6
C3 - Lighting	2.4	3.2	2.5	2.7
C4 - Sound, Noise	8.1	11.4	8.3	10.1

In interpreting the figures in Table 7, one should keep in mind that students' evaluation of their secondary school experience was made several weeks before they took the ACT tests. Though the proportion of students critical of their testing environment is comparatively small, ranging from 3 to 11 percent depending on the specific feature, it is evident that these are the students who also are more likely to be dissatisfied with key aspects of their secondary school experience, suggesting that some students are in general more inclined than others to be critical of circumstances in their lives, including the conditions that surround them when they take the ACT examination.

Other Background Factors

The study at hand is exploratory in nature. It is not designed as a test of well founded hypotheses but seeks, rather, to identify relationships that exist between students' opinions of certain aspects of the environment in which they took the ACT Assessment and a number of background characteristics which the authors selected for investigation as possible factors in shaping these opinions.

Given the prevailing interest on the part of educators in the validity and meaning of standardized test results for handicapped students (Casey, 1987), the study separated out and examined reactions of students who identified themselves as having "a physical handicap or diagnosed learning disability." It should be noted, however, that a separate, individualized administration of the ACT tests is available for handicapped students who request it. Accordingly, the number of handicapped students who elected to take the examination by regular administration is quite small. The total study sample of approximately 27,000 students includes only 214 handicapped individuals. The reaction of this group of test-takers to the test-room conditions differs very little from that of non-handicapped students, although the handicapped individuals tended to be slightly more accepting of the two conditions that otherwise were most frequently criticized, writing space and noise level.

Much attention has been devoted to the persistent differences in test scores of individuals from different racial or ethnic backgrounds. It was of interest, therefore, to compare responses to the Student Review for different racial groups. The comparison reveals that the responses for the three largest racial or ethnic subgroups, Blacks, Caucasians and Mexican-Americans, are very similar, all falling within the range of 6.0-6.5 percent negative responses. Asian-American and American Indian students tended by a small margin (7.3 percent negative reactions) to be more critical of the testing conditions.

The 3800 test centers operated by ACT range in size from single-room centers located mostly in high schools to multi-room centers at large universities. In the case of the latter, some rooms used for testing may feature seating and desk arrangements that are different from what most high school students are accustomed to, i.e., a science auditorium with tablet side arms instead of individual desks. It is perhaps not surprising, therefore, that students in multi-room test centers tended to be somewhat more critical of crowding in the test room (4.9 percent negative reaction vs. 3.6 percent in single room centers), and about the adequacy of the writing surface provided (11.5 percent vs. 8.1 percent).

Summary and Conclusions

The purpose of the study reported here springs from the truism that all measurement is subject to error, especially mental measurement. The physical condition under which students take tests, in this case the ACT college entrance tests, represents one source of error that is recognized but rarely researched. Immediately upon completing the ACT tests, the candidates are asked to respond to a Student Review section which includes four questions about the adequacy of the writing surface available, the spacing of seats, the lighting, and the sound or noise level in the test room. The purpose of the study was to assess the overall level of satisfaction with these conditions and to identify relationships between the test-takers' reactions and some 10-12 student characteristics, including sex, racial background, academic performance in high school and on the ACT tests, degree aspirations, type of college choice, and level of satisfaction with the secondary school experience.

A 5 percent random sample of over half a million students who took the ACT tests in April and October of 1987 was used. The study findings may be summarized as follows:

1. The large majority of test takers found no fault with the testing conditions being evaluated. The proportion of students who found the conditions inadequate ranged from 2.5 percent who criticized the lighting to about 10 percent who considered the available writing surface to be inadequate and the noise level too high.
2. Female students tended to be slightly less critical of the test-room environment than their male counterparts.
3. Students who identified themselves as handicapped were equally accepting of the test conditions as non-handicapped students or more so.
4. Test conditions were evaluated very similarly by Black, Caucasian and Mexican-American students, the three major racial/ethnic subgroups in the population studied.
5. Students whose academic achievement and educational aspiration le-

vels were above average tended to be more critical of the conditions under which they took the tests.

6. Students whose evaluation of their high school experience (quality of classroom instruction and number and variety of courses offered) was negative tended also to be more critical of the test-room conditions, lending support to a theory of negative pre-disposition as a generalized trait.

The practical implications of the findings include a suggestion that lighting conditions in schools and college facilities used for ACT testing appear to be sufficiently uniform and adequate so as not to need continuous monitoring. Sound or noise, as a potential factor in students' test performance, on the other hand, should remain a matter of keen attention. Not only is distracting noise difficult to anticipate and control as it usually emanates from outside the test room proper, but it may well be the one element of the testing environment most liable to subjective interpretation as a distractor. It is a well-known phenomenon that what is normal sound to some is distracting noise to others and that total silence is a source of uneasiness and tension to certain individuals. Further research on sound level as a factor in mental concentration in general and test taking in particular is warranted.

References

American College Testing Program (1987). *Assessment Student Information, High School Course/Grade Information, Interest Inventory, ACT Student Profile Section*, Iowa City: American College Testing Program.

American College Testing Program (1988). *Assessment Program Technical Manual*, Iowa City: American College Testing Program.

American College Testing Program, (1988). *Preparing for the ACT Assessment, Iowa City*.

American Educational Research Association, American Psychology Association and National Council on Measurement in Education (1985). Standards for Educational and Psychological Testing, (pp. 83-84), Washington, D.C.: American Psychological Association.

Boggs, D.H. & Simon, J.R., (1968). Differential Effect of Noise on Tasks of Varying Complexity. *Journal of Applied Psychology, 52,* 148-153.

Casey, E., (1987). Accommodating Testing to Disabled Students, In. Bray, F., Belcher, M.J. (Eds.), *Issues in Student Assessment,* Jossey-Bass, San Francisco.

Ingle, R.B. & De Amico, G. (1969). The effect of physical conditions of the test room on standardized achievement test scores. *Journal of Educational Measurement, 6,* 237-240.

Laing, J., Sawyer, R. & Noble, J., (1987, July). *Accuracy of Self-Reported Activities and Accomplishments of College Bound Students,* (ACT Research Report Series 87-6), Iowa City.

Sawyer, R., Laing, J. & Houson, M., (1988, March). *Accuracy of Self-Reported Activities and Accomplishments of College Bound Students,* ACT Research Report Series 88-1, Iowa City.

Traxler, A.E. & Hilkert, R.N., (1942). Effect of Type of Desk on Results of Machine-Scored Tests. *School and Society, 56,* 277-279.

Valiga, M., (1986, November). *The Accuracy of Self-Reported High School Course and Grade Information,* (American College Testing Program Research Report Series, 87-1), Iowa City.

Part 4:

Occupational Tests

11

When Applicants Rate the Examinations: Feedback from 2,000 People[1]

Roger Davis

Abstract

Very high rates of satisfaction with their job tests are experienced by employment applicants, as is evident from a series of studies conducted by the King County Civil Service Commission from 1980 to 1986. Almost 2500 job applicants were sampled, including people applying for entry-level jobs as well as current employees applying for promotion. The author, in his capacity as Chief Examiner, conducted 18 Quantified Feedback studies for the Commission. The types of tests covered included nationally standardized paper-and-pencil aptitude tests, written ability tests, assessment centers, and a physical performance test. Overall, the author found 94.9% of the King County applicants stating positively that they felt the test they received was fair (vs. unfair), and 93.6% of the respondents stating positively they felt the test they received was job-related. The two dimensions of fairness and job-relatedness were combined to a single index, labeled a Satisfaction Quotient. The final weighted index, or Satisfaction Quotient, for all tests studied indicated 94.2% of all 2,440 employment applicants sampled were positive about and satisfied with their job test. The results hold true for professionally developed tests only, not for all selection/promotion procedures. Results were generally consistent across time, and independent of test specificity. There were indications that results were consistent across race. Results were generally comparable across type of test and regardless of whether or not the applicants were seeking entry-level jobs or promotional opportunities. Because these re-

---

1   This chapter was originally presented to the Tenth Conference of International Personnel Management Association, San Francisco, 1986.

sults have important implications for voter-taxpayer/elected official relations and for labor-management relations, studies in Quantified Feedback from job test applicants should be continued, with further analysis
conducted on the obtained data.[2]

Introduction

Actually the present number of subjects in the study is considerably
greater than the aggregated 2000 when the topic title was written. The
present number of subjects is closer to 2500. But the results continue in
the established direction and essentially remain the same.

What makes this study, and my "test data", different and worth reporting
is that in this study I do not use a job test or tests on employment applicants to evaluate them for work. In this study I submit the job tests to the
applicants for their evaluation. It is the tests themselves that are evaluated.

The fact that this has not been done systematically before, only means
that as professionals in testing we still have much to learn - not least from
the testees themselves.

Since applicants are not professional evaluators of employment tests, I
do not interpret the information collected from them as definitive about
the quality of a given test. Important characteristics of test quality, like reliability and validity, are independent of ordinary opinion. Nevertheless
the information collected from the "consumers" in the form of feedback
opinion in this study is quantified data, not verbal anecdotes, and it
derives from all the job applicants, not just small samples. Therefore, I
suggest that quantified feedback from 100 out of almost 2500 people, is
weighty information and deserves attention.

This report presents the raw data, a set at a time, and describes both the
job and the job test to which each set applies. One problem is that in interpreting this information we have no standard of comparison.

At the beginning of this paper a simple poll was taken among specialists,
and the general notion seemed to be that in a quantified feedback study,
one might find a 60-65% positive response to a given test from job appli-

---

2   Findings and conclusions reached herein are the author's and do not necessarily ex-
     press those of the Commission. Quotations permissable with attribution and, after De-
     cember 1, citation to Proceedings, 1986, Assessment Council, I.P.M.A., Alexandria,
     Va.

cants. This study shows that in King County (metropolitan Seattle), Washington, the local Civil Service Commission found much higher rates of positive responses from job applicants to tests it administered for several different jobs in the five-year period 1981-86. These high rates of positive response were discovered through systematic Quantified Feedback analyses, a program that has developed some surprising information.

Data and Commentary

Table 1

1. Do you feel the test was fair?		
A. Yes	476	94.8 %
B. No	26	5.2 %

2. Was two and a half hours enough time for you?		
A. Just about what I needed	177	35.2 %
B. Not enough	4	.2 %
C. More than I needed	322	64.1 %

3. How much of the study book were you able to complete before the test?		
A. All of it	327	65.5 %
B. Almost all of it	115	32.1 %
C. About half	35	7.0 %
D. Just a little bit	22	4.4 %
E. None	0	

4. Do you feel the test was job-related?		
A. Yes	480	95.6 %
B. No	22	4.4 %

The applicants are applying for jobs as police officers. The test is a civil service police test. Specifically the test is the new I.P.M.A. Police Officer examination which I chose for use in King County in 1985. It is a 2 1/2 hour, multiple-choice, paper-and pencil test of police officer aptitudes. There is a magazine-length "study book" which candidates must use to properly prepare for the test. This study book is free to the applicant, but insincere applicants tend to screen themselves out of the selection process by not appearing for the test if they have not prepared in advance.

This is an excellent test, no matter what candidates think of it. A small-scale, local validity study would probably show that this test has a high validity, at least .5 or .6, against Training Academy performance, and perhaps better. But what do candidates think of this test?

If we combine the (A) responses in items 1 and 4 in Table 1, we can compute a Satisfaction Quotient of 95.2% for the applicant population taking this test in 1985. That is, more than 95% of the people who actually sat for the test felt that it was fair and job-related.

This response is not completely anonymous. Candidates marked their responses on the same optically-scanned answer sheet on which they took the test proper. This sheet had the candidate's I.D. number on it. But the candidates were responding after 140 questions and 2 1/2 hours of testing, and I believe they answered this survey with a sense of complete anonymity. We have respected their honesty by analyzing this data only at the level of groups and not down to the level of any individual.

Perceived Job-Relatedness in Entry Level Exams

The question may arise as to why the candidates were not simply asked whether or not they liked the test, instead of whether they felt it was fair. The answer is that since nobody likes very much to be tested, nobody really "likes" any given test. For someone to "like" or say he likes a particular test would only mean that the respondent felt the test challenged him within the limits of his capability.

When we request feedback it is neither meaningful nor useful to ask if the candidates "liked" the test. It is useful to know, if their perception was that the test was job-related. (Actual jobrelatedness, of course, is determined through sophisticated analysis. Perceived job-relatedness, or face-validity, is impression and reaction, not analysis.)

226

Similarly, we do not ask if the applicants thought the test was job-related, as if to imply a concept, or even a mis-conception. We only need to know if the candidates felt the test was job related, or not, or if they felt the test was fair.

A similar but different test, an excellent one produced by the educational Testing Service and distributed from 1982 to 1985 is about 50 questions and one hour longer than the previous one. It is also a police officer multiple choice test. It is no longer available and these data are from its 1984 administration in King Country. Its Satisfaction Quotient is 93.8%.

Table 2

Do you feel this test was job-related

A. Yes	401	95.5%
B. No	19	4.5%

Do you feel this test is fair?

A. Yes	388	92.2%
B. No	33	7.8%

Like the previous test (Table 1), there were no reviews or challenges to this test on the part of anyone in the 422-person applicant population, but there is an interesting, subtle, and important difference between this set of data and those in the second set (Table 2), a difference not apparent so far.

In the first, the shorter I.P.M.A. test, 71 percent of the testees described it as at least "hard." In the case of the longer E.T.S. test 84 percent of the candidates described it as at least "hard." More people thought the ETS test was hard because it really was harder: it produced lower mean scores.

The respective Satisfaction Quotients (SQ) for the two tests, however, are these:

IPMA	ETS
N = 504	N = 421
SQ = 95.2%	SQ = 93.8%

The percentages do not reflect an appreciable or important difference. "Hardness" or the difficulty of a test thus does not affect the willingness of the applicant test-takers to describe the test with extreme agreement as fair or job-related. The capacity of the applicants to describe a test as fair and job-related is independent of the perceived, or actual, difficulty of the test.

One should not hesitate from giving hard tests. Candidates may be highly satisfied with a test even though most think it is difficult.

Responses of Minority Compared With White Candidates

Let us consider the difference, if any, between the responses of Minority and White candidates. This is important, although shortage of staff prevented us from fully analysing all the data collected so far. Yet from a sample of police officer applicants taking the ETS test in 1983 we find this composition:

Minorities	31	11.7%
Whites	2.35	88.3%

Do you feel the test was job-related?

	Minorities		Whites	
A. Yes	29	(93.5%)	224	(95.3%)
B. No	2	(6.5%)	11	(4.7%)

How difficult was the test?

	Minorities	Whites
A. Hard/Too hard	24%	50%
B. Easy/Too easy	6%	3%
C. Just about right	70%	47%

Comparable percentages of Minorities and Whites felt the test was job-related, but far more Whites thought it was "hard."

In fact the test was moderately hard. How accurate are candidate perceptions about test difficulty?

	Minorities	Whites
$\bar{X}$ test scores	65.7%	72.6%

Perceived Job-Relatedness and Fairness in Promotion Exams

To be "pure," test feedback, like challenges and protests, has to be elicited from candidates uninfluenced by possible personal consequences for themselves. We may obtain information regarding current employees, when they take promotion exams: In a test for police sergeants

applying for police lieutenants in 1985, their responses to it were not markedly different form those of the entry-level applicants to theirs:

Do you feel the written test was job-related:

A. Yes	33	80.5%
B. No	8	19.5%

The numbers are fairly small, like the Minority candidates above, compared with the large numbers of entry-level police officer applicants.
This was also a written test, 120-item, multiple-choice, covering local department procedures and some popular general management books such
as *The Pursuit of Excellence and The One-Minute Manager.*
Although 80 percent of the candidates felt the test was job-related, test
performance in fact correlated with peer job performance appraisals only
$r = .19$ and with managers' job performance appraisals only .22. (The
same peer appraisals correlated $r = .60$ with assessment center scores.)
Next we observe employee reactions to two different job tests given for
promotion. Both are sergeant examination written tests, given in 1981
and 1983, and the respondents were current, experienced police officers
at King County:

Do you feel the written test was job-related:?

	1981		1983	
A. Yes	71	(80.7%)	179	(87.3%)
B. No	4	(4.6%)	15	(7.3%)
C. Maybe	13	(14.7%)	11	(5.4%)

The data sets are comparable and the response patterns similar. The 1983
test was slightly more preferred by its candidate population. But, it
should be borne in mind that these were police officers taking consecutive sergeant exams, so many were the same individuals. (The 1981 group
is much smaller than the 1983 group because the former was a sample responding to a mail survey while the latter responded at the test site.)

The tests are similar but not the same; they were liked about equally. The 1981 test is a nationally standardized police sergeant test produced by Personnel Decisions, Inc., one of the most respected test consulting firms in the country. It is a multiple-choice, critical incident test with differently weighted item response alternatives. This is a content-valid and criterion validated test, whose validity has been upheld by the State Supreme Court of Iowa. It was the first time this type of test was used for a Sergeant examination at King County, and the second time this type of test had been used for Sergeant in the Pacific Northwest. There were no challenges or protests in King County to this test when used.

The 1983 test is a locally standardized police sergeant test produced by a small Pacific Northwest consulting firm, K.M.B. Associates. Its format is exactly the same as the previous test. It is content-valid. As to its criterion-relatedness, test scores for the more than 200 candidates had a slight negative correlation (or orthagonal relationship) with a content-valid peer appraisal procedure developed by the same consultant. This test produced a small but fierce storm of protests despite the broad candidate satisfaction documented above.

The levels of strong satisfaction underlying a test administration, and revealed by the Quantified Feedback procedure, suggest why tests are not more widely challenged. A small group of protestors may be especially intense without providing a true picture of the broad candidate acceptance of a test.

Perceived Fairness and Influence of Assessment Centers

All the Quantified Feedback studies recounted above were conducted in written tests. The data suggest that candidates are likely to respond as positively in other kinds of tests also.

Since 1980 King County has been conducting Management Assessment Centers as required parts of police promotional exams. Before a King County police officer can get promoted to any rank, it has been my plan that s/he must score high on both a written test and at an assessment center.

In the last six years, nine Management Assessment Centers have been conducted, covering three ranks, and evaluating well over 100 King

County employee candidates for managerial promotion (N = 134).
Summing all these respondents across time and rank, one can see this pattern:

	Aggregate 1980 - 1985
A. Yes	134
B. No	0

The King County Civil Service Commission has not experienced any challenges, appeals, or protests to any of its Management Assessment Centers.

Since assessment centers have been new experiences for many of the employees, in our Quantified Feedback program.[3] we also asked this question:

Were you positively or negatively influenced by your exposure to an assessment center?

	Aggregate 1980 - 1985	
A. Positive	134	(88%)
B. Neutral	13	(10%)
C. Negative	2	(2%)

It should be observed that about 20 of these respondents failed in the assessment center process. Some were reticent and shaded their opinion toward the neutral part of the spectrum; others in the sample were honest, no matter how poorly they did relative to other competitors, and were satisfied that they had been fairly tested.

---

3   With credit to assessment center consultant Jack Clancy and Associates, Sacramento, California

Even people in the middle range of scores showed their satisfaction with the fairness of the test, for the majority of the 118 candidates did *not* get promoted; less than 50 did.

Perceived Fairness and Difficulty of Performance Tests

The acquisition of very high satisfaction rates in feedback from testees serves many purposes. For example, after elaboration of a new testing program, like the assessment centers started in 1980, a pattern of Satisfaction Quotients of 94-95 percent positive for *all* respondents will confirm the usefulness of the new tests. If the tests are content-valid or predictively-valid, even though hard, new and unfamiliar, resource costly, or with some other feature that calls their use into question, their high level of acceptance by the test-takers themselves is extremely valuable more valuable than costly. Depending on the questions, it can also be determined how comfortable the applicants were within the time limits of a power test and future schedules may be adjusted accordingly. These are but a few of the purposes for quantified feedback information.

Written tests such as the I.P.M.A. police test or the E.T.S. police test have a measurable per capita cost of about 8 dollars but their extremely high validity and high acceptability to entry level job applicants make such tests more valuable than cheaper, less valid, and less acceptable forms of testing. The same is true of Management Assessment Centers, eventhough their per capita costs are over 500 dollars, on account of their moderately high validity and extremely high acceptability to current employees.

The following is a physical ability test for entry-level police officer job applicants. It is another example of a non-written test with high applicant feedback. It is a performance test, not a paper-and-pencil test. It is also difficult. An eight-year testing program of almost 2000 applicants has produced an overall pass/fail ratio of 65/35 percent when about one-third of the applicants tested were young women. Pass/fail rates for young women are about 55/45 percent and for young men about 70-75/25-30 percent.

With that high a proportion of failures for a job such as this, which young people often feel a strong desire to obtain, challenges and appeals, while not frequent, are nevertheless not uncommon. Therefore giving and getting a fair test administration is important:

Did you get a fair test administration today?

A. Yes	176	98%
B. No	4	2%
C. No response	4	

Do you feel this test was a fair evaluation of your physical ability for being a police officer?

A. Yes	146	82.5%
B. No	31	17.5%
C. No response	7	

Considering the above data, we must ask why thirty-odd applicants felt that the test itself had not been a "fair" (i.e., thorough) evaluation even though the test administration had been fair. The answer probably lies in this feedback item:

How difficult was this test, as a whole?

A. Too hard	0	
B. Hard	12	6.5%
C. Just about right	104	56.5%
D. Easy	63	34.2%
E. Too easy	5	2.8%

Thirty-six percent of the applicants thought an objectively difficult test, in terms of its pass/fail rate, was an Easy or Too easy test, probably because it did not tax them to capacity. Therefore it presumably did not seem to these applicants, to have been a "fair evaluation" of them. (meaning that the test was not fair to them because it did not tax and fail more of the other, less competent applicants).

It also has to be observed that this particular test is not a content valid test. All the other measures upon which I have collected Quantified Feedback and reported the results here are content-valid tests. One of the reasons the applicant Satisfaction Quotients are so high is that the previous tests are content-valid, and therefore reflect considerable face validity. Content-valid tests could be expected to get higher Satisfaction Quotients than equally construct valid, but not content-valid, tests.

The physical ability test, entitled the Police Officer Physical Efficiency Battery, has little face validity. It is a simple battery of three rather abstract exercises and one passive measure. Since the sub-tests do not highly intercorrelate with each other, when combined in a weighted battery they provide a broad-spectrum index of the general, overall health and physical condition of the subject. From more than 300 hires among nearly 2000 tests in the last eight years, there has been only one false positive. (If there is a high pass rate, a low selection rate, and a low number of Type 1 errors, then Type II errors will not themselves appreciably mitigate the utility of a test for an employer.) Such a measure as this has high test utility for the employer, so regardless of its amount of validity (this test does have high construct validity) the Police Officer Physical Efficiency Battery[4] satisfies a documented business necessity of the employer.

It is a tough test, highly accurate on the positive side, and one that can be evenly and fairly administered to hundreds of applicants, who respect it. But it is not a test that the mostly highly physically-qualified individuals really enjoy. Presumably they find more appealing those fence surmounts, body drags, and quarter-mile runs.

Persistence Over Time of Perceived Job-Relatedness and Fairness

The last set of data concerns the new I.P.M.A. police test.

If my estimates of high candidate satisfaction with our tests are true, the

---

4   The principle author of the Police Officer Physical Efficiency Battery is Dr. Marcella D. Woods of Kirkland, Washington.

results should persist over time. Above, it was noted that 95.6 percent of the applicants were positive on the *job relatedness* and 94.8% positive on the *fairness* of the I.P.M.A. police test in 1985 in Seattle. The responses of a slightly larger group in May, 1986 were:

Do you feel the test was job-related?

A. Yes	602	95.0%
B. No	32	5.0%
C. No response	6	

Do you feel the test was fair?

A. Yes	598	94.7%
B. No	33	5.3%
C. No response	9	

The data remain consistent. If we combine the two groups we find?

	Job-related		Fair	
A. Yes	1082	95.2%	1074	94.8%
B. No	54	4.8%	59	4.8%

The combined 1985-1986 Satisfaction Quotient was 95.0% for the use of the new International Personnel Management Association/A.R.R.O. police officer test in metropolitan Seattle.

Conclusions

It is quite common in training settings for the trainer to collect evaluative feedback information from the participants, i.e., the students. The process seems to start around college, skips over graduate school, and then reappears in professional training programs and short courses.

On the other hand, in testing situations it is almost universal for us not to collect feedback. We do not want it. We are not sure what we would do with it if we got it. But I suggest that we as testmakers have not pursued feedback because we are reluctant to receive it. We want to avoid it.

There are a lot of pretexts: they, the applicants, wouldn't know a good test if they saw one; it is an exercise merely in face validity; the purpose of a test is to sort out by job qualifications, so why should we assume that those who are poorly qualified for the job have anything of value to say about a highly job-related test, etc. While these notions are true they cut us off from potentially useful information that is quite easy to collect and not as painful as we expect. We probably avoid quantified feedback out of a fear of what candidates think of their tests/our tests and what they might say given the chance. True, competitive tests are not typically pleasant. At best they are challenging, but people basically do not like to undergo somebody else's test. Since we force people to do so, we could expect a lot of hostility in candidate feedback. The civil service tradition of our testing even prepares us for that: the system of reviews and challenges to testing implies that protesting is only the tip of the real iceberg of what candidates actually feel about their job tests.

The truth, based on new evidence, is the reverse. Candidates perceive our tests to be much better than what we imagine them to feel about these measures.

Sum of all Studies (N = 18)

Do you feel the test was job-related?

A. Yes	2283	93.6%
B. No	157	6.4%

2,440 applicants

237

Sum of all Studies (N = 14)

Do you feel the test was fair?

| A. Yes | 1772 | 94.9% |
| B. No | 96 | 5.1% |

1868 applicants

The weighted Satisfaction Quotient for the tests studied is 94.2%.
These eighteen Quantified Feedback studies from entry-level and promotional job applicants have important implications for labor/management
relations and for voter-taxpayer/elected official relations. For labor and
management certain critical questions unavoidably arise. Since the results obtained on applicant satisfaction with impartial, competitive selec-
tion/promotion tests contrast sharply with (are much higher than) employee satisfaction over most organizations' employee job performance
evaluation systems, we are forced to face this question: *Why are individuals so much more satisfied that their tests are fair and job-related than they
are that their performance evaluations are fair and jobrelated?*
We are not begging the question or operating on a false assumption;
countless employee attitude surveys have well established the high dissatisfaction among employees with their performance appraisals.
This leads us to the important second question: *If it is possible to make the
selection and promotion tests so fair and job-related, why are not the performance evaluations programs made so?*
Quantified Feedback is also important for voters, taxpayers, and elected
public officials. All have a right to expect and know that jobs in the public
service are meted out on the basis of impartial and job-related criteria
(fairness and job-relatedness) that can be connected with future productivity and efficiency (the validation of those criteria) in the government
workforce. This leads us to one of the uses and applications of Quantified
Feedback programs: the results reported here suggest that voters, taxpayers, and their elected leaders, with a vital interest in and need for cer-
tainty that jobs are awarded on the basis of merit, can be assured that the
job applicants themselves are overwhelmingly satisfied they have been
treated with respect and that the proper standards of merit in hiring have
been applied to them equally.

12

Is There a Dilemma between Validity and Acceptance in the Employment Interview?

Heinz Schuler

Abstract

Literature survey shows that most of the relevant studies report low (empirical) validity for the eployment interview. On the other hand this same seletion device has high acceptance among potential employees. This chapter describes and discusses this discripancy and provides some suggestions for researech and application which are based on studies performed at the University of Hohenheim.

Introduction

Among the many methods used for occupational selection and counseling the interview is given special weight. Unlike most or all of the other selection and counseling tools, the functions of the interview are not limited to predicting the applicants' future occupational or academic success. The interview may also provide information to the applicants about the organization, the job, the tasks and the task requirements; it may elicit information on applicants' expectations and the labor market; it results in personal acquaintance, contact and liking, identification and commitment; it "sells" the organization and negotiates individual employment conditions.

The multiplicity of these functions shows, that the employment interview is an indispensable component of the selection procedure even if its predictive validity may be insufficient. This may be the reason for the ubiquitous use of the interview by American (Miner and Miner, 1978) British (Robertson and Smith, 1989) and German business organizations (Schulz, Schuler and Stehle, 1985).

At the same time, the style of the interview and the person of the interviewer seems to be important variables: A study by Schmitt and Coyle (1976) reported, that the interviewer was a highly important source of influence on the acceptance of an employment offer by qualified applicants. Compared with other methods of personnel selection or occupational counseling, the employment interview may be seen in advance regarding acceptance by applicants if performed well. On the other hand, validity research shows low mean validity when future occupational success has to be predicted (Schuler and Funke, 1989a). Hence, a dilemma may arise between the goals of validity and acceptance when choosing an appropriate selection method. And, while there are many empirical data demonstrating low predictive validity of the conventional employment interview, the evidence for its high acceptance is more anecdotal in nature. In this article the latter aspect is given priority, presenting some empirical results of the Hohenheim research group. But to be in a position to discuss how the so-called dilemma situation may be overcome it is useful first to briefly summarize validity research.

Interview Validity

In early studies the low predictive validity of the employment interview was already reported (Scott, 1916). In a few reviews (e.g., Wagner, 1949; Mayfield, 1964; Schmitt, 1976) validity estimations of roughly $r = .05$ to $r = .25$ were given. More recent summaries (Reilly and Chao, 1982; Arvey and Campion, 1982; Webster, 1982) also report values around $r = .20$. Hunter and Hunter's (1984) meta-analysis, summarizing 15 single studies, resulted in an r of .14 when supervisors' ratings were taken as criteria; validity was even lower ($r = .08$) when compared with occupational promotion. Predictions of academic success tend to be still lower, i.e., hardly better than chance (Trost, 1986).
These are the mean values for the traditional, mostly unstructured, kind of interview. In contrast, validities of more elaborated and controlled selection tools are typical in the thirties and forties (Schuler and Funke, 1989a). The interview seems therefore to be a highly deficient method. However, it has recently been argued that the interview's validity was underestimated by most validations, representing only an incremental validity component (Hunter and Hirsh, 1987) that in content might resemble the non-achievement component usually included in criterial per-

formance assessment. Moreover, Dreher, Ash and Hancock (1988) pointed out that consideration of individual rating tendencies - e.g., halo, which lowers inter-individual but not intra-individual rating consistency - would result in markedly higher values.

Standardization or structure as well as job relatedness were discovered as powerful moderating determinants of validity, Wiesner and Cronshaw (1988) reported a mean validity coefficient of r= .13 for unstructured interviews, but one of r= .40 for structured interviews. McDaniel, Whetzel, Schmidt, Hunter, Maurer and Russel (1986) calculated mean values of r= .30 for job-related interviews and r= .21 for traditional psychological interviews.

Schuler and Funke (1989b) conducted a construct validation of a multimodal interview. This highly structured interview was developed on a job analytical basis for a large German banking organization. Correlations of interview results with cognitive ability test scores were low, but there were high correlations of several interview components (r= .40 to .73) with ratings from a role-structured group discussion. Sex proved to be of no influence on interview results, thus attesting to the fairness of this interview as a selection tool. But a multitrait-multimethod analysis of two interview components - biographical and situational questions - resulted in very low correlations in questions intended to represent the same task dimensions (convergent validity). Also, discriminant validity proved to be low. Factor analysis of biographical and situational questions including comparable dimensions did not result in a common factorial structure for these two types of question.

In further construct analyses of this multimodal interview (Schuler, 1988), correlations of interview components with assessment center exercises and, even more, with personality tests showed plausible convergencies and discriminations. Some general personality factors like extraversion, dominance, inhibition, activity and self-acceptance as well as components of achievement motivation proved especially well measured by the biographical component of this interview. Moreover, a test constructed to measure customer orientation (Schuler and Funke, unpublished) showed virtually the same correlation pattern with personality test scores as the biographical interview component. Substantial improvement of the employment interview can thus be expected as has already been demonstrated by structuring the interview, defining different standardized components, basing it on job analyses, and conducting construct validations. These steps or principles should increase predictive validity of the employment interview, i.e., the "technical" component of its usefulness. On the other hand, the important question if acceptance, well-being or other parameters determining the applicants' evaluation of selection situations and instruments are similarly positive has to be explored independently. At best, this side of the evaluation is independent of validity; at worst, a dilemma could result from technical improvements that make the interview less accepted the more it is technically suitable. Results reported by Latham (1989) and by Robertson (personal communication), for example, suggest that a structured interview consisting only of situational questions was not well accepted by applicants.

Interview Acceptance

Rynes, Heneman and Schwab (1980) summarize some results concerning the acceptance of employment interviews. Glueck (1973) and Alderfer and McCord (1970) found, like Schmitt and Coyle (1973), that recruiters were a major reason for acceptance of a job offer, the latter two studies adding that interviewer characteristics significantly contributed to this effect. Also, recruiter knowledge of jobs turned out to be a critical variable. It has been reported that candidates had an especially bad impression of their interviewers if these seemed not to be acquainted with their resumes. Higher status, such as "Recruiting Director", and identification by name improved candidates' impressions of their interviewers (Rogers and Sincoff, 1978). Glueck (1973) and Downs (1969) found that applicants dislike interviewers who talk at length. Also the use of stress questioning is distinctly disliked by candidates (Downs, 1969; Alderfer and McCord, 1970). It has been reported several times that "face-valid" selection procedures - interviews as well as other tools - are preferred to those not apparently related to the job requirements. Rynes et al. (1980) suppose that this preference is due to applicants' concerns over invasion of privacy in the recruiting process (Rosenbaum, 1973).
Rynes et al. (1980) complain that most research in this field has been done without any specific theoretical framework. In terms of the concept of "social validity" or "social quality" Schuler and Stehle (1983) Schuler, (1989) suggested four components as presumably the most important to make socially acceptable situations out of selection procedures: relevant information about task requirements and organizational characteristics

(including social and psychological characteristics such as organizational culture and leadership style); direct or representative participation in the development and the execution of the assessment program - in the wider sense the possibility of exerting control over the situation; transparency of the situation, of the assessment tools, and of the judgmental evaluation; and content as well as mode of communication of the results, i.e., feedback in an honest, considerate and comprehensible manner.

The employment interview could be considered to fulfill the demands of this concept more than most other selection instruments: in principle all four aspects can be fulfilled in a high degree - but of course, this is not obligatory; moreover, in many cases, candidates might tend to overestimate the social qualities of interviews, for example, in respect of their possible situational control. On the other hand, the opportunities presented by the interview often may not be fully exploited by the interviewers or the recruiting organizations, for example, by not informing candidates about the aspects of their future jobs actually relevant to their decision, giving them instead economic details which cannot be retained in this highly activating situation and narrowed motivational set.

Recent Research

In a current research program at Hohenheim University we are investigating participants' reactions to a variety of selection instruments and processes, trying to quantify the importance of the different independent variables (situation aspects) for the candidates' decisions, performance, and well being. A summary of the studies and results so far is given by Schuler (1989). In the present context the report is restricted to some special studies on reactions to the employment interview.

In a study reported by Fruhner and Schuler (1988), 605 German students of different academic subjects were asked for their experience with and attitudes towards employment interviews compared with psychological tests. On a five-point-scale global evaluations were more positive for the interview than for tests (M_1 2,2; M_T= 3,2). This difference was somewhat smaller for people already experienced in selection situations than for those without any experience. While 85 percent of the experienced respondents would agree to undergo an interview once again, only 44 percent of the test participants would be willing to take a test again. Given the fictitious choice between different selection instruments in the case of their next application, subjects ranked eight instruments in the following order:

1. Interview
2. Work sample
3. Practical training
4. School grades
5. Psychological tests
6. Curriculum vitae
7. Handwriting
8. Chance

This sequence of preferences proved quite stable for different groups when Fruhner, Schuler, Funke and Moser (in press) enlarged the total sample to $N = 1207$ students from different fields of study. What the interview has in common with work samples and with practical training are three factors which may be responsible for the candidates' preferences: (1) all allow for behavioral and situational control (at least according to the applicants' subjective impressions); (2) they measure present performance (in contrast to past performance as represented, for example, in school grades); (3) they inform applicants about relevant job characteristics and requirements.

Subjects' ratings of selection instruments on a semantic differential resulted in three factors: general evaluation, stress, and transparency. In addition to the semantic differential, separate ratings were performed. Among other results, interviews were seen to be more informative concerning job demands and more suitable for measuring the relevant abilities. Respondents judged their achievements as good in both instruments with a slight advantage for the interview, while the difference was substantial for the presumed possibility of influencing one's own results (a form of situational control).

Among the biographical variables moderating this result were experience - experienced subjects rating the interview higher than unexperienced ones, while there was no difference for tests in overall evaluation - and sex, unexperienced women expecting more stress in test situations than experienced ones.

In a multiple regression, single ratings were used as predictors of global evaluations. Suitability for measuring one's own abilities and possibility of influencing one's own results proved sufficient predictors of global evaluations for the test. For the interview two components were added:

presumed own performance and information about job demands. With a questionnaire similar to that used by Fruhner et al. (in press), Rüdiger Schmidt (1988) asked 31 applicants in three different companies for their reactions to the employment interviews. Results again indicated largely positive attitudes towards this selection instrument, multiple regression showing subjective control of the situation to be the most important determinant of the evaluation.

As a step in the construction of a biographical inventory we compared responses to the same items presented in written or in oral form respectively. Stehle (1983) asked 26 members of the target group and seven union members to rate each item according to its acceptability in both ways of presentation.

Generally, more items were rated as acceptable when put in oral than in written form. Items belonging to the areas "family" and "childhood" were especially rejected if included in a questionnaire.

In a study conducted together with Zehelein (Zehelein, 1985) 96 student subjects (48 males and 48 females) rated their impressions of interviewers by listening to an audiotape of an employment interview and completing a questionnaire. On the audiotapes a male or a female interviewer applied a directive or a non-directive interviewing approach. The styles were based on dimensions used in client-centered psychotherapy (Tyler, 1969) and the theory of defensive communication in small groups (Gibb, 1961).

The results of this study were as follows. Subjects saw both types of interviews as highly relevant for their decisions to accept or reject a job offer. They assumed high accuracy of job interviewers' assessments. The job of an employment interviewer was seen as masculine rather than feminine. Male and female subjects did not rate differently. Subjects had no preference regarding the sex of the interviewer but they saw a better chance of a job offer from an opposite-sex interviewer. The male interviewer was characterized as more appropriate and precise than the female interviewer.

Comparing the two interview forms, subjects indicated they had more favorable impressions of non-directive interviewers, liked them more, thought that it would be easier to talk to them and that they would feel comfortable with them. They trusted a nondirective interviewer more than a directive interviewer; the nondirective male interviewer more than the non-directive female interviewer, but the non-directive female interviewer more than the directive female interviewer. (Regarding differences related to sex, each sex was represented by one person only, so the difference may be person-dependent and not generalizable). Nondirective interviewers were seen to fit the picture of the ideal interviewer better and to be more easily influenced (the female more than the male) by words as well as physical appearance and eye contact. The non-directive interviewers were deemed more accurate in their assessments and the directive interviewers (the male interviewer more than the female). Non-directive interviewers also were characterized as having greater acumen as employment interviewers than the directive interviewers. The overall ability of the male and the female interviewer was not judged differently. Finally, the non-directive approach was perceived as more appropriate for a job interview than the directive approach.

A Solution for the Dilemma

This is in accordance with results reported by Latham (1989) and Robertson (personal communication) concerning the rather negative reactions to interviews consisting only of situational items. On the other hand, as summarized above, structured and job related interviews are more valid than traditional unstructured interviews. To overcome this potential dilemma the multimodal interview noted above (Schuler, 1988; Schuler and Funke, 1989) is so constructed that highly standardized components alternate with open and unstructured sections. All the questions in this interview were not only tested according to psychometric principles but were examined and selected for acceptability (e.g., for not invading privacy). In addition, the interviewers are trained to establish a friendly and warm climate of interaction. Among the thousands of practical applications of this interview so far there has been virtually not one case of explicitly negative reaction to it (although there have been negative reactions to and withdrawals from the testing procedure used by the same banking organization).
We may conclude that a potential conflict between validity and acceptance in the employment interview indeed exists: while task relatedness is suitable to improve both aspects, structure tends to heighten validity but lower acceptance. But as may be demonstrated with the multimodal interview, it is to combine both requirements and thus make the employment interview both a potentially valid and a well-accepted selection instrument.

References

Alderfer, C. & McCord, C. (1970). Personal and situational factors in the recruitment interview. *Journal of Applied Psychology, 54,* 377-385.

Arvey, R.D. & Campion, J.E. (1982). The employment interview: A summary and review of recent research. *Personnel Psychology, 35,* 281-322.

Downs, C.W. (1969). Perceptions of the selection interview. *Personnel Administration, 32,* 8-23

Dreher, G.F., Ash, R.A. & Hancock, P. (1988). The role of the traditional research design in underestimating the validity of the employment interview. *Personnel Psychology, 41,* 315-328.

Fruhner, R. & Schuler, J. (1988). Bewertung eignungsdiagnostischer Verfahren zur Personalauswahl durch potentielle Stellenbewerber. In G. Romkopf, W.D. Frölich, and I. Lindner (Eds.), *Forschung und Praxis im Dialog* (Bd. 1) (pp.107-111). Bonn: Deutscher Psychologen Verlag.

Fruhner, R., Schuler, J., Funke, U. & Moser, K. (in press). *Zum Erleben von psychologischen Tests und Vorstellungsgesprächen.*

Gibb, J.R. (1961). Defensive communication. *Journal of Communication, 11,*141-148.

Glueck, W. (1973). Recruiters and executives: How do they affect job choice? *Journal of College Placement, 28,* 99-102.

Hunter, J.E. & Hirsh, J. (1987). Applications of meta-analysis. In C.L. Cooper and I.T. Robertson (Eds.), *International review of industrial and organizational Psychology 1987* (pp.321-357).

Hunter, J.E. & Hunter, R.F. (1984). Validity and utility of alternative predictors of job performance. *Psychological Bulletin, 96,* 72-98.

Latham, G.P. (1989, May). *Situational interviews and perceived fairness form the vantage point of managers, interviewees and lawyers.* Paper presented at "The Individual and Organizational Side of Selection and Performance Evaluation and Appraisal", Hohenheim University, R.F.G.

248

Mayfield, E.C. (1964). The selection interview - A reevaluation of published research. *Personnel Psychology, 17,* 239-260.

McDaniel, M.A., Whetzel, D.L., Schmidt, F., Hunter, J.E., Maurer, S. & Russel, J. (1986). *The validity of employment interviews: A review and meta-analysis.* Unpublished manuscript, US Office of Personnel, Washington, DC.

Miner, M.G.& Miner, J.B. (Eds.) (1978). *Employee selection within the law.* Washington: Bureau of National affairs.

Reilley, R.R. & Chao, G.T. (1982). Validity and fairness of some alternative employee selection procedures. *Personnel Psychology, 35,* 1-62.

Robertson, I.T. & Smith, M. (1989). Personnel selection methods. In: M. Smith and I.T. Robertson (Eds.), *Advances in selection and assessment* (pp.89-112). Chichester: Wiley.

Rogers, D. & Sincoff, M. (1978). Favorable impression characteristics of the recruitment interviewer. *Personnel Psychology, 31,* 495-504.

Rosenbaum, B.L. (1973). Attitude toward invasion of privacy in the personnel selection process and job applicant demographic and personality correlates. *Journal of Applied Psychology, 58,* 333-338.

Rynes, S.L., Heneman, H.G. III & Schwab, D.P. (1980). Individual reactions to organizational recruiting: A review. *Personnel Psychology, 33,* 529-542.

Schmidt, R. (1988). *Das Vorstellungsgespräch aus der Sicht des Stellenbewerbers. Eine Feldstudie.* Unpublished Masters Thesis, University of Bielefeld.

Schmidt, N. (1976). Social and situational determinants of the interview decision: Implications for the employment interview. *Personnel Psychology, 29,* 79-101.

Schmidt, N. & Coyle, B. (1976). Applicant decisions in the employment interview. *Journal of Applied Psychology, 61,* 184-192.

Schuler, H. (1988, August). *Construct validity of a multimodal employment interview.* Paper presented at the XXIV International Congress of Psychology, Sydney, Australia.

Schuler, H. (1989). *Social validity of selection situations: A concept and some empirical results*. Paper presented at "The Individual and Organizational Side of Selection and Performance Evaluation and Appraisal", Hohenheim University, F.R.G.

Schuler, J. & Funke, U. (1989a). Berufseignungsdiagnostik. In E. Roth (Ed.), *Organisationspsychologie. Enzyklopädie der Psychologie D/III/e* (pp.31-42). Göttingen: Hogrefe.

Schuler, J. & Funke, U. (1989b). The interview as a multimodal procedure. In G.R. Ferris and R.W. Eder (Eds.), *The Employment Interview: Theory, Research and Practice* (pp.). Newbury Park: Sage Publications.

Schuler, J. & Stehle, W. (1983). Neuere Entwicklungen des Assessment-Center-Ansatzes - beurteilt unter dem Aspekt der sozialen Validität. *Psychologie und Praxis. Zeitschrift für Arbeits- und Organisationspsychologie, 27*,33-44.

Schulz, C., Schuler, J. & Stehle, W. (1985). Die Verwendung eignungsdiagnostischer Methoden in deutschen Unternehmen. In H. Schuler and W. Stehle (Eds.), *Organisationspsychologie und Unternehmenspraxis: Perspektiven der Kooperation* (pp.126-132). Stuttgart: Hogrefe/Verlag für Angewandte Psychologie.

Scott, W.D. (1916). Selection of employees by means ofquantitative determinations. *Annuals of the American Academy of Political and Social Science, 65*.

Stehle,W. (1983). *Zur Konzeption eines Personalauswahlverfahrens auf der Basis biographischer Daten*. Unpublished doctoral dissertation, Hohenheim University, Stuttgart.

Trost, G. (1986). Die Bedeutung des Interviews für die Diagnose der Studieneignung. Darstellung der internationalen Forschungsergebnisse. In R. Lohölter, K. Hinrichsen, G. Trost and S. Drolshagen (Eds.), *Das Interview bei der Zulassung zum Medizinstudium*. Stuttgart: Schattauer.

Tyler, (Ed.). (1969). *The work of the counsellor*. New York: Appleton-Century-Croffs.

Wagner, R. (1949). The employment interview: A critical summary. *Personnel Psychology, 2*, 17-46.

Webster, E.C. (Ed.). (1982). *The employment interview*. Schomberg, Ontario: SIP Publications.

Wiesner, W.H. & Cronshaw, S.F. (1988). A meta-analytic investigation of the impact of interview format and degree of structure on the validity of the employment interview. *Journal of Occupational Psychology, 61,* 275-290.

Zehelein, (1985). *Students' judgements of interviewers: The influence of gender and communication style.* Unpublished Masters Thesis, University of Erlangen-Nuremberg.

13

Psychological Selection Tests as Viewed by the Testees Five Years Later

Amir Rozen

Abstract

The use of Psychological Selection tests (before study options in school, before conscription, entering college, taking on a new job) is constantly expanding all over the world. Much effort and time have been devoted to investigating the psychometric qualities of these tests, but seldom have the researchers approached the testees themselves to ascertain their attitudes after experiencing such tests.

Such an approach seems justified for two reasons:

a) *The public point of view*: Today's testees may in some years, become the main users of the tests, either as decision makers deciding on hiring job applicants or promoting employees, or as parents educating a generation of children born into a period when such tests are a legitimate and accepted process.

b) *The psychometric point of view*: Testees who see the tests as suitable and fair, and trust in the accuracy of their measurements, will approach them with less hostility and fear and will be far more willing to cooperate, thus actually contributing to the enhancement of the reliability and validity of the test.

In this article we introduce our method of approaching testees who have been tested in the past in a psychological testing system, the object being to determine their attitude and feelings toward the test. The aim is to evaluate the effect of the testing experience on the testees in retrospect.

Introduction

Most selection and classifying tests are conducted in two areas: study and employment. The few studies concerned with the viewpoint of the testees have focused on three groups:
1) School pupils, who are continually tested for both comparative and standard knowledge and ability before moving to a higher level of studies (higher class, group, stream etc.)
2) University students, who are selected by entrance examinations for studies toward the first degree or for specialization toward the second degree.
3) Adult workers, who undergo the selection tests for hiring purposes.
In all three groups the act of taking the test is of great significance for the testee because of the great impact of its results on his academic or professional career. The research conducted so far is as follows.

School pupils

Tesser (1968) examined the exposure of American high school students to various types of examinations and their beliefs and attitudes toward tests. Scruggs et al. (1985) presented a questionnaire that they developed (TAS) to observe the difference in attitude to examinations between regular students and students with behavioral problems. Lerner (1986) reviewed responses in American public opinion polls in 1980 on the standardized achievement tests. Goslin (1967) presented teachers' opinions of standard achievement tests. Zeidner (1988) compared the attitude of Israeli sixth grade students toward special ability tests with that toward the regular school examinations.

University students

Baird (1977) studied the attitudes of 4000 candidates toward the entrance examination to universities in the US. Lerner (1986) surveyed answers to public opinion polls held among students in the US in 1977 on the Scholastic Aptitude Test (SAT). Baird (1987) examined the influence of examination results on the academic career of students studying towards the first, and second degree. Nevo & Sfez (1985) developed an Examinees Feedback Questionnaire (EFEQ) for use in psychometric tests for studies in institutions of higher learning. The answers to the questionnaire were processed and published by Nevo (1988) and in NITE reports

(1984-1988). Oren (1988) reported on answers to feedback questionnaires given to Israeli examinees in their studies toward the second degree in psychology (GRE psychology test). They were requested to express their feelings and beliefs concerning the test.

Working adults

In this category we found only one research paper. Fiske (1967) asked 600
adults to take part in selection tests, to recall the last testing situation they
experienced, and to report their feelings and express beliefs and opinions
about the process. The replies were compared according to the type of selection test taken by the participants. In these studies the testees were
asked for three kinds of replies:
a) *Beliefs and opinions about the tests*: Is the test fair? Are its measurements accurate? Is it a valid tool to measure what it is supposed to
measure (face validity)? Is the test of any value in helping to determine
the direction of a future career? What is the practical validity of its results? To what extent is it possible to accept the series of tests as the sole
factor in the selection? Can it forecast future success in life? Can the test
reveal things the testee does not want revealed? Etc.
b) *Emotional feelings toward the tests*: Feelings of fear or anxiety before
the test; of difficulty, stress, worry, nervousness and tension during it;
sense of frustration, disappointment or failure at the end of it; and
general feelings not associated with the test, such as boredom, restless-
ness, excitement, challenge, interest, etc.
c) *Behavior related to the tests*: The test registration procedure; preparation process for test; previous experience with various tests and their frequency; exposure to background information about test; estimate of success after test; influence of environmental conditions on test; attitude to
testors, their attitude and presentation of the instructions of the test; test
characteristics (total duration of test and sub-tests, guessing possibilities); receiving results and explanations, etc.
The three reaction facets of testees in a selection system are very similar
to the three components of the term "attitude," defined by Lindzey and
Aronson (1985), as a set of cognitions, beliefs, opinions and facts, all of
which through the inclusion of emotional evaluations (positive or negative) describe the subject or the items that is the object of the attitude. In
short, *knowledge* and *feelings* determine "persons" behavior. These
authors note that the world of knowledge is loaded with complicated details and facts and that the world of feelings is much more simple and auth-

entic. Nevertheless, they recognize that the emotional factor is the dominant among the three. They point out that an opinion is generally formed as a result of influence parents' images, meaningful friends and colleagues, ideology of the institute in which one studies, laws and the media. There is no doubt, however, that an opinion can be formed as a result of even a single meaningful experience.

The view that people become aware of their positions through observing their open behavior during a meaningful experience is strengthened by Bem and McConnel (1970), Miller et al. (1975), support this, noting that people express beliefs and opinions that are based on meaningful past experiences.

If so, then how is the *attitude* of a testee toward a selection test formed? In the language of attitude we speak of accumulation, *over time* , of real test experiences. Each such experience leaves behind sensory impressions, strengthens actual *behavior* in the test conditions he experienced. The emphasis is on the *personal experience*.

Since selection tests are a familiar and significant experience for adults and youth alike (in Israel for example almost every adult has experienced at least two to four selection tests, at least one of which is very important for him), and knowing that the actual performing of the test is important for determining the positions toward selection tests, the test authors and the testing consumers have a greater interest in making the test more acceptable to the testee. To this end we define (a) the aim of the approach to the testee (research aims) and (b) the form of the approach (research tools).

Research aims

We have already mentioned the few studies in Israel and the world where testees were asked to provide feedback on the system by which they were tested. The present study indicates the missing elements and endeavors to provide them, and also to add new ones, which are as follows.

The time elapsed between test and feedback

So far testees have been asked their opinions on tests, without reference to any possible selection test experience or to any concrete test event (Lerner, 1986; Tesser, 1968); they have been asked immediately following the end of the test (Baird, 1987); or they have been asked to recall the last classifying test they experienced. The average time elapsed for all those asked turns out to be fourteen years (Fiske, 1967).

This study seeks to examine how the testee regards the test in the perspective of time that has enabled him to adopt a position on the test during or following his educational or professional development. Feedback, therefore, is sought *five years* after the test was taken (for comparison the complete questionnaire will also be given to a sample of testees who took the test *three years* before and to a sample of testees who have just finished the test).

Scope of feedback

Apart from the EFEQ questionnaire (Nevo & Sfez, 1985) no suitable instrument adapted to provide feedback on a classifying system has been constituted. The EFEQ refers to the three elements of attitude, but concentrates on the behavioral part and on examining the opinions. There is hardly any reference to the emotional part. In the framework of this study we have constructed an instrument (EFEQTIV) that refers to the three elements of attitude. Its questions are directed at obtaining opinions about the test, feelings about it, and at recalling behavior throughout the experience: before the test (preparing for it), during the test (remembering the contents of the test, reference to environmental conditions) and after the test (receiving the result and reference to it). There are also questions on changes in attitudes toward tests as a result of the test experience.

Examining attitude as expressed in feedback vis-â-vis a "hard" index

Until now most studies have asked the testee for his opinion, and left it at that. In comparisons made in some studies the result of addressing different groups experiencing a similar test (high school students' views compared with high school teachers' views; first degree students' views compared with second degree students' views), No effort was made to typify different profiles of respondents within the same group. "Hard" variables such as the nature of the test's results, consequent acceptance or rejection, the number of previous experiences of selection tests - all may shed light on the positions expressed in the feedback questionnaire, but they were not checked against the answers of respondents. The exception is a study that examined the connection between the success of the testee in a GRE test and the perception of the test as fair (Baird, 1987).

Our study examines the connection between the retrospective observations of the testee (his opinions, feelings, the recollection of what took place), and his grades, his success in being accepted in the selection process, his experiences in psychological classifying tests, his scholastic and professional stability, and background variables - sex, age and education.

Comparison of attitudes of testees in selection tests in different selection systems:

One comparison was made between people tested in three different spheres joining the Army, enrolling in a university, and beginning work (Fiske, 1967). No such comparison has been made in the last 20 years.
This study will compare people being tested by the selecting body for tertiary studies and those tested by the classifying body for employee recruitment. This comparison is important because of the basic difference between some of the test's elements:
1) *Composition of test*: A test comprising an ability to check by means of paper and pencil tests, in contrast to one comprising checks of ability, interests and personality, with an interview as part of the process as well as situational simulation at times.
2) *Duration of test*: About three hours in contrast to about eight hours.
3) *Type of interaction with testing body:* Contact with the testee beyond the test situation - mailing of preparation handbook, notification of results and comments about them - in contrast to contact with testee in the test situation only.
4) *Possibility of improving results*: The chance of taking the test again within one year in contrast to one test only with no option for improvement.
5) *Significance of results*: Results that allow possible alternatives to be chosen even in case of rejection, in contrast to results indicating a specific job, and rejection being clearcut and final.
The aim of this study is to compare retrospective consideration by testees in two important classifying systems (classification prior to admittance to institutions of higher learning and classification prior to job recruitment). Retrospective consideration is limited to a fixed and significant time span (five years) as compared with shorter periods (three and 0 years). The opinions and feelings expressed in the feedback do not remain on the subjective determining level only but are put to the test vis-à-vis "hard" indices (quality of results, number of test experiences, etc.).

Study assumptions

Results of the feedback studies show that there is cognizance of the value of the selection tests. The test experience is unpleasant (stress, tension) and reactions and feelings vary according to objective outcome. Nevertheless, the research questions as defined in the section on aims have never been asked before, and hence it was not possible to conjecture the direction of the assumptions, beyond intuitive feeling.

From the answers on the questionnaire, comparisons will be made within each of the two testing bodies participating in the study: the effect of time passed since taking the test; the effect of subjective feeling of success; and the effect of objective measure of success.

Comparison will be made between the institutions: the effect of time and diversity of tests; difference in face validity of the various classifying devices; and the effect of relevant variables (previous experience with tests, level of education, etc.).

Research tools

The EFEQTIV questionnaire (Examinees' Feedback Questionnaire over Time Interval) was composed to enable the testee in the classifying system to express his opinion, retrospectively, about the experience he underwent. The ideas for questions came from three sources:

a) Existing feedback questionnaires: principally Nevo and Sfez's EFEQ (1985); in the area of emotional reference, Jäger's CLEDS (1986); and the semantic differential published in Zeidner's study (1988).

b) Questions concerning opinions and beliefs of testees on selection tests which have appeared in studies listed in the review of the literature.

c) Questions derived from the practical experience of the author.

The questions concern three position determining elements (questions from the questionnaire appear in the Appendix):

The cognitive element

This part deals with opinions and beliefs about the tests (14 statements). Seven statements concern the personal significance of the test (the desire to receive detailed results, to receive feedback from an expert, the test's contribution to self cognizance and career development, change of atti-

258

tude towards this type of test in particular and toward psychology in general, as a result of the test). These are measured by the Likert Scale comprising seven grades, from 1 (not at all) to 7 (considerably). The seven remaining statements concern general opinions about tests of the kind they have experienced and about tests in general (fairness of test, confidence in its validity, confidence in its reliability, its usefulness for society, the connection between its results and the worth of the person). All are measured by the 7-grade Likert Scale, with one exception: the questions on evident validity, which attempts to give a weight to 10 measuring tools according to their usefulness as classifying devices in a test like that taken. The possible weight for each tool is from 1 (very unsuitable) to 5 (very suitable).

The affective element

Feelings about the test are surveyed by 12 measures. These are polar measures with 7 distance units between them. The testee marks the degree of his proximity to one of the poles in every measure. The principle for choosing them and the method of their presentation are similar to the form known as the semantic differential (Osgood et al. 1957); there are measures of evaluation (complicated - simple; interesting - uninteresting), measures of force (easy - difficult, deep - superficial), and measures of action (repulsive - attractive, creative - routine).

The behavioral element

This part consists of six questions.
One question deals with the preparation for the test (practicing for it, resting before it, learning techniques for coping with test). The testee is not required to report if he did so, but were he to take the test today if he would change anything in his preparation procedure. The answers are on the 7-grade Likert Scale and in an open question.
Three questions deal with taking the test itself (satisfaction with environmental conditions, remembering length of test and type of sub-test). Satisfaction is marked on a 5-grade Likert Scale, from 1 (bad) to 5 (excellent). Questions pertaining to memory are open.
Two questions deal with reference to test results (disappointment or pleasant surprise, regarding the test as contributing to being accepted). Answers are given in 3-graded statements.
The 32 questions in the questionnaire appear in a certain order. They begin with the actual performance of the test (prior preparation, the tests

themselves), continue with feelings during test and beliefs held after it, and conclude with the test's results. At the end there is one general open question.

References

Baird, L.L. (1977). What graduate and professional school students think about admissions tests. *Measurements in Education, 7(3),* 1-7.

Baird, L.L. (1987). Do students think admissions tests are fair? Do tests affect their decisions? *Research in Higher Education, 26(4),* 373-388.

Bem, D.J. & McConnell, H.K. (1970). Testing the self perception of dissonance phenomena. *Journal of Personality and Social Psychology, 14,* 23-31.

Fiske, D.W. (1967). The subject reacts to tests. *American Psychologist, 22,* 287-296.

Goslin, D.A. (1967). *Teachers and Teaching.* New York: Russell Sage Foundation.

Jäger, R.S. (1986). Measuring examiner and examinee reaction to each other and the psychodynamic situation. In B. Nevo & R.S. Jäger (Eds.), *Psychological Testing - The Examinee Perspective* (pp. 129-146). Toronto: Hogrefe.

Lerner, B. (1986). Representative democracy - 'Men of Zeal' and testing legislation, in B. Nevo & R.S. Jäger (Eds.), *Psychological Testing - The Examinee Perspective* (pp. 5-20). Toronto: Hogrefe.

Lindzey, G. & Aronson, E. (1985). *The Handbook of Social Psychology* (Vol. 1, 2). (3rd ed.). New York: Random House.

Miller, R.L. & Brickman, P. & Bolen, D. (1975). Attribution versus Persuasion as a means for modifying behavior. *Journal of Personality and Social Psychology, 31,* 430-441.

National Institute for Testing and Evaluation (1984-1988). *Feedback Reports* No. 18, 22, 30, 36, 40,44, 47, 55, 56, 58, 63, 66, 77. Jerusalem.

Nevo, B. (1988). The practical and theoretical value of examinees' feedback questionnaires. *Applied Psychology - an International Review.* (in press).

260

Nevo, B. & Cohen, Y. (1988). *Selected Problems in Evaluation and Measurement*. Jerusalem: National Institute for Testing and Evaluation.

Nevo, B. & Sfez, J. (1985). Examinees' feedback questionnaires, *Assessment and Evaluation in Higher Education, 10,* 235-243.

Oren, C. (1988). MKAL as a model for building National Achievement Test. in B. Nevo & Y. Cohen, (Eds.), *Selected Problems in Evaluation and Measurement*. Jerusalem: National Institute for Testing and Evaluation.

Osgood, C.E., Suci, D.J. & Tannenbaum, P.H. (1957). *The Measurement of Meaning*. Urbana: University of Illinois Press.

Scruggs, T.E., Mastropieri, M.A., Tolfa, D. & Jenkins, V. (1985). Attitudes of behaviorally disordered students toward tests. *Perceptual and Motor Skills, 60,* 467-470.

Tesser, A. & Leidy, T.R. (1968). Psychological testing through the looking glass of youth. *American Psychologist, 23,* 381-384.

Zeidner, M. (1988). Sociological differences in examinees' attitudes towards scholastic ability exams. *Journal of Educational Measurement.* (in press).

APPENDIX

Feelings about the test

1) Emotional reaction to test

Before you are adjectives, connected to the test you took about 5 years ago. At the two extreme ends of the scale, words are listed in opposing pairs. If you agree very much with the word on the right side mark an x next to it; if you agree very much with the word on the left side, mark an x next to it; all the others are intermediate positions and the direction of your feelings will be indicated by the position of your x.

```
profound– – – – – – –|– – –|– – –|– – –|– – –|– – –|– – –|– – – superficial
easy – – – – – – – – –|– – –|– – –|– – –|– – –|– – –|– – –|– – – difficult
known – – – – – – – –|– – –|– – –|– – –|– – –|– – –|– – –|– – – unknown
complicated – – – – –|– – –|– – –|– – –|– – –|– – –|– – –|– – – simple
intelligent – – – – – –|– – –|– – –|– – –|– – –|– – –|– – –|– – – unintelligent
scientific – – – – – – –|– – –|– – –|– – –|– – –|– – –|– – –|– – – unscientific
interesting – – – – – –|– – –|– – –|– – –|– – –|– – –|– – –|– – – boring
prohibitive, repelling–|– – –|– – –|– – –|– – –|– – –|– – –|– – – attractive
soothing – – – – – – –|– – –|– – –|– – –|– – –|– – –|– – –|– – – frightening, creates tension
frustrating – – – – – –|– – –|– – –|– – –|– – –|– – –|– – –|– – – not frustrating
outdated – – – – – – –|– – –|– – –|– – –|– – –|– – –|– – –|– – – innovative
creative – – – – – – –|– – –|– – –|– – –|– – –|– – –|– – –|– – – routine
```

2) Opinions about test

a) To what extent do you agree with the following statements (circle the
number which conforms to your opinion)

	not at all					very much	
– Were I to take this test today the results would be better	1	2	3	4	5	6	7
– The final result was not enough. I was interested in getting detailed test results	1	2	3	4	5	6	7
– I feel the test helped me to know myself better	1	2	3	4	5	6	7
– The feeling that the test helped me in furthering my career (academic/professional)	1	2	3	4	5	6	7
– This kind of test is fair to various kinds of examinees	1	2	3	4	5	6	7
– This kind of test is suitable for examining functioning ability (professional and personal)	1	2	3	4	5	6	7
– This kind of test is suitable for examining mental ability	1	2	3	4	5	6	7
– This kind of test is beneficial to society	1	2	3	4	5	6	7
– This kind of selection test is a reliable and accurate measuring device	1	2	3	4	5	6	7
– There is a connection between the worth of a person and the results of his tests (he who gets higher marks is worth more)	1	2	3	4	5	6	7

b) Following the psychological selection test that you took, your opinion of (your
evaluation of) these tests has

decreased very much		not changed			improved very much	
1	2	3	4	5	6	7

c) Following the psychological selection test that you took, your opinion of (your
evaluation of) psychology in general has

improved very much		not changed			decreased very much	
1	2	3	4	5	6	7

Attitude to test results

1) I received the results of the selection tests

   ☐ from the employer who hired me (my boss or the personnel department)

   ☐ by my own initiative (I checked with the institute or my employer)

   ☐ I did not receive them, but I am able to estimate them

   ☐ I did not receive them and am unable to estimate the results (Move to question 3)

2) The results of the selection tests –

   ☐ Disappointed me (they were lower than I expected)

   ☐ Matched my expectations

   ☐ Pleasantly surprised me (they were higher than I had expected)

3) Did the selection test you took *help* or *harm* your chances of being hired for the job you were applying for?

   ☐ The test helped

   ☐ The test neither helped nor harmed

   ☐ The test harmed and caused rejection

Open question

If you wish to add anything about the test you referred to in this questionnaire, please do it here:

_____

_____

_____

_____

_____

Part 5:

The Psychodiagnostic Context

14

Measuring Reactions of Examiner and Examinee to Each Other and to the Psychodiagnostic Situation

Reinhold S. Jäger

Abstract

This chapter and its appendices present two instruments which have been developed in order to assess the attitudes and reactions of examinees concerning the psychodiagnostic process. Our argument is based on the theory that (a) every testee either has some prior knowledge and personal predispositions concerning psychological testing, or develops them in the course of examination itself; and (b) these predispositions have an effect on the client's test behavior. In the first two sections of this chapter we have tried to demonstrate the validity of these hypotheses and to show the value of systematic feedback data. In psychodiagnosis, two individuals (the client and the tester) cooperate, each of them acting from within his or her own perspective. Each perspective must be measured separately - hence the need for two questionnaires. The third section of this chapter describes the questionnaires, which are reproduced in full in the appendices.

Introduction

In this chapter we address the question of how the psychodiagnostic process and its results are affected by conditions associated directly or indirectly with the process itself, especially the client's past experience with testing. The diagnostic process was defined as "the orderly application of testing devices so as to provide the person making the referral with assistance in decision making, or to bring about a decision " (Jäger, 1983, p. 9). The examinee's experience of the diagnostic procedure consists of emotions, attitudes, and cognitions produced and shaped by (a) the diagnostic goals of the psychologist; (b) external conditions; and (c) the internal predisposition brought to the process by the client. Table 1 contains some representative factors pertaining to these three categories.

Table 1

Factors Influencing Examinee's Experience Within the
Psychodiagnostic Context

Goals of Testing	Examinee's Predispositions	External Conditions
General goals	Previous experience with psychological testing	Examiner's behavior
Specific diagnostic questions	Attitude about being tested	Physical conditions
Strategies and techniques	General psychological state	Specific order of tests

The table sets out only a few of the complex factors that influence the examinee's reactions, internal as well as external, to the testing experience. A systematic study of these responses is necessary for practical reasons, and represents a promising direction for future research. Indeed it constitutes the main subject of our concern in this chapter. Let us however first consider a number of issues connected with examinee feedback and psychological testing in general.

Standardization of Testing

In their review of the literature dealing with standardization, Sader and Keil (1966) concluded that strict standardization in psychodiagnosis cannot be guaranteed. Discussing the same theme, Eckel (1978) concluded that a specific psychological testing situation cannot be accurately replicated, either in a test-retest situation for one individual or across different examinees. These differences within and between individuals should not be treated as contaminating variables, but rather as legitimate topics of research.

Validity

a) Face validity: During the diagnostic experience the client may formulate ideas concerning the purpose of testing and the mechanisms of scoring and interpretation. While most of the perceptions will be false, they may nevertheless influence the examinee's reactions during the diagnostic process and thus lead to a biased response. It is the responsibility of the testing psychologist to evaluate these perceptions and to estimate the bias accordingly.

b) Construct validity: Psychodiagnostic instruments are normally based on theoretical frameworks that are geared toward specific practical applications and designed to be used with particular client populations. Any attempt to apply the tests to purposes or populations other than those prescribed by the manual would require additional empirical support (Jäger, 1978).

Effect of Previous Experience on Examinee Reactions

Many experts would agree with the statement that past experience with testing is an important determinant of examinee test responses (Anastasi, 1976; Sader & Keil, 1966; Spitznagel, 1982). In practice, however, psychodiagnosticians do not give due consideration to this premise and behave as though they assumed stochastic independence of test items and battery parts. It is our view that single-case studies in diagnostics, even more than group statistics, will reveal significant effects of experience with testing. Unfortunately, however, there is a dearth of research in both areas.

The Test User

In many cases the person requesting psychological testing is not the examinee. Psychiatrists refer their patients, psychotherapists refer their clients, and employers refer their prospective job candidates for psychological evaluation. This situation may lead to legal difficulties (Jäger, 1983) as well as clinical problems. The weaker the consent of an examinee to undergo psychodiagnosis, the greater will be the conflict. To study this issue, feedback must be obtained from clients in a systematic way.

Evaluation of Psychodiagnostic Experiences

The goal of a diagnostic process defines the frame of reference within which actual testing takes place. We distinguish between two different kinds of goals:
a) Selection: the goal of testing is to optimize decisions regarding acceptance or rejection of applications for various positions.
b) Modification: diagnosis is aimed at optimizing decisions concerning the modification of the examinee's behavior.

These two goals are not mutually exclusive, and are often combined in a single diagnostic evaluation.

The diagnostic question specifies and operationalizes the general goal. The term "question" refers to the specific purpose of the selection (in terms of the criterion), the selection ratio, the applicant's intake and so on.

Strategy can be defined as the application of diagnostic tools for the purpose of answering the diagnostic questions.

Four dimensions have been suggested for the categorization of diagnostic strategies; a fifth dimension was added by Jäger (1982, 1983) and by Jäger and Booth (1982). These five dimensions of diagnostic strategies are presented in Table 2:

Table 2

Dimensions of Psychodiagnostic Strategies

a) diagnosis of the individual in a static state	– diagnosis of the individual as a dynamic entity
b) norm inference approach	– criterion reference approach
c) quantitative approach	– qualitative approach
d) diagnopstic orientation	– prognostic orientation
e) individual assessment	– group-oriented assessment

Any application of psychological testing may be classified according to these five dimensions. Goals, questions, and strategies will vary from one testing situation to the next, and the testees will react differently to each variation. It is important that detailed feedback from the individuals being tested should be gathered within the context of each combination of goals, questions, and strategies.

Conflict vs. Shared Interest between the Examinee and the Examiner

Test motivation may be directly affected by the level of shared interest between the diagnostician and the client. Three examples are presented below:

a) The psychologist and the client share the same interest, as in the case of a client who seeks diagnosis of his or her own accord. Here one may expect to find high motivation and strong ego involvement.

b) Conflicting interests may occur in situations in which an external authority, such as a court of law, advises or requests that a client submit to psychological examination. In this circumstance, clients may exhibit a lack of motivation and involvement.

c) Psychodiagnostics may take place within the framework of a learning experience (e.g. in the case of clinical psychology students) or of a research project. In these instances examinees are usually volunteers, and their motivation may vary from very high to nil.

One may hypothesize that examinees in different categories will have different attitudes toward the testing procedure, and will consequently have different responses to the test items. The influence of motivation on performance in ability tests is exemplified in the reverse U-shaped function which is derived when individuals are repeatedly tested under different induced levels of motivation (Foppa, 1968).

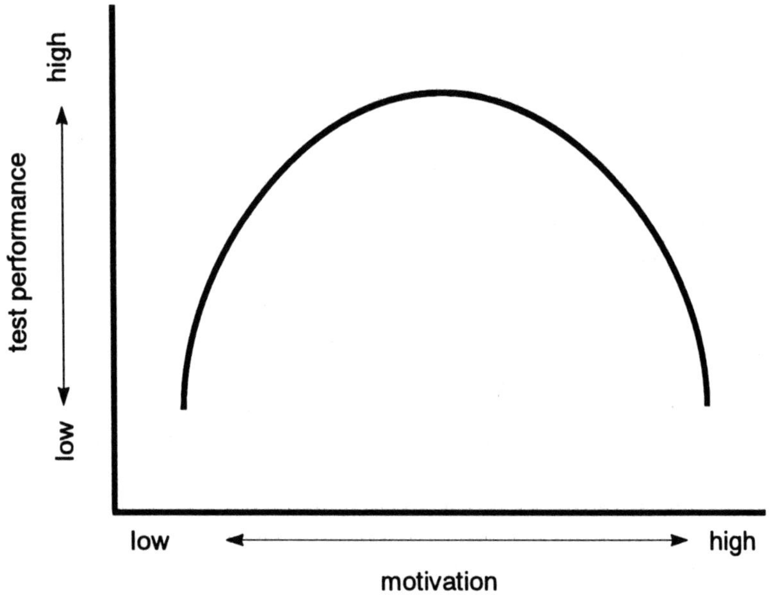

Fig. 1: U-Shaped Function Between Test
Performance and Motivation

It is therefore crucial to discover the client's basic attitudes toward testing. In the absence of this information test performance may be incor-
rectly interpreted.

Internal Predispositions

Motivation is only one of the factors apt to influence the reaction to the
testing situation and the performance of examinees. Other factors which
should also be taken into consideration when interpreting test results are
willingness to cooperate, test anxiety, and familiarity with the testing situation. These variables - referred to as "internal predispositions" - develop within the individual prior to and during testing. The major internal
predispositions are listed in Table 3.

Table 3

Major Internal Predisposition

1. General psychological state
2. Previous experience with psychodiagnostics
3. Acceptance of the need for testing
4. Attitudes toward the psychodiagnostican
5. Attitudes toward the diagnostic instruments

Gathering Feedback Data

In order to evaluate these factors systematically, two questionnaires have been devised to serve as feedback mechanisms. These are discussed in the concluding paragraphs below.

Questionnaire I: The Examinee's Perspective

This device is filled out by the examinee after the test, and relates to the client's attitudes toward psychodiagnosis. We confine ourselves here to a general description of the questionnaire. The reader will find it reproduced in its entirety in Appendix A.

Part I: The items here refer to the examinee's previous experience with psychodiagnosis (e.g. Was he tested before? When? How many times? Under what circumstances).

Part II: The client is asked to describe, by means of an adjective check list, his general psychological state before and after the testing.

Part III: The client is asked to rate the test administrator. A series of pairs of contrasting descriptions is presented from which the client is asked to choose the most appropriate description in each pair.

Part IV: The items are meant to reveal the examinee's attitude toward the psychological instruments by a method which is identical to that used in Part III.

Questionnaire II: The Psychodiagnostician's Perspective

Appendix B contains the complete version of Questionnaire II, which is to be filled out by the diagnostician. Although basically similar to Questionnaire I, it contains additional items for obtaining information about issues such as the examiner's perception of the use of language, and the visual-motor ability of the examinee.

Interpretation of Responses to Questionnaires I and II

At this stage no standard approach to the interpretation of the examinee's responses is recommended. Empirical data must be collected and norms established, before objective scoring methods and standard interpretations can be employed. Much can be learned, however, from a qualitative analysis of the examinee's feedback, including information about the diagnostician and the tools of diagnosis. Comparison of data from Questionnaires I and II may provide interesting material, especially as regards those items in which gaps or discrepancies are detected between the perceptions of the psychologist and the client. These questionnaires should be viewed as proposed models rather than imposed instruments, and diagnosticians may add or omit items according to their own needs.

References

Anastasi, A. (1976). *Psychological testing. (3rd. ed.)* New York: Macmillan.

Eckel, K. (1978). Das Sozialexperiment: Finales Recht als Bindeglied zwischen Politik und Sozialwissenschaft. *Zeitschrift für Soziologie, 7,* 39-55.

Foppa, K. (1968). *Lernen, Gedächtnis, Verhalten: Erbegnisse und Probleme der Lernpsychologie (3rd ed.).* Cologne: Kiepenheuer & Witsch

Jäger, R.S. (1978). *Differentielle Diagnostizierbarkeit in der Psychologischen Diagnostik. Theoretische und empirische Untersuchungen mit Moderatoren.* Göttingen: Hogrefe.

Jäger, R.S. (1982). Strategien und Zielsetzungen in der pädagogischen Diagnostik: Eine Analyse verschiedener Randbedingungen. In K. Ingenkampo, R. Horn & R.S. Jäger (Eds.), Tests und Trends: *Jahrbuch der pädagogischen Diagnostik* (pp. 119-145). Weinheim: Beltz.

Jäger, R.S. (1983). *Der diagnostische Prozeß: Eine Diskussion psychologischer und methodischer Randbedingungen.* Göttingen: Hogrefe.

Jäger, R.S., & Booth, J.F. (1982). Selzione o modificazione? Una esame delle strategie a degli ogettivi nella diagnostica della maturitâ scolastica. In F. Lunette & R.S. Jäger (Eds.), *La problematica psicodiagnostica della maturitâ scolastica* (pp. 19-58). Padua: Cedam.

Sader, M., & Keil, W. (1966). Bedingungskonstanz in der psychologischen Diagnostik *Archiv für die gesamte Psychologie, 118,* 279-308.

Spitznagel, A.F. (1982). Die diagnostische Situation. In K.J. Groffman & L. Michel (Eds.), *Grundlagen psychologischer Diagnostik Enzyklopädie der Psychologie: Vol. 1 Serie Psychologische Diagnostik* (pp. 284-294). Göttingen: Hogrefe.

APPENDIX A

Check List for Examinees in a Diagnostic Situation (CLEDS)*

Instructions

You have just participated in a psychological examination. We should like to learn in a more systematic way about your feelings and attitudes toward the testing experience, the diagnostician who administered the examination, and the test instruments.

Please answer the questions on the following pages or indicate your choice of the appropriate answer with an X. If you have made a mistake in placing the X, you may correct it by drawing a circle around it.

Please take note of the following:

1. Answer the questions just as you feel now, or as you felt before or during the test. It is important for us to know how you felt in this specific situation, rather than how you feel generally.
2. Do not think about which answer gives the best impression. It is important that we know your immediate response, so don't think for too long.
3. If you can't find an answer immediately, please indicate the answer which best describes you or how you feel.
4. Do not omit any questions.

PERSONAL INFORMATION

Name: _____
Address: _____   City: _____
Age: _____
Sex: _____
Date: _____

For the use of the tester:

_____
_____
_____
_____
_____
_____
_____
_____
_____

278

I. Previous Experience and/or Knowledge about Psychological Testing:

1. Have you ever participated in a psychological examination before?

Yes 0   No ..... 0 (If not, please go on to question 9.)

2. How many times have you been tested?

		times

3. How was the test administered to you?

verbally 0   written 0   verbally and written 0

don't remember 0

4. With what type of psychological test were you tested? (More than one answer is possible.)

development test .... yes 0   no 0

school readiness test .... yes 0   no 0

intelligence test .... yes 0   no 0

special aptitude tests (e.g. for music or

technical comprehension) .... yes 0   no 0

interest questionnaire (e.g. job interest) .... yes 0   no 0

attitude questionnaire (e.g. attitude on

political issues) .... yes 0   no 0

personality test .... yes 0   no 0

cannot define type of test 0

do not remember type of test 0

5. If you remember the name of the test, please write it down here:

_____

_____

6. Please record the occasions on which you were tested:

   1. year _____

      circumstances _____

      where _____

   2. year _____

      circumstances _____

      where _____

   3. year _____

      circumstances _____

      where _____

7. From your own personal experience, do you feel that psychological tests can provide valuable diagnostic information?

                                            yes 0   no 0

8. Did you get the results of your psychological examination?

                                            yes 0   no 0

9. Where did you get your past ideas about psychological tests?

   professional literature . . . . yes 0   no 0

   lectures or courses . . . . yes 0   no 0

   actual test materials . . . . yes 0   no 0

   participation in psychological testing . . . . yes 0   no 0

   magazines . . . . yes 0   no 0

   other sources of information (name them) . . . . yes 0   no 0

   cannot define type of test 0

   do not remember type of test 0

II. **Your Psychological State before and after the Test:**

1. How did you feel *before* the psychological examination?

I felt:

a) hostile	0	j) numb	0
b) energetic	0	k) able to concentrate	0
c) calm	0	l) tired	0
d) self-confident	0	m) not confident	0
e) apprehensive	0	n) cheerful	0
f) restrained	0	o) nervous	0
g) friendly	0	p) dejected	0
h) exited	0	q) depressed	0
i) passive	0	r) ill	0

2. Now, *after* the psychological examination, I feel:

a) hostile	0	j) numb	0
b) energetic	0	k) able to concentrate	0
c) calm	0	l) tired	0
d) self-confident	0	m) not confident	0
e) apprehensive	0	n) cheerful	0
f) restrained	0	o) nervous	0
g) friendly	0	p) dejected	0
h) exited	0	q) depressed	0
i) passive	0	r) ill	0

III. Attitudes Toward the Diagnostician:

What is your impression of the person who administered the examination? (Choose the more appropriate of the two possibilities in each line.)

a) confident 0   not confident 0

b) sympathetic 0   unsympathetic 0

c) condescending 0   not condescending 0

d) critical 0   uncritical 0

e) active 0   passive 0

f) penetrating 0   superficial 0

g) expert 0   inexpert 0

h) communicative 0   uncommunicative 0

i) good at explaning 0   bad at explaning 0

IV. Attitudes Toward Psychodiagnostic Instruments:

How did you perceive the psychodiagnostic instruments (test and/or questionnaires) to which you were exposed? (Choose the more appropriate of the two possibilities in each line.)

a) penetrating 0   superficial 0

b) easy 0   difficult 0

c) familiar 0   unfamiliar 0

d) appropriate 0   inappropriate 0

e) complicated 0   uncomplicated 0

f) direct 0   indirect 0

g) general 0   specific 0

h) intelligent 0   unintelligent 0

j) scientific 0   unscientific 0

k) interesting 0   uninteresting 0

l) comprehensive 0   not comprehensive 0

m) stimulating 0   repelling 0

n) professional 0   unprofessional 0

282

APPENDIX B:

Check List for Diagnosticians for Behavior Rating of Examinees in
a Diagnostic Situation (CLBEDS) *

Instructions

This check list will help you rate the examinee's work habits and obtain a clearer understanding of the conditions under which the examinee participated in this psychological examination. When data from this check list is combined with the CLBEDS, valuable information emerges. Please note that this instrument can be applied only to individual examination and not to groups.

PERSONAL DATA OF THE EXAMINEE

Name: _____

Address: _____   City: _____

Date of Testing: _____

Examined by: _____

Psychological State of the Examinee

I.   How do you rate the psychological condition of the client?

a) hostile	0	j) numb	0
b) energetic	0	k) able to concentrate	0
c) calm	0	l) tired	0
d) self-confident	0	m) not confident	0
e) apprehensive	0	n) cheerful	0
f) restrained	0	o) nervous	0
g) friendly	0	p) dejected	0
h) exited	0	q) depressed	0
i) passsive	0	r) ill	0

II. How do you rate the client's work habits and cooperation during the test? (Check the most appropriate of the contrasting adjectives in each line.)

a) quick	0	slow	0
b) precise	0	imprecise	0
c) concentrated	0	not concentrated	0
d) calm	0	restless	0
e) hestiant	0	confident	0
f) tense	0	relaxed	0

III. How did the examinee react to failure in the examination? (Check the most appropriate of the contrasting adjectives in each line.)

a) calmly	0	nervously	0
b) resigned	0	animated	0
c) depressed	0	cheerful	0
d) making excuses	0	not making excuses	0

IV. How did the client react to positive feedback during the examination? (Check the most appropriate of the contrasting adjectives in each line.)

a) gratefully	0	indignantly	0
b) tried harder	0	became careless	0
c) concentrated better	0	same concentration	0
d) calmly	0	nervously	0

V. How do you rate the language of the examinee? (Check the most appropriate of the contrasting adjectives in each line.)

a) fluent 0   hesitant 0
b) clear 0   unclear 0
c) direct 0   indirect 0
d) spontaneous 0   not spontaneous 0
e) eccentric 0   realistic 0

VI. How do you rate the visual motor behavior of the examinee? (Check the most appropriate of the contrasting adjectives in each line.)

a) quick reaction 0   slow react 0
b) trial and error 0   well planned 0
c) fluent 0   awkward 0
d) impulsive 0   controlled 0
e) coordinated 0   uncoordinated . . . .
f) appropriate gestures 0   inappropriate gestures 0

VII. Global ratings of examination

a) valid 0   not valid 0
b) reliable 0   not reliable 0

VIII. Other ratings or comments:

15

The psychodiagnostic experience: Reports of subjects

Hagit Benziman & Amira Toder

Abstract

Clinical psychologists administer psychological tests not for selection and classification but to help the individual. By means of these tests they attempt to peer into the secret recesses of his heart, to understand his difficulties and troubles, and to evaluate his abilities. The individual administration of tests is often the first meeting of the person with the mental health authorities, yet not enough consideration has been given to the understanding and analysis of this situation, or to attempts to learn from the subjects what they experience during and after the administration of these tests.

This chapter attempts to survey, both theoretically and through interviews with 30 subjects, children and adults, the residues of the diagnostic experience.

The picture obtained is that the examination experience is not simple, and psychologists do not contribute enough toward making it easier. A number of practical suggestions emerge from the results: greater preparation of the subjects, giving feedback, some changes in the test process itself, and others.

Introduction

One may speak roughly of two principal uses of psychological tests. One is for classification and selection, the second is for a deeper understanding of the individual.

When psychological tests are administered for classification and selection, their purpose is to serve a particular framework, educational, professional, military or other. Frameworks set up certain demands and admission requirements, and the psychological tests administered to candidates are supposed to decide which of the subjects satisfy them. The test is generally administered to groups, and the performance of each subject is compared with a criterion and with the performance of other candidates. The decision is then made in the light of these comparisons. When psychological tests are administered in such a context the examiners have no interest in the subject himself but only in the degree to which he suits the requirements of the classifying framework.

The other use of psychological tests is that by clinical psychologists, who are interested in the individual and try, with these diagnostic tools, to peer into the secret recesses of his heart, to understand his difficulties and troubles, and to evaluate his abilities and resources, in order to recommend the best ways of helping him. In this context the subject himself is the center of interest, concern and attention.

It would seem natural for clinical psychologists, who are sensitive to the feelings and experiences of the individual, to concern themselves with the examinee's experience while the psychological tests are being administered, his perception of the very fact of his being sent for testing, and the residues that remain after the tests. In fact, few clinical psychologists (Klopfer, 1964; Shafer, 1954) have dealt with these questions.

The more sensitive psychologists probably feel intuitively that the experience of "being an examinee" is not pleasant or simple. They try to talk to the subject before administering the tests, and they use means which they believe will somewhat relieve the anxiety of the diagnostic process. From discussions with many tens of psychologists, however, we gain the impression that even the more sensitive ones do not attribute great importance to this experience. The more experienced they are, and the more routine the diagnostic work becomes, the less sensitive do they become to this matter; in any event, they are not worried about the residues and ramifications of the test experience.

Theoretical and experimental exploration

We have attempted to analyze the "examinee experience" theoretically, on the basis of studies and papers dealing with parallel experiences, which seem relevant. We have also attempted to approach people who have undergone psychological examinations and to hear about the experience from them. Finding these people was not easy and the assistance of clinics and mental health centers was required. But, the willingness of the latter to cooperate in this research was extremely limited. The refusal of the psychologists to permit the interviewing of their examinees was derived from various considerations. Among other reasons, the psychologists justified their opposition as protection of their clients. "Isn't it enough that they underwent these tests? Do they also have to be interviewed about them?" Without doubting the sincerity of these justifications, it seems to us that their unwillingness to help us was derived not only from their wish to protect the examinees but also from their need to protect themselves or other examiners. It seems that the psychologists were uneasy at the prospect of a direct encounter between us and their clients and that they perhaps felt that their performance as examiners would be criticized in this context.

After much effort, and thanks to a number of psychologists who expressed interest and willingness to help, we were able to interview examinees, children and adults, and to hear from them about the experience of psychological examination. Obviously we took care to explain to the interviewees that this discussion with them was not an additional test, and that anything we heard from them would remain confidential and would not be reported to anyone using their names.

Theoretical discussion
Moment of crisis

In the vast majority of cases, psychological tests are administered when the subject arrives at the mental health center. Whether he has come on his own initiative or has been sent by others, it may be assumed that this is a point in time that expresses a moment of crisis, a moment of admitting the existence of problems that the person himself has failed to cope with on his own. At this difficult moment he is supposed to hand himself over to an examiner who will diagnose his problems, determine the severity of his situation, and even recommend or decide upon his future. This is a sensitive, tense situation that arouses anxiety. It may be compared with the situation of a person suffering from physical pain who has avoided being examined by a doctor. He has tried to ignore, deny, and devalue the pains. But when, at a given moment, for whatever reason, he decides to go for an examination. This examination acquires a decisive significance for him and he is filled with anxiety and tension while awaiting its results.

Identified patient

The parallel between the patient who goes or is sent to a doctor and one who is sent to a psychologist is only partial. When a person goes to a doctor it is entirely obvious that his pains are his own and no one else's. However, when the referral is for a psychological examination matters are not always so unequivocal. One of the criticisms leveled by the system therapy proponents (Haley, 1976; Minuchin, 1974) against therapists practicing individual therapy is the fact that the family or social system point to a certain individual and see in him the focus of the pathology; such focusing does not necessarily reflect the objective truth. Often, the referred person is only a scapegoat of the entire system, which itself possesses the pathology. The referral of a certain individual for a psychological examination gives a kind of seal of approval to the claim that he is the focus of the problem and that the pathology is in him and not in his environment. This fact is likely to arouse unpleasant feelings, guilt, anger, inadequacy and the like. This is especially evident in cases where children are referred to a psychologist. After getting to know the child and his parents and after administering the psychological examination, the psychologist may sometimes conclude that the source of the problem is not in the child himself but in the entire family system. Sometimes he will recommend family therapy or therapy for the parents alone. However, these are conclusions that are reached after the psychological examination and so do not concern us in this context. At the time when the child is sent for a psychological examination he is regarded, in his own eyes and in the eyes of others, as the problematic person in the system.

Test anxiety

Evaluative situations arouse tension and anxiety (Palmer, 1970). "Test anxiety" is a well-known concept that has been much studied, and it is known that this sort of anxiety increases with the importance of the evaluation and with the seriousness and significance of the evaluating framework in the eyes of the subject. There are studies showing that test anxiety at a certain level can raise motivation and make for more efficient performance, but at a higher level the quality of the performance is affected and there is an increase of negative self perception within the examinee.

Despite the familiar denials on the part of examinees in the context of psychological tests ("It's all nonsense!" "It's not scientific!") it seems reasonable to assume that test anxiety is involved to a non-negligible extent in psychological testing as well.

The ambiguity factor

Test anxiety increases whenever it is impossible to prepare for the tests. It seems that what is relevant in this connection is the ambiguity factor. It is known that ambiguity increases anxiety and arouses the need for an intensive search for ways of alleviating it. In their studies of behavior in situations of ambiguity Festinger (1954) and Schachter and Singer (1962) found that in such situations people lose their belief in their ability to judge reality, and they have a greater tendency to approach one another and to search for interpersonal cues to guide their behavior.

The person who is supposed to come for a psychological examination is therefore presumably caught in a situation of anxiety. He is unable to prepare for this examination, he does not really know what he is facing, and he is also unable to consult anyone else, as he has been sent for testing as an individual and there are no other participants. Even if he knew someone else who had undergone such a test, it is doubtful that he would turn to him for clarification. This would involve giving away his secret, whereas the stigma of differentness still besets the field and there is no openness in talking about it. At the time of the testing, both because the projective tests are based on ambiguity and because the examiner is required to sustain the ambiguity and not to provide any directive cues, the situation remains ambiguous. This situation, it may be surmised, does not change even after the psychological examination because the examinee does not have the opportunity for "social comparison," which would be likely to relieve his anxiety feelings somewhat. The giving of contentual professional feedback is likely to restore his feelings of security to a certain extent and to relieve the ambiguity and the accompanying anxiety.

Invitation to regression

The invitation to regression constitutes an additional component of test situations. The psychoanalytic school sees regression in the therapy situation as an intermediate process that permits an encounter with infantile contents and feelings, and results in growth and maturation. This regression undermines the equilibrium between primary and secondary ma-

292

terial, between drives and defenses, and exposes the person to unpleasant contents and feelings which are supposed to be worked through during the therapy. Projective tests also constitute an invitation to regression, but in contrast with what occurs in therapy the examinee must cope by himself with the effects of the regression. The testing situation does not permit or pretend to permit the working through of this material with the examinee.

It is clear, that the strength of the regression that occurs during psychoanalytic therapy is much greater than that occurring during a psychological examination. Nevertheless, Schafer (1967) stressed the many common characteristics of the two situations and the particular difficulty that characterizes the testing situation. This situation brings about intimate exposure in the presence of a stranger and so arouses feelings of rough penetration, anxiety, threats to privacy and helplessness.

The relationship with the examiner

The literature dealing with psychotherapy contains many references to the relationship with the therapist, the development of this relationship in the course of therapy, and the reactions of the client to the end of this relationship and the separation from the therapist. There are practically no references to the feelings of the examinee toward the examiner. The test situation is short, one-time, and ostensibly does not arouse feelings and expectations. However, there were those who pointed out that a complex system of feelings is aroused even toward the examiner, especially in children (Palmer, 1970). Similar feelings to those that arise in the therapeutic situation - inspection, apprehension, approach, difficulty in ending, feelings of abandonment, frustration and anger, were identified in children in test situations as well. Children who were sent for therapy frequently showed aggressive behavior that was associated with their disappointment with the examiner, disappointment because he left them and "preferred another child."

It seems reasonable to assume that in the test situation positive feelings are also likely to be aroused, the challenge of coping, the excitement of insight, and others. However, it is not by chance that we extended the discussion precisely about the difficulties of the situation and the negative residues it is likely to leave. Positive experiences do not require particular attention, but if the test situation does actually leave negative residues the examiners must know about this and try to moderate them as much as possible.

The research procedure

To get to know the examinees' experiences in psychological testing we selected the phenomenological method. The examinees were interviewed in a semi-structured interview. At the beginning and end of the interview they were asked to discuss the test experience freely. During the interview they were requested to answer structured questions that we had prepared ahead of time and that referred to points arising from the theoretical analysis. All the examinees were asked questions with identical content, but the formulation differed according to the subject's age and level of understanding.

The structured questions dealt with the following points:

1) How did the examinee understand the fact that he was sent for testing? What did he see as the purpose of the testing, and to what extent, in his opinion, was this purpose achieved?
2) Which of the components of the examination does the examinee tend to remember? What does he remember as likable and what as hateful?
3) What did the examinee understand about himself during the testing and how did this understanding affect him?
4) To what extent did the examinee continue to be concerned about the tests after he had completed them? Did he find an answer to the questions that were bothering him and, if so, how?
5) To what extent did openness or concealment characterize his performance on the tests?
6) How much feedback did he receive during or after the examination?
7) What were the examinee's feelings about the confidentiality of the tests, and how did this factor affect his performance?
8) What was his attitude towards the examiner?
9) What was the effect of the examination experience on his willingness to receive psychological help in the future?

We interviewed 15 children and 15 adults who had undergone psychological testing within a range of not more than half a year before the interview.

Results

Unpleasant feelings

Almost all the subjects experienced difficult and unpleasant feelings during the testing. The test situation was described as frightening and

anxiety-arousing. Both children and adults referred to the difficulty arising from the ambiguity of the test, from the feeling that there was no way
of knowing what was wanted and expected of them. The adults added the
feeling of passivity and smallness, the feeling of the lack of opportunity to
plan, to change and to react, and the absolute control of the examiner
over the situation. Some of them mentioned the fact that to the best of
their knowledge not everyone who goes to a mental health center is
referred for testing. The referral for psychological diagnosis therefore ac-
centuated their feeling of differentness and aroused anxiety in them
about the severity of their situation.

The lack of sufficient preparation

More than half the interviewees claimed that they had not received a
prior explanation about why they had to undergo psychological testing
and about the nature of these tests. The adults attempted to understand
this on their own by reading professional literature in the areas of psychology and education or by asking psychologist friends. The children were
forced to use more problematic sources. A third of them received explanations from their parents that were sometimes only partial or wrong and
gave them the feeling that they were being punished for underachieve-
ment at school. Others were told that they were being brought to play
with the examiner. A number of children received explanations from
other children who had undergone testing, but some of them were left
without any explanation at all and explained to themselves that psychological tests are a type of school test. As the age of the children increased,
they showed a more accurate understanding of the nature of the tests.

Distressing and excessive ambiguity

A third of the examinees felt that the tests were meant to serve mainly the
examiner and not the examinee. Some of the students who had undergone psychological tests felt that the tests were designed only to allow psychology students to practice and learn, and they left with the unpleasant
feeling of having been guinea pigs. More than half the interviewees related that the psychological examination continued to disturb them quite
a lot even after it was over. The adults among the examinees were especially concerned. It was clear that most of them wanted to discuss the
tests with someone, both to share the experience and to get a criterion for
comparison and an estimate of their performance relative to others.

Those subjects who expressed unwillingness to discuss the test with anyone justified this by feelings of shame and the fear of stigma.

Wariness of exposure and regret after the fact

Most of the interviewees claimed that during the testing they had avoided full exposure and/or had been sorry afterwards about things they had said. This selectivity derived mainly from embarrassment about discussing certain topics like sex, aggression, family problems and "negative" personality traits. A few examinees claimed that they avoided discussing certain topics out of fear that talking about them would aggravate the problem. Some of the adults had been given "advice" before the testing about what "should" and "should not" be said.

The adults who revealed things and later regretted it expressed anger toward the examiner and toward the situation which had "extracted" intimate details from them. They were distressed by the feeling of intimate exposure in the presence of an anonymous examiner.

Children who were distressed about their performance on the tests generally mentioned wrong answers they had given, which fits their general perception that the tests are connected with school tests and are mainly examining their abilities.

Preferences and dislikes among the tests

The most memorable test for the subjects was the Rorschach. The adults remembered it as the most significant test and had mixed feelings about it. The children had unpleasant feelings about it. The children preferred the drawing tests, while the adults described the drawing as a hateful task. The request for drawing confronted them with the need to prove themselves using a tool they were not skilled with, and they felt small and ridiculous. The Bender Gestalt test was hardly remembered by the interviewees.

The lack of feedback

Twenty-seven of the interviewees expected to be given feedback, a summarizing discussion or a diagnosis. Nine of the adults told us that they had not received any feedback. Six of the adults said that the results of the examination had been reported to them, but four of these claimed that this was a superficial and unsatisfying report. Surprisingly, all the children claimed that they had received no feedback whatsoever.

The interviewees were divided on the question of who they would have preferred to get the feedback from. It is interesting to note that the children expressed an absolute desire not to get the feedback from their parents.

Some of the adults, who had undergone the psychological examination during the course of therapy, preferred, because of the nature of their relationship with the therapist, to get the feedback from him rather than from the examiner.

The lack of confidence in secrecy

Most of the interviewees, nearly all the adults and about 60 percent of the children, were worried about the problem of the secrecy of the results of the tests and expressed apprehension that the material might not be safe guarded and might reach the hands of different people in different frameworks, school, army, family and even the Dean of Students in the university. Much concern was expressed in this connection, and five of the adults went even further and worried that the psychological examination might affect their chances of obtaining work in the future.

The effect of the examiner

When the subjects were asked about attitude toward the examiner, 12 of them spoke about the pleasant atmosphere at the time of the examination, but the rest reported an unpleasant and heavy atmosphere. Especially for the children there was something oppressive in the encounter within the rigid framework of the tests.

Nine of the adults and six of the children claimed that the behavior of the examiner affected their performance on the tests. Some of them reported that the encouragement and caring of the examiner helped them to perform better and to get more from themselves, while others claimed that the strangeness, indifference and formal attitude of the examiner prevented them from expressing themselves on the tests and made things more difficult for them

. Some adults complained about the use of a stopwatch and about the fact that the examiner was occupied taking notes the whole time. His writing, they claimed, gives the examinee the feeling of an experimental experience and not of a person who is really interested in them. Some of them said that it would be better to use a tape recorder rather than writing materials.

A non-negligible number of the interviewees mentioned that the sex of the examiner affected their performance on the tests and that they would rather have a female than a male examiner (this claim was heard from people of both sexes). Women spoke about the difficulty of being tested by a man, especially if he was attractive. The presence of a man prevented the women from expressing sexual material.

The age of the examiner also constituted a significant factor. University students claimed that the examiner's youth aroused in them a feeling of discomfort, a feeling that they were being confronted by a friend and not by a person of authority.

To give some idea of the authentic expressions of the interviewees we will quote the words of one of the female subjects:

"This was a very significant experience that leaves many residues and arouses many thoughts and gives the impression that the authorities or the professional people do not relate to it seriously but see it as like any other examination, like an X-ray where you come, are X-rayed and leave. As if it is something that does not require depth and personal involvement. Something very technical. And it is not like that, because you invest a lot of mental energy and many open questions remain for which you do not always get an answer."

The interviewees also mentioned some positive aspects of the testing situation and the examiners, but we did not describe them in detail because they do not require special attention or a thorough change.

Discussion

Psychological tests are generally the first encounter between an individual and the mental health authorities. If we can judge by the reports of 30 interviewees who shared their experiences with us, it seems that the first greeting of the psychologists is not remarkable for its sensitivity to psychological distress.

The results attest that the test experience arouses unpleasant feelings. It seems likely that during and after the examination procedure the examinees are engaged in "self-analysis" and there is a need to stop or to moderate this process by giving feedback. According to their reports most of the examinees did not receive feedback or received superficial and unsatisfying information. It does not seem likely to us that all the interviewees who reported the lack of feedback were giving a factually accurate report. Nevertheless, the very fact that they do not remember the summarizing discussion demonstrates that this was done partially and in an unsatisfying way. Even the preparation for the tests and the explanations about them and about their confidentiality were not conducted properly. Why is this? Do the psychologists have no respect for the examinees? Are they unaware that every psychological test constitutes a complex experience? Are they afraid to speak to the examinees about this, to prepare them in advance and to tell them where they stand? This is not the place to speculate on the motivations of psychologists, but it is clear that this examination of the test experience should arouse action and change.

Different tests have a different impact on the examinees. Children have more difficulty in ambiguous situations and find drawing easier, while adults find drawing tests very difficult. These findings bring up the question of whether it might not be worthwhile to make the order of administering the tests more flexible, to take the preferences of the subject into consideration and to try to begin and end the examination with test that create a positive feeling.

Perhaps it would also be possible to find an alternative to taking notes during the examination.

If not, it is certainly important to accompany the note-taking or the use of a stopwatch with a reassuring explanation. The fact that psychological tests require the examiner to act in a standard manner and to follow instructions does not mean that he has to behave mechanically and to lose his feelings and his flexibility. He needs to find the golden mean and to be a sensitive psychologist even in the test situation. That, after all, is why we speak of a psychodiagnostician and not of a testologist.

References

Festinger, L. (1954). A theory of social comparison processes. *Human Relations, 7,* 114-140.

Haley, J. (1976). *Problem solving therapy: New strategies for effective family therapy.* San Francisco: Jossey-Bass.

Klopfer, W.G. (1964). *The psychological report: Use and communication of psychological findings.* New York: Grune & Stratton.

Minuchin, S. (1974). *Family and family therapy.* Cambridge, MA: Harvard University Press.

Palmer, J.D. (1970). *The psychological assessment of children.* New York: John Wiley.

Schachter, S. and Singer, J.E. (1962). Cognitive, social and psychological determinants of emotional states. *Psychological Review, 69,* 379-398.

Schafer, R. (1954). *Psychoanalytic interpretation in Rorschach testing.* New York: Grune & Stratton.

Schafer, R. (1967). *Projective testing and psychoanalysis.* New York: International Universities Press.

References

Adams, S. (1950). Does face validity exist? *Educational and Psychological Measurement, 10,* 320-328.

Alderfer, C. & McCord, C. (1970). Personal and situational factors in the recruitment interview. *Journal of Applied Psychology, 54,* 377-385.

Arvey, R.D. & Campion, J.E. (1982). The employment interview: A summary and review of recent research. *Personnel Psychology, 35,* 281-322.

Allen, M. J. & Yen, W. M. (1979). *An introduction to measurement theory.* Monterey, CA: Brooks/Cole.

American College Testing Program (1987). *Assessment Student Information,* High School Course/Grade Information, Interest Inventory, ACT Student Profile Section, Iowa City: American College Testing Program.

American College Testing Program (1988). *Assessment Program Technical Manual,* Iowa City: American College Testing Program.

American College Testing Program, (1988). *Preparing for the ACT Assessment,* Iowa City.

American Educational Research Association, American Psychology Association and National Council on Measurement in Education (1985). *Standards for Educational and Psychological Testing,* pp. 83-84, Washington, D.C.: American Psychological Association.

American Psychological Association. (1954). *Standards for educational and psychological tests.* Washington, DC: Author.

American Psychological Association. (1974). *Standards for educational and psychological tests (3rd ed.).* Washington, DC: Author.

Anastasi, A. (1954). *Psychological testing.* New York: Macmillan.

Anastasi, A. (1976). *Psychological Testing. (4th ed.)* New York: Mcmillan.

Anastasi, A. (1982). *Psychological testing (5th ed.).* New York: Macmillan.

302

Anderson, S.B., Ball, S., & Murphey, R.T. (1974). *Encyclopedia of educational evaluation*. San Francisco: Jossey-Bass.

Applebaum, M. I. & Cramer, E.M. (1974). Some problems in the nonorthogonal analysis of variance. *Psychological Bulletin, 81*, 335-343.

Arsenian, A. (1942). Own estimate and objective measurement. *Journal of Educational Psychology, 33*, 291-302.

Bailey, R.C. & Bailey, K.G. (1971). Perceived ability in relation to actual ability and academic achievement. *Journal of Clinical Psychology, 27*, 461-463.

Bailey, K.G. & Lazar, J. (1976). Accuracy of self-ratings of intelligence as a function of sex and level of ability in college students. *Journal of Genetic Psychology, 129*, 273-290.

Baird, L.L. (1977). What graduate and professional school students think about admissions tests. *Measurements in Education, 7(3)*, 1-7.

Baird, L.L. (1987). Do students think admissions tests are fair? Do tests affect their decisions? *Research in Higher Education, 26(4)*, 373-388.

Barnes, E.T. (1972). Cultural Retardation or Shortcomings of Assessment Techniques. In: Jones, R.L. (Ed.) *Black Psychology*. New York: Harper & Row.

Bartussek, D., Raatz, U., Stapf, K.H. & Schneider, B. (1984), (1985), (1986). *Die Evaluation des Tests für medizinische Studiengänge*. 1. Zwischenbericht 1984, 2. Zwischenbericht 1985, 3.Zwischenbericht 1986, Abschlußbericht 1986. Bonn: Sekretariat der Kultusministerkonferenz.

Beam, J. (1953). *Construction of educational and personnel tests*. New York: McGraw-Hill.

Bem, D.J. & McConnell, H.K. (1970). Testing the self perception of dissonance phenomena. *Journal of Personality and Social Psychology, 14*, 23-31.

Berdie, R.F. (1971). Self-claimed and tested knowledge. *Educational and Psychological Measurement, 31*, 629-636.

Berk, R.A. (Ed.) (1982). *Handbook of Methods for Detecting Test Bias*. Bmore: John Hopkins Press.

Blum, F., Hensgen, A. & Trost, G. (1985). *Beratungstests für Oberstufenschüler und Abiturienten.* Bonn: Institut für Test- und Begabungsforschung.

Boggs, D.H., Simon, J.R., (1968). Differential Effect of Noise on Tasks of Varying Complexity, *Journal of Applied Psychology, 52,* 148-153.

Boren, D.L. & Levin, C. (1980, May 28). Regulating Federal Regulators, *New York Times.*

Brim, O.G., Goslin, D.A., Glass, D.C. & Goldberg, I. (1964). *The use of standardized ability tests in American secondary schools and their impact on students, teachers, and administrators.* New York: Russell Sage Foundation.

Brim, O.G., Neulinger, J. & Glass, D.C. (1965). *Experiences and attitudes of American adults concerning standardized intelligence tests.* New York: Russell Sage Foundation.

Brim, O.G.M., Neulinger, J. & Glass, D.C. (1969). *American Beliefs and Attitudes Towards Intelligence.* New York: Russell Sage Foundation.

Brown, F.G. (1983). *Principles of educational and psychological testing (3rd ed.).* New York: Holt, Rinehart & Winston.

Campbell, D.T. & Fiske, D.W. (1959). Convergent and discriminant validation by the multitrait-multimethod matrix. *Psychological Bulletin, 56,* 81-105.

Carkhuff, R.R. (1964). Toward a comprehensive model of facilitative interpersonal processes. *Journal of Counselling Psychology, 14,* 67-72.

Carter, H.D. (1955). Importance and significance of objective test items. *California Journal of Educational Research, 6,* 61-71.

Casey, E., (1987). Accommodating Testing to Disabled Students, In. Bray, F., Belcher, M.J. (Eds.), *Issues in Student Assessment,* Jossey-Bass, San Francisco.

Cattell, R.B. (1944). Psychological measurement: Normative, ipsative, interactive. *Psychological Review, 51,* 292-303.

Cohen, J. (1977). *Statistical power analysis for the behavioral sciences.* New York: Academic Press.

Cole, M. & Bruner, J.S. (1971). Cultural Differences and Inferences About Psychological Processes, *American Psychologist, 26,* 867-876.

Cronbach, L.J. (1949). *Essentials of psychological testing.* New York: Harper & Row.

Cronbach, L.J. (1971). *Essentials of psychological testing (3rd ed.).* New York: Harper & Row.

Cronbach, L.J. (1984). *Essentials of psychological testing (4th ed.).* New York: Harper Institute.

Davis, R. (1987, June). *When applicants rate the examinations: Feedback from 2,000 people.* Paper presented at the 10th Conference of International Personnel Management Associations, San Francisco.

Denisi, A.S. & Shaw, J.B. (1977). Investigation of the uses of self-reports of abilities. *Journal of Applied Psychology, 62,* 641-644.

Deter, B. (1982a). Beziehungen zwischen Testleistungen und Merkmalen des außerschulischen Bildungsweges beim zweiten Einsatz des TMS. In G. Trost et al., *Modellversuch "Tests fur medizinische Studiengänge".* Bonn: Institut für Test- und Begabungsforschung.

Deter, B. (1982b). Weitergehende Analysen der Beziehungen zwischen den Antworten auf den Fragebögen zur Begleituntersuchung und den durchschnittlichen TMS-Leistungen der Teilnehmergruppe vom August 1980. In G. Trost et al., *Modellversuch "Tests für medizinische Studiengänge".* Bonn: Institut für Test- und Begabungsforschung.

Deter, B. (1982c). Beziehungen zwischen Testleistungen und Merkmalen des außerschulischen Bildungsweges beim dritten Einsatz des TMS. In G. Trost et al., *Modellversuch "Tests für medizinische Studiengänge".* Bonn: Institut für Test- und Begabungsforschung.

Deter, B. (1983). Beziehungen zwischen Testleistungen und Merkmalen des außerschulischen Bildungsweges beim vierten und fünften Einsatz des TMS. In G. Trost et al., *Modellversuch "Tests für medizinische Studiengänge."* Bonn: Institut für Test- und Begabungsforschung.

Deter, B. & Ebnet, U. (1981). Beziehungen zwischen Testleistungen und Merkmalen des außerschulischen Bildungsweges. In G. Trost et al., Modellversuch "Tests für medizinische Studiengänge". Bonn: Institut für Test- und Begabungsforschung.

Deutch, M. et al. (1967). Guidelines for Testing Minority Group Children. In: Passow A.II. (Ed.), *Education of the Disadvantaged.* Holt, Rinehart Winston, Inc.

Dinkmeyer, D.C., & Munro, J.J. (1971). *Group counseling: Theory and practice.* Itaksa, IL: Peacock.

Downs, C.W. (1969). Perceptions of the selection interview. *Personnel Administration, 32,* 8-23.

Dreher, G.F., Ash, R.A. and Hancock, P. (1988). The role of the traditional research design in underestimating the validity of the employment interview. *Personnel Psychology, 41,* 315-328.

Ebel, R.J. (1972) *Essentials of educational measurement.* Englewood Cliffs, NJ: Prentice-Hall.

Eckberg, D.L. (1979). *Intelligence and Race: The Origins and Dimensions of the I.Q. Controversy.* Praeger Publishers.

Eckel, K. (1978). Das Sozialexperiment: Finales Recht als Bindeglied zwischen Politik und Sozialwissenschaft. *Zeitschrift für Soziologie, 7,* 39-55.

Educational Testing Service (1985). *ETS Guide to Administering Tests,* 1985-86. Princeton, New Jersey.

Educational Testing Service (1987). *ETS Standard for Quality and Fairness.* Princeton, New Jersey.

Eells, K. et al. (1951). *Intelligence and Cultural Differences.* Chicago: University of Chicago Press.

English, H.B. & English, A.C. (1958). *Psychological and psychoanalytical terms.* New York: McKay.

Epps, E.G. (1974). Situational Effects in Testing. In: Miller, L.P. (Ed.), *The Testing of Black Students.* New York: Prentice-Hall.

306

Evans, R.A. (1974). Psychology's White Face. In: Gartner, A. et al. (Eds.) *The New Assault on Equality*. New York: Harper & Row.

Fay, E. (1984). Beziehungen zwischen Leistungen im TMS und Merkmalen des außerschulischen Bildungsweges beim sechsten und siebten Testtermin. In G. Trost et al., *Modellversuch "Tests für medizinische Studiengänge."* Bonn: Institut für Test- und Begabungsforschung.

Fay, E. (1985). Vorbereitungsmöglichkeiten auf den "Test für medizinische Studiengänge": Was gibt es? Wie wird es genutzt? Nutzt es? In G. Trost et al., *Modellversuch "Tests für medizinische Studiengänge"*. Bonn: Institut für Test- und Begabungsforschung.

Fay, E. (1986). Die Rolle der Psychodiagnostik bei der Zulassung zum Studium der Human-, Tier- und Zahnmedizin. Psychologie und Praxis. *Zeitschrift für Arbeits- und Organisationspsychologie, 30,* 68-76.

Festinger, L. (1954). A Theory of Social Comparison Processes. *Human Relations, 7,* 114-140.

Feuerstein R. & Shalom, H. (1967). Learning Potential Assessment of Culturally and Socially Disadvantaged Children, *Megamot, 15,* 174-187.

Feuerstein, R. et al. (1979). *The Dynamic Assessment of Retarded Performers*. Baltimore: University Park Press.

Fiorina, M.P. (1977). Congress: *Keystone of the Washington Establishment.* New Haven: Conn.: Yale University Press.

Fiske, D.W. (1967). The subjects react to tests. *American Psychologist, 22,* 287-296.

Fiske, D.W. (1971). *Measuring the concepts of personality*. Chicago: Aldine.

Flaugher, R.L. (1978). The Many Definitions of Test Bias, *American Psychologist, 33,* 671-679.

Foppa, K. (1968). *Lernen, Gedächtnis, Verhalten: Ergebnisse und Probleme der Lernpsychologie (3rd ed.)*. Cologne: Kiepenheuer & Witsch.

Freeman, F.S. (1950). *Theory and practice of psychological testing*. New York: Holt, Rinehart & Winston.

Friedman, M. & Friedman, R. (1980). *Free to Choose: A Personal Statement*. New York: Harcourt Brace Janovitch.

Friedman, H.S. (1983). On shutting one's eyes to face validity. *Psychological Bulletin, 94*, 185-187.

Fruhner, R. & Schuler, H. (1987). *Bewertung eignungsdiagnostischer Verfahren zur Personalauswahl durch potentielle Stellenbewerber*. Vortrag, gehalten beim 14. Kongress für Angewandte Psychologie des Berufsverbandes Deutscher Psychologen, 24.-27.9.1987 in Mainz.

Fruhner, R., Schuler, J., Funke, U. and Moser, K. (in press). Zum Erleben von psychologischen Tests und Vorstellungsgesprächen.

Gee, H.H. (1957). The student view of the medical admissions process. *Journal of Medical Education, 32*, 140-152.

Gellman, E.P. & Stewart, J.P. (1975). Faculty and students as admission interviewers: Results of a questionnaire. *Journal of Medical Education, 50,*626-628.

Gibb, J.R. (1961). Defensive communication. *Journal of Communication, 11,*141-148.

Gilmor, T.M. & Reid, D.W. (1978). Locus of control, prediction, and performance on university examinations. *Journal of Consulting and Clinical Psychology, 46*, 565-566.

Ginsburg, H. (1972). *The Myth of the Deprived Child*. New York: Prentice-Hall.

Glueck, W. (1973). Recruiters and executives: How do they affect job choice? *Journal of College Placement, 28*, 99-102.

Goslin, D.A. (1967). *Teachers and Teaching*. New York: Russell Sage Foundation.

Grondlund, N. E. (1976). *Measurement and evaluation in teaching. (3rd Ed.)*.New York: Macmillan.

Guttman, L. (1980). Integration of test design and analysis: Status in 1979. *New Directions for Testing and Measurement, 5*, 93-98.

Guttman, L. & Levy, S. (1980). Two structural laws for intelligence. *Megamot*, *25*, 421-438 (In Hebrew with English abstract).

Gynther, M.D. (1979). Do face validity items have more predictive validity than subtle items? The case of the MMPI and Pd scale. *Journal of Consulting and Clinical Psychology*, *47*, 295-300.

Haase, H. (1978). *Tests im Bildungswesen. Urteile und Vorurteile.* Göttingen: Hogrefe.

Haley, J. (1976). *Problem Solving Therapy: New strategies for effective family therapy.* San Francisco: Josey-Bass.

Harris, J.R. (1975). *A primer of multivariate statistics.* New York: Academic Press.

Havighurst, R.J. (1970). Minority Subculture and the Law of Effect, *American Psychologist*, *25*, 313-322.

Hensgen, A. & Blum, F. (1988). Vergleiche einzelner Teilnehmergruppen beim zweiten Termin des besonderen Auswahlverfahrens: zahlenmäßige Anteile, Test- und Schulleistungen. In G. Trost (Hrsg.), *Tests für medizinische Studiengänge (TMS): Studien zur Evaluation (S. 22-91).* Bonn: Institut für Test- und Begabungsforschung.

Hertzig, M.E. et al. (1968). Ethnic Differences in the Responsiveness of Pre-School Children to Cognitive Demands, *Monographs of the Society for Research Child Development*, *33*, pp.117.

Holden, R.R. & Jackson, D.N. (1979). Item subtlety and face validity in personality assessment. *Journal of Consulting and Clinical Psychology*, *47*, 459-468.

Hunter, J.E. & Hirsh, J. (1987). Applications of meta-analysis. In C.L. Cooper & I.T. Robertson (Eds.), *International review of industrial and organizational Psychology 1987* pp.321-357.

Hunter, J.E. & Hunter, R.F. (1984). Validity and utility of alternative predictors of job performance. *Psychological Bulletin*, *96*, 72-98.

Ingle, R.B. & De Amico, G. (1969). The effect of physical conditions of the test room on standardized achievement test scores. *Journal of Educational Measurement*, *6*, 237-240.

Ivey, A.E. (1980). *Counseling and psychotherapy: Skills, theories and practice.* Englewood Cliffs, N.J.: Prentice-Hall.

Jensen, A.R. (1980). *Bias in Mental Testing.* New York: Free-Press.

Jäger, R.S. (1978). *Differentielle Diagnostizierbarkeit in der Psychologischen Diagnostik. Theoretische und empirische Untersuchungen mit Moderatoren.* Göttingen: Hogrefe.

Jäger, R.S. (1982). Strategien und Zielsetzungen in der pädagogischen Diagnostik: Eine Analyse verschiedener Randbedingungen. In K. Ingenkamp, R. Horn & R.S. Jäger (Eds.), *Tests und Trends: Jahrbuch der pädagogischen Diagnostik* (pp. 119-145). Weinheim: Beltz.

Jäger, R.S. (1983). *Der diagnostische Prozeß: Ein Diskussion psychologischer und methodischer Randbedingungen.* Göttingen: Hogrefe.

Jäger, R.S. (1986). Measuring examiner and examinee reaction to each other and the psychodynamic situation. In B. Nevo & R.S. Jäger (Eds.), *Psychological Testing - The Examinee Perspective* (pp. 129-146). Toronto: Hogrefe.

Jäger,R.S., & Booth, J.F. (1982). Selzione o modificazione? Unaesame delle strategie a degli ogettivi nella diagnostica della maturitá scolastica. In F. Lunette & R.S. Jäger (Eds.), *La problematica psicodiagnostica della maturitá scolastica* (pp. 19-58). Padua: Cedam.

Janowitz, M. (1978). *The Last Half-Century: Societal Change and Politics in American.* Chicago: University of Chicago Press.

Katz, I. (1967). The Socialization of Academic Motivation in Minority Group Children. In: Levine, D. (Ed.), *Nebraska Symposium on Motivation, 133-192.*

Kirchenkamp, T. & Mispelkamp, H. (1988). Beziehungen zwischen Leistungen im Test für medizinische Studiengänge und verschiedenen Vorbereitungsmaßnahmen, Einstellungen zum Vergabeverfahren sowie links- bzw. rechtshändiger Schreibweise. In G. Trost (Hrsg.), *Test für medizinische Studiengänge (TMS): Studien zur Evaluation (S. 248-279).* Bonn: Institut für Test- und Begabungsforschung.

Kirk, B.A. & Sereda, L. (1969). Accuracy of self-reported college grade averages and characteristics of non and discrepant reporters. *Educational Psychology Measurement, 29,* 147-155.

310

Klopfer, W.G. (1964). *The Psychological Report: Use and Communication of Psychological Findings.* New York: Grune & Stratton.

Kooker, E.W. (1974). Changes in ability of graduate students in education to assess own test performance as related to their miller analogies scores. *Psychological Reports, 35,* 97-98.

Kultusministerkonferenz. (Hrsg.). (1985). *Die Hochschulzulassung ab Wintersemester 1986/87, insbesondere zu den medizinischen Studiengängen. Informationsbroschüre.* Bonn: Sekretariat der Kultusministerkonferenz.

Labov, W. (1970). The Logic of Non-Standard English. In: Williams, F. (Ed.). *Language and Poverty.* Chicago: Markham Publ. Co., 153-187.

Laing, J., Sawyer, R., Noble, J., (1987, July). *Accuracy of Self Reported Activities and Accomplishments of College Bound Students,* (ACT Research Report Series 87-6), Iowa City.

Latham, G.P. (1989, May). *Situational interviews and perceived fairness form the vantage point of managers, interviewees and lawyers.* Paper presented at "The Individual and Organizational Side of Selection and Performance Evaluation and Appraisal", Hohenheim University, R.F.G.

Lerner, B. (1979). Test and Standards Today: Attacks, Counterattacks and Responses. In: R.T. Lennon (Ed.), *New Directions for Testing and Measurement.* San Francisco: Jossey Bass.

Lerner, B. (1980). The War on Testing: David, Goliath and Gallup. *The Public Interest, 60,* 119-147.

Lerner, B. (1986). Representative democracy - 'Men of Zeal' and testing legislation, in B. Nevo & R.S. Jäger (Eds.), *Psychological Testing - The Examinee Perspective* (pp. 5-20). Toronto: Hogrefe.

Lifshitz, H. (1987). *Reports of EFeQ Findings* (Report Nos. 36, 40, 41). Jerusalem: National Institute for Testing and Evaluation.

Lindzey, G. & Aronson, E. (1985). *The Handbook of Social Psychology (Vol. 1, 2). (3rd ed.).* New York: Random House.

Linke, R., Chalmers, J. & Ashton, J. (1981). A survey of opinion among different occupational groups toward selection of medical students. *Medical Education, 15,* 414-421.

Mabe, P.A. & West, S.G. (1982). Validity of self-evaluation ofability: A review and meta-analysis. *Journal of Applied Psychology, 67,* 280-296.

Madison, D.R. (1961). Paper No. 52. In: R.P. Fairfield (Ed.), *The Federalist Paper.* Garden City: N.Y. Doubleday.

Mayfield, E.C. (1964). The selection interview - A reevaluation of published research. *Personnel Psychology, 17,* 239-260.

Mayhew, D.R. (1974). Congress: *The Electoral Connection.* New Haven, Conn.: Yale University Press.

McDaniel, M.A., Whetzel, D.L., Schmidt, F., Hunter, J.E., Maurer, S. and Russel, J. (1986). *The validity of employment interviews: A review and meta-analysis.* Unpublished manuscript, US Office of Personnel, Washington, DC.

Meadow, A., Parnes, S.J., & Reese, H. (1959). Influence of brain storming: Instructions and problem sequence on a creative problem solving test. *Journal of Applied Psychology, 43,* 413-416.

Miller, A.H. (1974). Political Issues and Trust in Government: 1964-1970. *American Political Science Review, 68,* 951-972.

Miller, R.L., Brickman, P. & Bolen, D. (1975). Attribution versus Persuasion as a means for modifying behavior. *Journal of Personality and Social Psychology, 31,* 430-441.

Mills, F.L. (1939). *Statistical methods.* New York: Holt, Rinehart & Winston.

Miner, M.G. & Miner, J.B. (Eds.) (1978). *Employee selection within the law.* Washington: Bureau of National affairs.

Minkowitch, A. et al. (1982). *Success and Failure in Israeli Elementary Education.* New York: New-Brunswick.

Minuchin, S. (1974). *Family and Family Therapy.* Cambridge, MA: Harvard University Press.

Mosier, C.I. (1947). A critical examination of the concepts of face validity. *Educational and Psychological Measurement, 7,* 191-206.

National Education Association. (1962). What do Teachers Think? *NEA Research Bulletin, 40,* 120-125.

National School Boards Association, (1977). School Board Attitudes Toward Standardized Testing. *NSBA Research Report, 1,* 25-29.

National Institute for Testing and Evaluation (1984-1988). Feedback Reports No. 18, 22, 30, 36, 40,44, 47, 55, 56, 58, 63, 66, 77. Jerusalem.

Nevo, B. (1985). Face validity revisited. *Journal of Educational Measurement, 22,* 287-293.

Nevo, B. (1986, July). *The practical value of Examinees Feedback Questionnaires.* Paper presented at the International Congress of Applied Psychology, Jerusalem.

Nevo, B. (1988). The practical and theoretical value of examinees' feedback questionnaires. *Applied Psychology - an International Review* (in press).

Nevo, B. & Cohen, Y. (1988). *Selected Problems in Evaluation and Measurement.* Jerusalem: National Institute for Testing and Evaluation.

Nevo, B. & Jäger, R.S. (Eds.). (1985). *Psychological testing: The examinee perspective.* Göttingen: Hogrefe.

Nevo, B., & Sfez, J. (1983). *Examinees' feedback questionnaire* (Research Rep. No. 61). Haifa: University of Haifa.

Nevo, B. & Sfez, J. (1985). Examinees' feedback questionnaires, *Assessment and Evaluation in Higher Education, 10,* 235-243.

Nevo, B. & Szef, J. (1986). Examinees' feedback questionnaire (EFeQ). In Nevo, B., and Jäger, R.S. (Eds.) *Psychological Testing: The Examinee Perspective.* Toronto: Hogrefe.

Nunnally, J.C. (1978). *Psychometric Theory.* New York: McGraw-Hill.

Oren, C. (1988). MKAL as a model for building National Achievement Test. in B. Nevo & Y. Cohen, (Eds.), *Selected Problems in Evaluation and Measurement.* Jerusalem: National Institute for Testing and Evaluation.

313

Osgood, C.E., Suci, D.J. & Tannenbaum, P.H. (1957). *The Measurement of Meaning.* Urbana: University of Illinois Press.

Palmer, J.D. (1970). *The Psychological Assessment of Children.* New York: John Wiley.

Poorman, D.H. (1975). Medical School applicant: A study of the admissions interview. *Journal of Kansas Medical Society, 76,* 29-8301.

Reilley, R.R. & Chao, G.T. (1982). Validity and fairness of some alternative employee selection procedures. *Personnel Psychology, 35,* 1-62.

Response Analysis Corporation. (1978). *High school students review the S.A.T. and college admissions process.* Princeton, NJ: College Board.

Riessman, F. (1974). The Hidden IQ. In: Gartner, et al. (Eds.), *The New Assault on Equality: IQ and Social Stratification.* New York: Harper & Row.

Robertson, I.T. & Smith, M. (1989). Personnel selection methods. In M. Smith and I.T. Robertson (Eds.), *Advances in selection and assessment* (pp.89-112). Chichester: Wiley.

Rogers, D. & Sincoff, M. (1978). Favorable impression characteristics of the recruitment interviewer. *Personnel Psychology, 31,* 495-504.

Rosenbaum, B.L. (1973). Attitude toward invasion of privacy in the personnel selection process and job applicant demographic and personality correlates. *Journal of Applied Psychology, 58,* 333-338.

Rynes, S.L., Heneman, H.G. III & Schwab, D.P. (1980). Individual reactions to organizational recruiting: A review. *Personnel Psychology, 33,* 529-542.

Sader, M., & Keil, W. (1966). Bedingungskonstanz in der psychologischen Diagnostik. *Archiv für die gesamte Psychologie, 118,* 279-308.

Samuda, R.J. (1975). *Psychological Testing of American Minorities.* New York: Harper & Row.

Sapington. A.A. & Farrar, W.E. (1982). Brain-storming vs. critical judgment in the generation of solutions which conform to certain reality constraints. *Journal of Creative Behavior, 16,* 68-73.

314

Sattler, J.M. (1982). *Assessment of Children's Intelligence and Special Abilities.* Boston: Allyn & Bacon, Inc.

Sawyer, R., Laing, J., Houson, M., (1988, March). *Accuracy of Self-Reported Activities and Accomplishments of College Bound Students,* ACT Research Report Series 88-1, Iowa City.

Scarr, S. (1981). *Race, Social Class and Individual Differences in IQ.* New York: Lawrence Erlbaum Associates.

Schmeiser, C.B. (1982). Use of Experimental Design in Statistical Item Bias Studies. In: Berk, R.A. (Ed.), *Handbook of Methods for Detecting Test Bias.* London: John Hopkins Press Ltd.

Schmidt, R. (1988). *Das Vorstellungsgespräch aus der Sicht des Stellenbewerbers.* Eine Feldstudie. Unpublished Masters Thesis, University of Bielefeld.

Schmitt, N. (1976). Social and situational determinants of the interview decision: Implications for the employment interview. *Personnel Psychology, 29,* 79-101.

Schmitt, N., Coyle, B.W. & Saary, B.B. (1977). A review and critique of analysis of multitrait-multimethod matrices. *Multivariate Behavioral Research, 12,* 447-478.

Schmitt, N. & Coyle, B. (1976). Applicant decisions in the employment interview, *Journal of Applied Psychology, 61,* 184-192.

Schuler, H. & Stehle, W. (1985). Soziale Validität eignungsdiagnostischer Verfahren: Anforderungen für die Zukunft. In H. Schuler & W. Stehle (Hrsg.), *Organisationspsychologie und Unternehmenspraxis: Perspektiven der Kooperation (S. 133-138).* Schuler, H. & Stehle, W. Stuttgart: Verlag für Angewandte Psychologie.

Schuler, H. (1988, August). *Construct validity of a multimodal employment interview.* Paper presented at the XXIV International Congress of Psychology, Sydney, Australia.

Schuler, H. (1989). *Social validity of selection situations: A concept and some empirical results.* Paper presented at "The Individual and Organizational Side of Selection and Performance Evaluation and Appraisal", Hohenheim University, F.R.G.

Schuler, J. & Funke, U. (1989a). Berufseignungsdiagnostik. In E. Roth (Ed.), *Organisationspsychologie. Enzyklopädie der Psychologie D/III/e* (pp.31-42). Göttingen: Hogrefe.

Schuler, J. § Funke, U. (1989b). The interview as a multimodal procedure. In G.R. Ferris and R.W. Eder (Eds.), *The Employment Interview: Theory, Research and Practice.* Newbury Park: Sage Publications.

Schuler, J. & Stehle, W. (1983). Neuere Entwicklungen des Assessment-Center-Ansatzes - beurteilt unter dem Aspekt der sozialen Validität. *Psychologie und Praxis. Zeitschrift für Arbeits- und Organisationspsychologie, 27,* 33-44.

Schulz, C., Schuler, J. & Stehle, W. (1985). Die Verwendung eignungsdiagnostischer Methoden in deutschen Unternehmen. In H. Schuler and W. Stehle (Eds.), Organisationspsychologie und Unternehmenspraxis: *Perspektiven der Kooperation* (pp.126-132). Stuttgart: Hogrefe/Verlag für Angewandte Psychologie.

Scott, W.D. (1916). Selection of employees by means of quantitative determinations. *Annuals of the American Academy of Political and Social Science, 65.*

Scruggs, T.E., Mastropieri, M.A., Tolfa, D. & Jenkins, V. (1985). Attitudes of behaviorally disordered students toward tests. *Perceptual and Motor Skills, 60,* 467-470.

Severson, R.A. & Guest, K.E. (1970). Toward the Standardized Assessment of the Language of Disadvantaged Children. In: Williams, F. (Ed.), *Language and Poverty.* Chicago: Markham Publ. Co.

Show, M.E. (1976). *Group dynamics: The psychology of small group behavior (2nd ed.).* New York: McGraw-Hill.

Shye, S. (Ed.). (1978). *Theory construction and data analysis in the behavioral sciences* (A volume in honor of Louis Guttman). San Francisco: Jossey-Bass.

Smith, F.T. (1936). The relationship between objectivity and validity in the arrangement of items in rank order. *Journal of Applied Psychology, 20,* 154-160.

Spence, J.T. & Helmreich, R.L. (1983). Beyond face validity: A comment on Nicholls, Licht and Pearl. *Psychological Bulletin, 94,* 181-184.

316

Spitznagel, A. (1982). Die diagnostische Situation. In K.-J. Groffmann & L. Michel (Hrsg.), *Grundlagen psychologischer Diagnostik. Enzyklopädie der Psychologie, Themenbereich B, Serie II, Bd. 1* (S. 248-294). Göttingen: Hogrefe.

Stahl, A. (1977). Language and Thought of Culturally Deprived Children in Israel. *Otsar HaMoreh*, (in Hebrew).

Stehle, W. (1983). *Zur Konzeption eines Personalauswahlverfahrens auf der Basis biographischer Daten.* Unpublished doctoral dissertation, Hohenheim University, Stuttgart.

Stetz, F.P. & Beck, M.D. (1979, April). *Comments from the classroom: Teachers' and students' opinions of achievement tests.* A paper presented at the annual meeting of the National Council on Measurement in Education. San Francisco.

Stevenson, D.K. (1981). Beyond faith and face validity. In A.S. Talner (Ed.), *Proceedings of the 1979 Teaching English as a Foreign Language Symposium.* Federal Republic of Germany, Munich.

Szalay, L.B. & Deese, J. (1978). *Subjective Meaning and Culture: An Assessment through Word Association.* New York: Lawrence Erlbaum Associates.

Tatsuoka, M.M. (1971). *Multivariate Analysis: Techniques for Educational and Psychological Research.* New York: John Wiley & Sons

Tesser, A. & Leidy, T.R. (1968). Psychological testing through the looking glass of youth. *American Psychologist, 23,* 381-384.

Thorndike, R.L. (1982). *Applied psychometrics.* Boston: Houghton Mifflin.

Thorndike, R.L. & Hagen, E. (1961). *Measurement and evaluation in psychology and education (2nd ed.).* New York: Wiley.

Thorndike, R.L. & Hagen, E. (1969) (3rd Ed.). *Measurement and evaluation in psychology and education.* New York: John Wiley

Traxler, A.E., Hilkert, R.N., (1942). Effect of Type of Desk on Results of Machine-Scored Tests, *School and Society, 56,* 277-279.

Trost, G. (1985). Pädagogische Diagnostik beim Hochschulzugang, dargestellt am Beispiel der Zulassung zu den medizinischen Studiengängen. In R.S. Jäger, R. Horn & K. Ingenkamp (Hrsg.), *Tests und Trends 4. Jahrbuch der Pädagogischen Diagnostik* S. 41-81. Weinheim: Beltz.

Trost, G. (1986). Die Bedeutung des Interviews für die Diagnose der Studieneignung. Darstellung der internationalen Forschungsergebnisse. In R. Loholter, K. Hinrichsen, G. Trost and S. Drolshagen (Eds.), *Das Interview bei der Zulassung zum Medizinstudium.* Stuttgart: Schattauer.

Trost, G. (1988). Ein psychologischer Beitrag zur Regelung des Hochschulzugangs. In F. Losel & H. Skowronek (Hrsg.), *Beiträge der Psychologie zu politischen Planungs- und Entscheidungsprozessen* (S. 213-224). Weinheim: Deutscher Studien Verlag.

Trost, G., Blum, F., Deter, B., Ebnet, U., Fay, E., Hensgen, A., Maichle, U., Mausfeld, R., Mispelkamp, H., Nauels, H.-U. & Stumpf, H. (1980-1987). *Modellversuch "Tests für medizinische Studiengänge." 3. bis 11. Arbeitsbericht.* Bonn: Institut für Test und Begabungsforschung.

Turner, C.B., & Fiske, D.W. (1968). Item quality and appropriateness of response processes. *Educational and Psychological Measurement, 28,* 297-315.

Turner, S.P. (1979). The concept of face validity. *Quality and Quantity, 13,* 85-90.

Tyler, (Ed.). (1969). *The work of the counsellor.* New York: Appleton-Century-Croffs.

Valiga, M., (1986, November). *The Accuracy of Self-Reported High School Course and Grade Information,* (American College Testing Program Research Report Series, 87-1), Iowa City.

Vernon, Ph.E. (1979). *Intelligence: Heredity and Environment.* San Francisco: W.J. Freeman & Co.

Wagner, R. (1949). The employment interview: A critical summary. *Personnel Psychology, 2,* 17-46.

Webster, E.C. (Ed.). (1982). *The employment interview,* Schomberg, Ontario: SIP Publications.

Wiesner, W.H. & Cronshaw, S.F. (1988). A meta-analytic investigation of the impact of interview format and degree of structure on the validity of the employment interview. *Journal of Occupational Psychology, 61*, 275-290.

Williams, R.L. (1972). Abuses and Misuses in Testing Black Children. In: Jones, R.L. (Ed.), *Black Psychology*. New York: Harper & Row.

Zehelein, (1985). *Students' judgements of interviewers: The influence of gender and communication style*. Unpublished Masters Thesis, University of Erlangen-Nürnberg.

Zeidner, M. (1983). *Some Situational Determinants of Group Performance on Standardized Tests of Scholastic Ability*. Unpublished doctoral dissertation. Jerusalem: Hebrew University.

Zeidner, M. (Chair). (1985, February). *Psychological testing: The examinee's perspective*. Symposium conducted at the annual meeting of the Israeli Psychological Association.

Zeidner, M. (1988). Sociological differences in examinees' attitudes towards scholastic ability exams. *Journal of Educational Measurement*. (in press).

Zeidner, M. (in press). Sociocultural differences in examinees' attitudes towards scholastic ability exams. *Journal of Educational Measurement*.

Subject Index